The Penguin Guide to Employment Rights

'Essential reading for those wanting to avoid costly mistakes in dealing
with employment law issues. The information in this book is easy to read
and should be distributed to all managers who have a responsibility for
managing people and their terms and conditions of service. I would
recommend this guide as a top three read to all HR staff and managers
irrespective of which sector they operate in.'

Bill Nuttall, Director of Human Resources, Amnesty International

'Excellent . . . it is definitely one that will find its way on to my "essential
management bookshelf" . . .'

Personnel Today, Rating *****

'*The Penguin Guide to Employment Rights* is a very user-friendly guide
with a good logical layout. Information is readily accessible and written
in an easy, jargon free style making it a portable handy reference tool for
busy HR professionals as well as employees.'

Sue Griffin, Head of ER, Ceridian Centrefile

'An invaluable book for HR practitioners.'

Anne Boënders, HR Manager, RHWL Architects

'This book is ideal. I particularly like some of the editorial features in the
book, such as "Key Questions", the "What if" scenarios, "tactics and tips"
and useful contact details.'

Lyn Stansfield, *Personnel Today*

'Excellent, straight to the point, essential reading for HR and line man-
gers. This is THE definitive guide on managing employee's issues fairly
and legally.'

Janet Shearer, Head of Human Resources, The Prince's Trust

Hina Belitz is a solicitor specializing in employment law. She is a partner and joint Head of the Employment Law Unit at her London-based law firm. She has many years of experience advising employees and employers on workplace issues, and has personally presented numerous claims at employment tribunals, including unfair dismissal and discrimination claims. Hina also regularly lectures and trains employees, managers and corporate executives on fair practices, rights and obligations at work, and how to avoid conflict in the workplace. Hina can be contacted at www.hinalegal.com

Dominic Crossley-Holland is Head of ITN's 24-hour News Channel. He joined Independent Television News in 1989 and has edited a range of programmes including *News at Ten* and the *ITV Nightly News*. An award-winning journalist, he has written for a number of publications.

The Penguin Guide to Employment Rights

Hina Belitz and
Dominic Crossley-Holland

PENGUIN BOOKS

PENGUIN BOOKS

Published by the Penguin Group
Penguin Books Ltd, 80 Strand, London WC2R 0RL, England
Penguin Group (USA) Inc., 375 Hudson Street, New York, New York 10014, USA
Penguin Group (Canada), 90 Eglinton Avenue East, Suite 700, Toronto, Ontario, Canada M4P 2Y3
(a division of Pearson Penguin Canada Inc.)
Penguin Ireland, 25 St Stephen's Green, Dublin 2, Ireland
(a division of Penguin Books Ltd)
Penguin Group (Australia), 250 Camberwell Road, Camberwell, Victoria 3124, Australia
(a division of Pearson Australia Group Pty Ltd)
Penguin Books India Pvt Ltd, 11 Community Centre, Panchsheel Park, New Delhi – 110 017, India
Penguin Group (NZ), cnr Airborne and Rosedale Roads, Albany, Auckland 1310, New Zealand
(a division of Pearson New Zealand Ltd)
Penguin Books (South Africa) (Pty) Ltd, 24 Sturdee Avenue, Rosebank, Johannesburg 2196, South Africa

Penguin Books Ltd, Registered Offices: 80 Strand, London WC2R 0RL, England

www.penguin.com

First published 2002
Revised edition published 2006
1

Copyright © Hina Belitz and Dominic Crossley-Holland, 2002, 2006
Preface copyright © Cherie Booth, 2002, 2006

Set in 9.5/11.5 pt Monotype Minion
Typeset by Rowland Phototypesetting Ltd,
Bury St Edmunds, Suffolk
Printed in England by Clays Ltd, St Ives plc

Contents

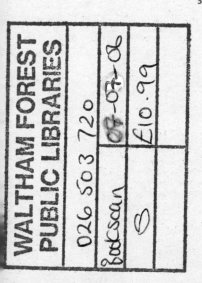

Your rights at work

Losing or giving up your job

It is often said that a person is defined not by what they are but by what they do. For many people their work is a crucial part of their identity. The right to work at a trade or profession without being unjustly excluded from it has been recognized by the common law[1] and, since 1971, has been expressly protected by statute.[2] This perception of the importance of the right to work is echoed in Article 23 of the Universal Declaration of Human Rights:

(1) Everyone has the right to work, to free choice of employment, to just and favourable conditions of work and to protection against unemployment.

(2) Everyone, without any discrimination, has the right to equal pay for equal work.

(3) Everyone who works has the right to just and favourable remuneration ensuring for himself and his family an existence worthy of human dignity, and supplemented, if necessary, by other means of social protection.

(4) Everyone has the right to form and to join trade unions for the protection of his interests.

If the right to work is to be properly protected workers need to know their rights. These rights extend far beyond the right not to be unfairly dismissed. Crucially, they cover the right not to be discriminated against on the grounds of race, sex or disability. By 2006 those rights will extend to sexual orientation, religion and age.[3]

But today there is an increasing realization that there needs to be a proper work–life balance. The long-hours working culture means that parents – and that means fathers as well as mothers – increasingly spend less time with each other and their children. The *Daily Mail* has pointed out in an article that, '88% of managers believed long working hours were damaging their relationships with their children.'[4] This situation is no longer acceptable to many men who are starting to challenge the assumptions in the workplace that the nurturing of children has nothing to do with them. The recognition that human beings are more than one-dimensional workhorses is long overdue.

Employers too are recognizing this and are reaping the economic benefits of adopting the work–life balance. Those employers who emphasize their commitments to the work–life balance are finding themselves reaping the benefits of being the employer of choice for many workers, enabling them to pick the best. A more committed and contented workforce leads to reduced rates of absenteeism and improved staff retention.

A wave of changes triggered by the signing of the Social Chapter in 1997 and the introduction of new employee-friendly policies have added to the ability of workers to enjoy a better work–life balance. The minimum wage, the new and improved rights to maternity leave, parental leave, the right to request flexible working and equal rights for part-time workers are all part of this trend. All these new rights are explained simply and clearly in this book.

The Penguin Guide to Employment Rights will help management and workers alike to navigate this increasingly complex and important area of law. Its user-friendly format and simple style will help all who are seeking to know their rights. I particularly welcome the fact that it does not impose a legal straitjacket on the world of work but organizes the chapters on the actual experiences of the world of work from recruitment to your rights at work to what happens if you lose your job. This Guide will prove indispensable to workers and their employers alike.

Cherie Booth

Notes

1 See *Nagle* v *Feilden* [1966] 2 QB 633 at 644–645, [1996] 1 All ER 689 at 693, CA, per Lord Denning MR. See also *McInnes* v *Onslow Fane* [1978] 3 All ER 211, [1978] 1 WLR 1520; *R* v *Barnsley Metropolitan Borough Council, ex p Hook* [1976] 3 All ER 452, [1976] 1 WLR 1052, CA; *Walker* v *Leeds City Council* [1978] AC 403, [1976] 3 All ER 709, HL; *Breen* v *Amalgamated Engineering Union* [1971] 2 QB 175, [1971] 1 All ER 1148, CA; *Edwards* v *Society of Graphical and Allied Trades* [1971] Ch 354.

2 Industrial Relations Act 1971 and its successors, currently the Employment Rights Act 1996.

3 Article 13 Directive on discrimination.

4. S. Doughty, 'The Price of Success', *Daily Mail*, Thursday 21 October, 1999, p. 7.

Part 1: Introduction

1

Introduction

This book is the essential guide to the workplace for everyone: it explains your rights at work in clear jargon-free language, offering an indispensable self-help handbook for everyone who works as well as a valuable reference source for employers. It also contains all you need to know to help keep workplace relations smooth, with legal and practical advice on how to tackle common problems at work. If it is necessary to take further steps, this guide gives you expert advice on how to take matters further.

Key features of this book include:
• snapshot overviews of the law, unravelling complexities to give you a practical understanding of your rights at work;
• answers to the most commonly asked questions at work 'Key Questions' with a useful Key Questions index at the end of the book;
• 'What if . . .' scenarios based on real cases to assist you with situations you may face at work;
• bullet point summaries of your rights at the end of each section;
• 'Tactics and Tips' to help you in general and specific situations;
• examples of useful documents and questionnaires;
• 'Contacts Points' to follow up if you do need to take additional steps;
• 'What Next . . .' navigates you around the various parts of the book which may also be relevant to your situation.

Employment law has expanded over the years to cover a huge range of situations, from parenthood to sickness, from the hours we work, to the way we work, and from sex, race and religious discrimination, to how much we are paid. And it is continuing to expand into new areas, such as the work–life balance and flexible working, the right to privacy in the workplace, to workers who blow the whistle about serious wrongdoings, and to job-related stress. And barely a week passes without news of some landmark judgment that affects us all, or a record compensation payout.

More of the UK population is in work than almost any other European country but perhaps the biggest change in the workplace in recent years is the huge rise in the number of women who work. In many respects this has forced the pace, putting the work–life balance onto the agenda, with an increasing need for jobs that can accommodate family life through more family-friendly and flexible work practices. The government's initiative aimed at achieving a proper balance between home and work is 'a prize for us all' both as a boost to the economy and to increase work and prosperity for everyone.

Many of our workplace rights have their origins in European Community law and the phenomenal growth in new laws in recent years has come from there. The new laws cover working hours, parental rights, equal opportunities, part-time and fixed-term workers – and there is much more to come, including new discrimination measures.

Whether within reach on your workstation, or in your pocket, access to the *Penguin Guide to Employment Rights* will undoubtedly help you succeed in your working life.

2

What everyone should know

Work–life realities

Many rights at work are explained in this guide, including rights on dismissal, redundancy, family-friendly laws, sickness and stress, as well as protection against discrimination. The law effectively sets a platform of legally enforceable standards that good employers achieve and exceed. While there are laws in place to cover most aspects of workplace life, legal action to enforce such rights should be taken only as a last resort. Most of the problems and conflicts that arise at work should be resolvable informally through discussion or compromise. Many solutions can, of course, derive from the law but it cannot be too heavily stressed that going to law over work issues should never be undertaken lightly.

Understanding the practical realities of the workplace includes being aware of all options available to you, whether they are purely legal solutions or a compromise between employer and employee, which makes both legal and commercial sense. In the real world of work it is as important to appreciate the bigger picture and commercial context, as it is to understand the law itself.

Even lawyers admit that no law is perfect and that it does not, in every instance, achieve fairness or the best solution in a particular situation. However, understanding employment law is an essential and invaluable tool enabling both employers and employees alike to achieve the best outcome for everyone. But good legal advice can be costly and it can be difficult for employees to know where to find the information and advice they need. This book is an essential guide for everyone at work whether employer or employee, freelance or part-time.

Workers denied rights at work *can* seek to put things right by raising a grievance or starting legal action. The uninitiated may believe fighting in court is the real purpose and best use of the law. While there will always be those who set out to have their 'day in court', the law is much more versatile than that and is often used to achieve resolution rather than conflict. Which is just as well as, unless you have experienced an employment tribunal first hand, it is difficult to appreciate what it is really like. The reality is that tribunals can involve legal expenses, time and energy, not to mention the stress of giving evidence and being ruthlessly cross-examined in front of members of the public and, sometimes, the media. And after all that you still have to deal with the uncertainty of whom the tribunal will find in favour. And tribunals do get it wrong – which is why appeals to the Employment Appeal Tribunal and higher courts take place. But to appeal requires determination and tenacity as it involves yet more time, money and uncertainty. Taking a matter to court when difficulties arise in the workplace should usually be your last option after you have exhausted all others.

It is important to be aware that not all employers comply with the law exactly as they should and some 'buy off' rights to fairness when dismissing employees – most commonly through a compromise agreement (explained in Chapter 28). They are able to do this because most employees will do a deal with their employer if they are offered adequate compensation. It is, in effect, a trade-off between fairness and money, and sometimes the pay-off may exceed the employee's entitlements if he or she had successfully complained to an employment tribunal. And even if it doesn't, there are factors to consider in deciding whether a pay-off should be made or accepted such as the irrecoverable legal costs, uncertainty, complexity of some legal issues and the sheer stress of pursuing your rights through the employment tribunals and courts.

So, everyone needs to understand their rights at work to appreciate a reasonable deal and what the law requires employers to do (*see* Chapter 28 for further guidance).

Are you protected?

Who employment law protects is a controversial area and reflects the struggle over the definition of an employee, which is evolving to include many types of worker that were never previously thought of as employees.

While laws such as the discrimination legislation had always extended its protection beyond employees, rights such as maternity and unfair dismissal protection apply to employees alone. But the fact is, there are millions of people who are not classed as employees because they are freelance, consultants or regard themselves as self-employed, who are entitled to a number of rights they may well be unaware of. These people generally provide their services personally, rather than hiring someone else to do it, and may work in exactly the same way and alongside employees in the organization for which they work. If this is so they could fall within the definition of 'worker', a term used to describe all but those that are genuinely self-employed. They will therefore be eligible for certain rights.

In other cases, the law may regard workers as employees even though the workers, or their employers, do not. The law focuses on the reality of the circumstances in practice to establish whether an individual is an employee. Rather unhelpfully no single factor is necessarily decisive although there is one essential component necessary to be an employee – there needs to be 'mutuality of obligation' which means that an employer must provide work to an employee and the employee should be obliged to do it. So the position with regard to who is an employee can be far from clear but to assist the assessment, it includes a consideration of the following issues.

More likely to be an employee if you:	More likely to be self-employed if you:
• Must do the work given to you	• Can decide if you will accept or reject work
• Are salaried or paid directly, and tax and national insurance contributions are deducted	• Invoice and are paid gross
• Do the work personally	• Can subcontract or send another to do the work
• Use computers and equipment provided to you	• Use your own computers or equipment
• Have limited control over how and when the work is done	• Control how and when work is done
• Are an integral part of the business	• Are not really integral to the business
• Have helpers hired by the company for you	• Hire and pay your own helpers
• Are not exposed to any financial risk	• Are exposed to financial risk
• Cannot profit or suffer loss from the work you do	• Can make a profit or loss

In addition to this, certain laws provide 'workers' with increased protection. For example, the Working Time Regulations (Chapter 8: Hours and Holidays), and whistleblowers' law (Chapter 21) protect 'workers' and not just employees (*see* Chapter 3).

 ## Tactics and Tips

'If only I had . . .' are common words when a dispute arises in the workplace or at employment tribunal. The sentence might conclude '. . . taken notes, sought advice, talked with my employer'. There are so many things both employer and employee can do to help smooth out a conflict; or make resolution easier. In some cases they may prevent a dispute even arising. Just a few careful steps can strengthen your position. Listed below are some fairly basic steps you can take to avoid conflicts or help resolve them.

Seek information

All sides should be open about making information about contracts and the terms of employment easily available. In most large companies there will be a staff handbook containing most of the relevant information, but be prepared to ask questions and seek clarification about your employment as this could prevent misunderstandings. All too often it is only when disputes arise that there is a scramble to find out such information, where it is kept and what it says.

Written records

For both employers and employees alike it is a really smart move to keep written records – almost like diary notes – as soon as possible or at around the time of any discussions. The notes do not need to be neatly typed up – handwritten notes are just as useful. A written record should be kept of what was discussed *and* the date it took place as well. If there is a dispute the notes will constitute strong evidence of what was agreed. This is called a 'contemporaneous note' (as it is made close to the time of the incident in question) and it will help make your position more robust if a case is taken to employment tribunal.

Missing terms and entitlements less than the legal minimum

Remember that there are many legal minimum entitlements in employment – holiday rights and wage levels, for example. If holiday entitlement is missing from an employment contract, a full-time employee is entitled to the legal minimum of 20 days per year.

Custom and practice

If there is no term (whether oral or in writing) in relation to something you regularly do, it may become a contractual entitlement by custom and practice. So, for example, if you always take Friday afternoons off and there is nothing in writing or orally agreed to say that you shouldn't, then it is possible that taking Friday afternoons off may become a term of your contract.

Reserve your rights

If an adverse change is imposed on you, you could choose to reserve your rights. This means that by formally registering your concern you effectively keep open the possibility of pursuing a claim either to restore your original position, or for compensation for your loss, rather than losing it. You should seek advice if this situation arises since you may not be able to successfully reserve your rights for an extended period of time.

Grievance procedure

If an employee is not satisfied with the way a matter is being dealt with at work he or she may be required to raise a 'grievance' before taking any more formal action. Raising a grievance is a way of making a formal complaint within a company. The minimum process is set out in the law and is also often set down in the employment contract or staff handbook, although a grievance may still be raised even if there is no procedure in writing. In most cases this merely means writing a letter raising the complaint.

Right to be accompanied at a disciplinary or grievance hearing

Every employee has the right to be accompanied to a disciplinary or grievance hearing. This is an important right for employees as it may assist an employee in what can be a difficult meeting. One further useful tip: if the companion is unable to attend the employee has the legal right to postpone the hearing by up to five working days.

Cutting a deal

Negotiations between employers and employees can often help resolve a problem or conflict: an alternative resolution to the matter can often be found. One frequently used option is for employees to sign away their rights to bring an employment law claim in return for a larger pay-off – both parties enter into what is called a 'compromise agreement' which is used to agree legally binding dismissal deals.

Dismissal just before you have enough service

If an employee is dismissed just before he or she has the legal right to bring a claim, for example, within a week before the qualifying period of one year's service for an unfair dismissal complaint, the termination date can be legally extended by a week, which will mean the employee will then qualify to bring a claim.

Right of appeal

The right to appeal against a decision to dismiss should always be given and is required by the law. Depending on the internal procedures of an employer it may also be possible to appeal against warnings under the disciplinary procedure. A dismissal that is not followed by the right of appeal could be unfair on that basis alone.

Notice entitlements

There are rights to minimum periods of notice if you have been dismissed, unless the dismissal is for gross misconduct. The entitlement is to a minimum of one week's notice for each complete year of continuous service, up to a maximum of 12 weeks for 12 or more years' service. If a contract specifies less entitlement than this, the term is invalid and the employee is entitled to the statutory minimum. If a contract specifies longer then the employee would be entitled to the longer period.

Your reputation

Whatever the reason for your departure it is best to depart on good terms wherever possible. If making allegations cannot change a situation then it may be better that they are not made in the first place. Although tempting, a melodramatic exit may not be in your best interest as prospective employers may hear about the manner of your departure.

References

Although there is no general obligation to provide a reference (except in certain situations such as in the financial services sector) the whole business of getting a helpful reference is obviously a particular worry for those facing dismissal or leaving on less than good terms. The wording of a reference can be agreed prior to an employee's departure and many employers will often agree to provide a basic factual reference stating start and end dates, and the duties undertaken. However, if an employer does provide a reference they are under an obligation to be both careful and honest and may be contacted for further information about the circumstances of a dismissal.

Making a claim

In most cases employees have only three months from the date of their dismissal in which to lodge a claim at employment tribunal although employees may be required to raise a grievance and appeal against a decision internally before they can claim. This may help resolve the problem – if not it will show the tribunal that the employee did everything possible to reach a resolution and thereby minimize losses before taking action, which could impact favourably on any compensation that may be awarded.

Guidelines and contact points

Make use of the information and organizations set out in Appendix B: Contact Points at the end of this book as they can provide you with further guidance and information. For example, the DTI produces useful guidance in many areas of employment law and codes of practice are available to give further insight. Tribunals may take such guidance into account although they are not strictly required to do so.

Take legal advice early

If you are thinking of taking further action or, as an employer, you face a claim by an employee, legal advice should be sought without delay. This book cannot anticipate every situation and new law is emerging all the time. Furthermore, rights can be lost or positions can become indefensible if matters are not dealt with in the correct way.

3

Your status

I am self-employed
Prince Philip, when asked about the nature of his work

The rights you have depend upon your status. We're not talking about how important you are, but the question is: are you an 'employee' or 'self-employed'. If you are self-employed then the question is: are you in fact a 'worker' or *genuinely* self-employed and in business on your own account?

Many different terms are used to describe those that are not employees, such as freelancer, consultant, independent contractor, self-employed, and so on. Such terms do not have precise legal meanings. Either you are an employee, a worker or genuinely running your own business. And the rights you get depend on which of these categories you belong to.

The law gives all workers basic rights. While there is an overlap between the rights of employees and workers, as an employee you have the right to a higher level of protection as well as more basic rights at work. For example, it is only if you are an employee that you have the right to a fair dismissal and compensation in the event of an unfair dismissal (*see* Chapter 22: Being dismissed).

Defining the exact limits of employee status is a hot legal issue. Furthermore, employment rights are gradually extending to cover those originally excluded from protection – this reflects the struggle over the definition of an employee, which is evolving, and may include many types of worker never previously thought of as employees.

To resolve this problem of definitions, much recent legislation, including the Working Time Regulations refer to 'workers' being protected. The term 'worker' has recently emerged as a new protected category. A worker is defined more widely than an employee and includes certain types of work traditionally viewed as a form of self-employment. Workers include all but those who are genuinely in business on their own account (self-employed) and, therefore, a consultant or freelancer may also be a worker.

If a person is not an employee or a worker, most employment law does not protect them. In reality it can be hard to differentiate those genuinely self-employed from workers and for this reason the tests below are used to assist.

There are some types of worker whose status falls somewhere between being employed and self-employed, and others who simply don't fit into the neat legal boxes that they are meant to. As a result the whole issue of employment status and the consequent legal protection has become somewhat confused. Over time, as the way we work has evolved, the distinction between employee and self-employed has become hopelessly blurred, and the law simply no longer fits the reality, for example, there are many independent business people who invoice for their services but who are in reality only working for one company on which they are entirely dependent – hence the introduction of the concept of a worker who enjoys a lesser, but very definite, measure of protection.

Employees

The legal position of an employee has its roots in the historical relationship between *master* and *servant*, terms actually used under the age-old legal system in England and Wales called the common law. As an employee you work under an employment contract – whether it is in writing or not.

You are either an employee or not, there is no middle ground. Although this seems a straightforward statement, in practice the exact position is often extremely difficult to determine for the reasons stated above.

Employees can be full-time, part-time, or work on fixed-term, flexible, temporary or even seasonal contracts.

Rights and obligations

All employees, whether full-time, part-time or temporary, have a large number of rights and obligations. Examples of these rights, which are covered in the different chapters of this *Guide* include:
- written terms of employment;
- rights relating to hours of work and holiday entitlement;
- a minimum wage;
- protection from various types of discrimination;

- the right to a safe place of work and to have reasonable care taken of your health and safety;
- maternity rights;
- time off in certain circumstances;
- statutory sick pay;
- equality of pay between the sexes;
- protection against being unfairly dismissed;
- redundancy payments;
- statutory minimum periods of notice.

As an employee you are required, among other obligations to:
- obey the reasonable orders of your employer;
- pay tax and national insurance contributions in a certain way;
- work faithfully for your employer.

Self-employed: freelancers and consultants

The self-employed typically include those we refer to as contract workers, freelancers and consultants. But many of these individuals are in fact under the control of those they provide their services to, and really only work for that one organization. In reality they may well be considered to be employees in the eyes of the law. There are numerous tribunal cases involving companies having terminated the engagement of someone they thought of as self-employed only to find they have to pay redundancy or unfair dismissal compensation to the individual as the courts have classified them as employees.

For a genuinely self-employed person (who is not a worker) the terms of the engagement including duration, charges, what happens in the event of sickness, etc., are a question of the commercial agreement negotiated between one business and another.

Employee or self-employed – the tests

The business of establishing who is genuinely self-employed is a light industry in itself! The basic question that must be answered is 'are you genuinely in business on your own account?' If you really do run the show, you will typically be able to profit from the management of your business, decide when and where to work, provide your own equipment, and invoice the firm you work for – you are then likely to be self-employed.

In many cases it may be clear that you are an employee or that you are self-employed. Difficulties arise if the way you work is a hybrid situation. If the following feels difficult to grasp it's because it is!

To qualify as an employee (who works under a contract of employment as opposed to a contract for services, consultancy agreement, etc.) the courts and tribunals take into account a variety of factors but the most important are listed below.

Both employer and individual must be under a mutual obligation

In other words your employer must be under an obligation to provide you with work and you must be obliged to accept it. So, if you are a casual worker engaged as and when required you would not be obliged to take up the offer of work and so would not be classed as an employee.

You have to undertake the work for your employer personally

You must do the work yourself rather than hire someone else to do it.

Other established factors that point to one status or the other include whether you provide your own equipment, invoice clients and dictate to them how you intend to do the work. If this is the case then you are probably self-employed.

Beware though as none of these factors, and those listed below, are conclusive of your status. The law in this area makes it plain that in reaching a decision you need to step back and look at the whole picture. Ironically the way you are categorized for tax purposes is also not conclusive of your employment status. What you understood to be the case and how you conducted yourself can be relevant, particularly where your contract is partly or fully agreed on the basis of oral terms.

Even if you set up as a limited company, you may still be held to be an employee!

The questions asked to determine if you are in business on your own account include:

1 *Does the firm for which you work control how and when you do the work?* If so then you are more likely to be an employee, if not it points to self-employed status.
2 *Are you an integral part of the business?* If so, you are more likely to be an employee.
3 *Do you supply your own tools and equipment or are they provided for you?* If you are supplied with them you are more likely to be an employee.

4 *Can you subcontract the work to other people?* This suggests self-employed status.

5 *Are you exposed to a degree of financial risk?* If you are exposed to financial risk in the work that you do you are more likely to be self-employed.

6 *Can you profit from the management and performance of your task?* If you have your own business the object is surely to be able to profit from it, so if this factor applies, it suggests self-employed status.

7 *Do you invoice or do you receive regular wages/salary?* Employees generally do not invoice but receive wages/salary with tax and national insurance deducted. But those that invoice have been held to be employees despite this practice.

8 *Are you paid for sickness absence?* If you are you are more likely to be an employee.

9 *Are you subject to the organization's disciplinary procedures?* Disciplinary procedures are normally for employees so if you are subject to them it suggests you are an employee. As a self-employed person working under a commercial agreement, a breach of discipline may well be dealt with by terminating the agreement for breach of a commercial term.

Rights and obligations

As a self-employed individual, you have the right:
- not to be discriminated against;
- to benefit from the contractual entitlements you agreed, such as fee and pay arrangements, and the timescale for the work you are undertaking;
- to be provided with a safe place and method of work;
- not to have any deductions made from your pay without your consent.

You must however:
- fulfil the obligations as agreed;
- work with due skill and diligently;
- pay tax and national insurance contributions as a self-employed worker.

Workers

Workers include employees. Of those that are self-employed, all but those who are genuinely in business on their own account will be classified as workers. There is limited guidance in law on the difference in practical terms between a worker and a genuinely self-employed person, in part, due to the recent introduction of the term. A worker is, however, a defined term. The definition broadly describes a worker as an individual who works under a contract of employment (an employee) or any other contract, such as a freelance contract, for example, under which he or she personally undertakes to do the work or provide services to another party. The contract does not need to be in writing. A specific exclusion applies to the definition in certain instances in relation to the status of that other party, which should not be a client or customer of a profession or business undertaking being carried on by the individual. So, for example, an accountant providing services personally to a client of his own accountancy practice will not become a worker of that client.

Clearly, many casual workers, freelancers and self-employed workers are covered. Many of the factors noted above are also relevant to an assessment of whether an individual is a worker.

The protection workers are afforded includes:
- working time, hours and holidays, etc. (Chapter 8);
- part-time work (Chapter 10);
- national minimum wage (Chapter 13);
- discrimination (Chapter 14);
- the right to be accompanied at a disciplinary or grievance hearing (Chapter 16);
- whistleblowing (Chapter 21).

Younger workers

Young workers are past school-leaving age but under the age of 18 years. There is special protection in place for young workers in relation to their health and safety at work, to the hours they work, to the amount of annual leave to which they are entitled, as well as a minimum wage. See the chapters on these areas for further details.

Part 2: Getting a job and starting work

4

Applying for a job

An estimated 9 million job vacancies arise each year
DTI

Whether applying for a job, changing jobs or ending one, we're all on the move at one time or another. Gone, it seems, is the notion of 'a job for life', if it ever really existed.

Getting the recruitment process right is also vital to employers if they are to select the best people for the jobs available, and unfair or discriminatory practices can cost employers time and money in defending legal claims.

Applying for a job is a very uncertain process with few uniform procedures or standards. Broadly speaking, most employment rights only apply once you are in a job, but you do have some important rights in the process of applying for a job. The most important right you have when applying for a job is not to be discriminated against on the grounds of sex, race, religion, sexual orientation, marital status, disability or trade union membership. And protection against discrimination will soon extend to age discrimination as well.

The codes of practice such as those issued by the Equal Opportunities Commission, the Commission for Racial Equality, and the Disability Rights Commission provide guidance to employers on best practice. While they are not legally binding, tribunals will take account of these codes in any discrimination claim. Your right to be protected against discrimination is detailed in Chapter 14.

This chapter looks at your rights at each stage of the application process from job advertisements, application forms and CVs through to interviews and the importance of references. You should also refer to the more detailed chapters on References (Chapter 6) and Discrimination (Chapter 14).

Job advertisements

While employers increasingly use the Internet and recruitment consultants for recruitment many still use the old-fashioned newspaper
advertisement, especially in the specialist trade press, as well as putting
advertisements in job centres.

Naturally job advertisements specify the need for certain skills and
qualifications as well as the requirement to submit an application form
by a certain date. But advertisements should not specify any requirement
that is discriminatory, for example, 'men only to apply' unless being male
is a genuine requirement for the job. Where such a requirement is
necessary it is referred to as a genuine occupational qualification and it is
lawful to discriminate in the advertisement. An example would be an
advertisement for a female attendant for the women's changing rooms at
a clothes store: being a woman is likely to be a genuine requirement
for the job. Similarly, if the distribution of a paper containing a job
advertisement is targeted at one race or sex, it may be discriminatory. A
note of caution to publishers – both the publisher and advertiser will be
guilty of the unlawful act, although as a publisher you do have a possible
defence if you can prove you relied on a statement from the advertiser
that the advert was not unlawful and that it was reasonable for you to
rely on that statement.

The use of gender-specific words describing jobs in advertisements,
such as 'waiter', 'salesgirl', 'postman' or 'stewardess' should be avoided as
it may indicate an intention to discriminate. An advertisement can make
it clear that the job is open to both men and women, by stating 'applications are invited from both men and women'. In a case on the use of such
words the court said the use of 'a bloke' with no further reference to
either sex was discriminatory but that 'manager' does not have a sexual
connotation although 'manageress' could be discriminatory, as could
'carpenter/handyman'.

...? What if . . .

- A charity places an advertisement in a national newspaper inviting a
black or Asian woman to work in their information centre. A woman
who is neither black nor Asian and has no intention of applying for the
job brings a discrimination claim to tribunal.

Outcome: A job advertisement is not an act of discrimination against an individual and an individual is not entitled to bring such proceedings. A job advertisement can indicate an intention to discriminate but only the relevant commission is competent to bring proceedings – in this case the Commission for Racial Equality.

• A newspaper advertisement is placed for a 'head waiter' with no further indication of whether both sexes were welcome to apply.

Outcome: This may be discriminatory as it implies that the job is available to male applicants alone.

 Key Questions

What is an advertisement?
The law recognizes every form of advertisement whether available to the public or internally within the company, in a newspaper or other publication, on TV, radio or on an employee notice board.

What about the phrase 'This company is an equal opportunities employer'?
As a means of demonstrating commitment to equality of opportunity, employers are encouraged to state that they are an equal opportunity employer in job advertisements although they are not required by law to do so.

What about positive discrimination? Some advertisements say applications are encouraged from women and ethnic minorities, etc?
Positive discrimination is not generally lawful except in limited circumstances. In the case of job advertisements it is lawful to encourage applications from, for example, a particular sex or race if, at a point in the last 12 months, the sex or race being encouraged was under-represented among the workers doing that work. There is no particular form of words that should be used. In the case of race discrimination it is lawful if that race is either under-represented among the workers doing that work or in the locality targeted for recruitment.

Do vacancies have to be advertised internally and externally?
There is no formal legal requirement to advertise job vacancies internally and externally, but there are risks associated with the manner of advertising. Restrictive methods of recruitment such as internal advertisements

or recruitment by word of mouth may have the effect of excluding or limiting opportunity to, for example, a particular sex, religion or race. It may then be discriminatory. Such recruitment practices do take place, mostly without experiencing any problems, but a note of caution should be sounded to any employer wishing to take such a short cut because, although small, a potential risk of a claim is associated with such recruitment practices.

What happens if an advertisement is found to be discriminatory?
The discrimination commissions are empowered to undertake formal investigations and issue non-discrimination notices. A non-discrimination notice requires the person to stop the discriminatory act which, in the case of advertisements, could mean its withdrawal. A register of non-discrimination notices is kept and is available for inspection to anyone who makes a request to any of the commissions.

What if I apply after the closing date?
Employers are entitled to impose closing dates and other rules relating to applications. It is, therefore, not unlawful. If you apply after the closing date, whether your application is allowed is at the discretion of the organization that placed the advertisement, but if they, for example, accept an application by a man after the closing date but reject a woman's application, it is possible they could then be accused of discrimination.

 Your Rights

You do not have any direct rights in relation to job advertisements, but if you think an advert is discriminatory, you should contact the Equal Opportunities Commission, the Commission for Racial Equality or the Disability Rights Commission who have the power to take action in relation to advertisements.

Application forms and CVs

Consider this. You call up about a job and state your name – Mr Patel. You are promptly told the job is no longer available. You call up another day quoting a different name, such as Mr Weatherly. Your details are immediately taken down so that an application form can be sent to you. You may have a discrimination claim on this basis alone. In fact a lawyer made a habit of doing just this, allegedly making a fortune from out of court settlements. He also submitted two identical CVs, one with an Indian and the other with an English name, and brought a claim immediately when one CV resulted in an interview while the other did not.

Application forms can vary widely, but most ask for much the same information, usually including details of your current job and salary, your employment history and education and training. Some also contain sections that ask you about the job you are applying for. You are under no legal obligation to answer all the questions on an application form, but if you fail to do so it might affect your chances of getting the job.

There are no absolute restrictions on what you can be asked in an application form although there should not be any questions on the form that could indicate an intention to discriminate. It is a question of whether answers you give are used by a prospective employer to unlawfully discriminate against you. Unlawful discrimination presently falls into these categories: discrimination on the grounds of sex, marital status, race, religion, sexual orientation or disability. This will soon be extended to include age (2006) (*see* Chapter 14).

If you fulfil all the criteria but are not selected for interview, you may suspect it is unjustified but direct evidence of discrimination can be difficult to obtain. Given the nature of recruitment processes you are unlikely to know for certain. Tribunals realize that direct evidence of discrimination is often unlikely to be available in a society that is aware that it can be sued if caught. So all the evidence, including indirect evidence, is considered and tribunals can infer discrimination. An employment tribunal could, on that basis, find that you were discriminated against.

Generally, CVs should give the same sort of information, but one note of caution: while many people exaggerate their qualifications or current levels of responsibility when applying for a job you should take care to provide accurate and truthful information. Lies on CVs and application forms can result in dismissal after you have been hired or retraction of an offer before you are hired, and may adversely impact on your future credibility in the job market.

How to find out whether a rejection was because of sex, race, religion, sexual orientation or disability

The obvious way is to make enquiries of the company to which you applied. There is, however, a formal way of doing this by sending a discrimination questionnaire to the company. This enables you to put a variety of questions to the company and ask for information and statistics that may help you decide whether to bring a claim. If there is no response to the questionnaire, that in itself may persuade a tribunal to draw an inference supporting the fact you may have been discriminated against (*see* Chapter 14).

 What if . . .

- People applying for manual jobs were required to complete application forms in their own handwriting. Two applicants could not read or write in English and claimed race discrimination.
  Outcome: Claimants in a similar case won their claim because the employer's requirement discriminated indirectly against foreign applicants.
- A candidate asks to submit an application form on tape, because he was blind and unable to write but still able to perform the job being advertised.
  Action: The prospective employer should agree to the proposed change in standard procedure as it is likely to constitute a reasonable adjustment under the Disability Discrimination Act (*see* Chapter 14).
- An employer had a policy of not accepting applications from or interviewing anyone who lives in an inner city area of Liverpool (where the majority of the population was black). A request by the Careers Service to consider an applicant for interview who lived in the inner city area is refused. The potential applicant claims race discrimination.
  Outcome: In a similar case the claimant won his claim because the employer's policy of not employing anyone from that area discriminated indirectly against black people.

Key Questions

What can I be asked at an interview or on an application form?
There are no strict legal rules on what you can and cannot be asked. Questions should be relevant to the position that you are applying for.

Does it matter if I omit certain facts?
If your omissions are significant and liable to mislead your prospective employer then it could be problematic. It is a judgement that you will have to make, but remember that you run the risk of an offer being withdrawn, being dismissed or disciplined on starting your new job if you have withheld important facts.

What if I have a criminal record?
As part of rehabilitating offenders, the law provides that after a period of time, people who have been convicted of certain criminal offences and have served their sentence should not be required to disclose their conviction. Their conviction becomes 'spent'. The length of time that must elapse before a conviction becomes spent depends on the conviction and sentence, but if a conviction is spent it does not need to be disclosed even if a direct question is asked on an application form (although there are exceptions to this rule for certain jobs such as lawyers and doctors). You could be disciplined or dismissed if your conviction is not spent and you do not disclose it.

Do I have to say if I've been to employment tribunal with a previous/ current employer?
There is no requirement for you to disclose this information unless you are asked.

Do I have to give the name of a referee?
Most offers are conditional on a satisfactory reference from your previous employer. If you fail to give details of a referee, your offer may be lawfully retracted.

Does data protection law protect the information I give on an application form?
The information that you give on your application is protected and the

Information Commissioner has set out the following benchmarks in Part 1 of the Code of Practice:

- the application form should state who you are providing information for and how it will be used (unless it is obvious);
- unnecessary personal information should not be sought;
- questions about criminal convictions should make it clear that spent convictions do not have to be declared (unless the job falls into one of the exceptions that require that spent conviction be disclosed, such as doctors, solicitors, accountants and police officers);
- the checks used to verify the information you give should be explained to you;
- if you are asked to provide sensitive personal information, the employer should explain how that information will be used. Sensitive personal information may refer to racial or ethnic origin, political opinions, religious beliefs, trade union membership, physical or mental health, sexual life, and offences committed or alleged to have been committed;
- a secure method of transmission of your application should be in place.

 Your Rights

1 Not to be discriminated against on grounds of sex, marital status, race, religion or belief, sexual orientation or disability. Age will be included in this list in 2006.
2 To request reasonable adjustments to the application process to accommodate you in the event that you have a disability.

Interviews and tests

The interview remains one of the most commonly used selection methods, but ability (or aptitude) tests and personality questionnaires are also widely used. A survey by the Institute of Personnel and Development on recruitment methods found that around half the companies it interviewed used ability tests, a third used personality tests, and two per cent said they used graphology – analysing candidates' writing!

It is perfectly legal to test potential recruits but any test must not be discriminatory unless it can be objectively justified. In one case job applicants had to pass a 15-minute test written in English. This could not be objectively justified as the job was catering for a major airline and so a high level of English proficiency was not necessary for the duties of the job. The effect of the test was to exclude applicants of a different race who had not been raised or educated in the UK.

Again there is no law to say how interviews should be conducted, but you do have a number of rights when at interviews and these include not being discriminated against because of your sex, marital status, race, religion, sexual orientation or disability.

There is often a further complication: when you apply for a job within the company you already work for, your boss or colleagues may be assessing your application. All the more reason to know your rights.

 What if . . .

- A job applicant with a good deal of experience is interviewed for the post of a butcher's assistant. At the interview, the shop manager makes it clear that he had no intention of employing a woman. When she calls later, she is told that the position was filled. She complains of sex discrimination.
  Outcome: In a similar case the job applicant won her claim. The shop manager had been discriminatory.
- An Indian is asked at an interview for the post of laboratory technician if he would have any trouble supervising a white workforce. He does not get the job. He later discovers a similar job being advertised and is discouraged from applying. He claims race discrimination.
  Outcome: In a similar case the job applicant won his claim. An inference was drawn from the remarks at interview that the applicant's colour was taken into account in rejecting him.
- A woman who suffers from photosensitive epilepsy that was being controlled by medication applies for a job. She mentions this on her CV. She is not contacted about any arrangements for the interview, but arrives at the interview with sunglasses around her neck. The room had bright fluorescent lighting and she comments on this, remarking that she might be disadvantaged. During the interview she does not use the sunglasses and does not tell the interviewer that she feels unwell. She fails to get the job. She then complains that the interviewer failed to make a reasonable adjustment to accommodate her disability by changing the lighting in the room and had therefore subjected her to disability discrimination.

Outcome: In a similar case the job applicant's claim failed. She had not been unlawfully discriminated against on the grounds of her disability as a result of a failure to make a reasonable adjustment to the physical features of the premises. The condition was rare and no reasonable employer could be expected to know without being told that the lighting would cause her a substantial disadvantage. In any event the interviewers were led to believe that she brought her sunglasses in case she needed them.

 ## Key Questions

Do I have the right to time off to go to an interview?
No, there is no general right to take time off to attend an interview unless you are under notice of redundancy (*see* Chapter 8: Rest Breaks and Time Off).

What rights do I have at interview?
You have the right not to be discriminated against on grounds of sex, marital status, race, religion, sexual orientation or disability in the arrangements made to determine who should be selected. This means, for example, that if you are disabled and have special needs with regard to an interview, these should be accommodated if it is reasonable and practical to do so. For example, if an applicant is deaf or hard of hearing somebody should be on hand to interpret sign language if necessary.

Is it legal to ask my age and marital status?
Yes. But you may be able to argue that the question was evidence of an intention to discriminate. Presently only discrimination relating to your sex, race, religion, sexual orientation, marital status or disability is prohibited by law. Although there is an age discrimination code of practice there is, presently, no direct protection against age discrimination. New law prohibiting such discrimination is due to come into force in 2006 (*see* Chapter 14).

Can I be asked if I'm pregnant or have a child in an interview?
You should only be asked questions that are relevant to your job. There is no rule against you being asked such questions but employers who do so are potentially laying themselves open to a discrimination claim if, after asking such questions, you are not offered the job.

Do I have to reveal my current salary?

There is no strict obligation on you to reveal your current salary, although your prospective employer may view you as being uncooperative if you refuse. You may wish to give a ballpark figure including benefits, or hold off the answer until a later stage in the process if this question bothers you.

What if I have a criminal record?

If you have a criminal record that is spent, you do not need to disclose it (although there are certain exceptions to this rule). This does not apply if your criminal record is not spent and, if asked, you are required to disclose it.

Are the rules different if I am an internal applicant?

The rules should not be different if you are an internal candidate, although the interview can be less formal as you already know more about the company than an external candidate.

I felt the interview was unfair and unnecessarily confrontational. What are my rights?

Just feeling the interviewer was aggressive or tough on you does not give rise to any claim: testing interviews may reveal more about you as a potential employee. You can only take action if you feel you have been discriminated against.

Who keeps a record of what went on – should a representative of Human Resources (HR) always be there?

Your interviewer should keep notes of the interview. Procedures vary a lot from one organization to the next. Some require HR to be there while others do not, or have inadequate HR resources to do this. If there is a dispute notes could be vital – you should keep your own record of the interview.

Should the interviewer reimburse my costs for attending an interview?

There is no requirement for them to do so.

Your Rights

1 Not to be discriminated against on grounds of race, sex, marital status, religion, sexual orientation or disability. Age will also be protected in 2006.
2 To have a reasonable adjustment made to the interview arrangements if you are disabled.

References

Most employers will ask for a reference before offering you a job. A reference is a means of getting evidence from an employer, school or college about your character, as well as an opinion about your capability to do a job. Employers often request a reference before taking you on, and job offers are usually conditional on a satisfactory reference being supplied. In an increasingly competitive job market your reference can make all the difference between getting a job and being passed over for it.

Legally, your employer does not in most cases have to provide a reference but if one is provided then it must be true, accurate, fair and not misleading. Failure to take reasonable care in writing a reference could lead you to lose a job and you could sue the employer for damages. In practice almost all employers provide references, and most will even write a basic factual reference for those dismissed for under-performance or misconduct. (For more on this *see* Chapter 6.)

 Contact Points

Commission for Racial Equality
Address: Elliot House, 10–12 Allington Street, London SW1E 5EH
Telephone: 020 7828 7022 **Customer service line:** 020 7932 5214
Website: www.cre.gov.uk

Disability Rights Commission – has offices in London, Manchester, Cardiff and Edinburgh
Helpline: 08457 622 633 **Textphone:** 08457 622 644

Address: 7th Floor, 222 Grays Inn Road, London WC1X 8HL
Telephone: 020 7211 4110 **Minicom:** 020 7211 4037
Website: www.drc-gb.org

Equal Opportunities Commission
Address: Arndale House, Arndale Centre, Manchester M4 3EQ
Telephone: 0161 833 9244
Scotland: St Stephens House, 279 Bath Street, Glasgow G2 4JL
Telephone: 0141 248 5833
Wales: Windsor House, Windsor Place, Cardiff CF10 3GE
Telephone: 029 2 0343552
Website: www.eoc.org.uk

Equality Commission (N Ireland)
Address: Andras House, 60 Great Victoria Street, Belfast BT2 7BB
Telephone: 028 90 500 600
Website: www.equalityni.org

National Association for the Care and Resettlement of Offenders (NACRO)
Address: 169 Clapham Road, London SW9 0PU
Telephone: 020 7582 6500
Website: www.nacro.org.uk

 What next . . .

If you need advice on applying for a job, the first thing you should do is note the tactics and tips every worker and employer should know in Chapter 2. If you need to take things further *see* Part 5: Taking things further. Details of other organizations that can assist you and further information are in Appendix B: Contact points.

5

Job offers

Congratulations! The phone goes, a letter drops through the box or your boss calls you in – you've been offered the job. After the initial celebration the practicalities suddenly come upon you thick and fast – whether to accept, how to negotiate pay and other terms and conditions, when to start . . .

Whether you have been headhunted or have applied for a job, once an offer has been made and you have accepted, a basic contract exists between you and your new employer even if you have nothing in writing. If the offer is withdrawn, which is not unknown (or you change your mind), this could amount to breach of contract and you could claim for damages.

In practice it is far better that you get an offer in writing because, if it comes to a dispute, it will only be your word against the prospective employer's. As the Hollywood mogul Sam Goldwyn put it 'a verbal agreement isn't worth the paper it is written on'! So make it a rule that you should not resign from your existing job until you have the offer in writing. Once you have the offer take time to look at the terms and conditions and contract details before accepting, and take legal advice if you are unclear. There are many clauses that could be helpful for you, or cause you problems (*see* Chapter 7 for details of the standard terms in a contract).

Some job offers are made subject to conditions such as passing a medical or providing satisfactory references, and employers are well within their rights to make such job offers conditional. The best advice is not to resign from your current job until your employer confirms you have satisfied these conditions, although in reality it may not always be possible.

Before resigning from your current job you should be sure there are no post-termination restrictions in your contract of employment preventing you from working with your prospective new employer. Although rare such restrictions are contained in restrictive covenants, and can legally prevent you working with the new employer for a period of time. This is covered in more detail in Chapter 7.

..? What if . . .

- You are offered a job and hand in your notice with your current employer after signing a copy of the offer letter. The company then phone you to say that due to a mix-up they are unable to take you on.

  Outcome: You have the right to claim breach of contract or wrongful dismissal but your damages claim will be limited to what you would have earned during your notice period. If the reason for your offer being retracted is on account of your sex, race, religion, sexual orientation or disability, you may also have a discrimination claim against the prospective employer.

- You have been offered a job and would like to start straight away. However, you have a two-month notice period and your current employer has not agreed to let you go early.

  Outcome: If you refuse to work your notice and just leave earlier then you are in breach of contract and could be taken to court. However, this is unlikely unless your early departure causes serious loss to your employer's business. Otherwise the main thing you risk is a bad reputation.

- You are offered a job, but when you start the terms and conditions are not as promised and the job itself is not as described.

  Outcome: The first thing to check is whether you were made this offer in writing or whether the agreement was reached orally. If it was oral, you should immediately write down everything you remember about what you were told, including the date on which the agreement was reached – don't just rely on your recollection because if you do need to go to court to establish what terms were agreed, this would be much stronger evidence than just your recollection at a hearing which may be months away. You should then raise your concerns with your employer – preferably in writing or both orally and confirmed in writing. Again – to protect yourself if you do need to go to court – it is much stronger evidence to have your concerns documented in writing and tribunal chairmen and judges love it! If you are still denied the terms agreed, you could take your employer to court, but make sure you have good evidence of what was agreed otherwise it will just be one person's word against another's.

Probationary periods

So you've got the job and have started work and been placed on what your contract refers to as a probationary period. The main purpose of this is to give both you and your employer the opportunity to 'test the waters' and see if you both feel you are suitable for each other. It does not affect your statutory rights concerning discrimination and unfair dismissal.

During the probationary period there is normally a shorter notice period of, for example, one week so that the relationship can be brought to a speedy end if things do not work out. Benefits such as pensions and bonuses can also be withheld during the probationary period.

To mark the end of a probationary period, employers normally hold a review meeting or appraisal, after which your appointment is confirmed or terminated. However, in many cases, time pressure and inefficiency can mean that it is postponed to a later date or not held at all. Your boss or line manager should confirm whether you have satisfactorily completed your probationary period. The measure of your performance would depend on the nature of your job – there are no official yardsticks.

Probationary periods can be extended and it is not uncommon for this to happen. If this happens to you, you should ask for the reasons why so that you are able to address your employer's concerns. Employers commonly have difficulty in telling their workers where they are falling short of the required standard, but it is better all round for everyone to be open about such things. If your boss is not a good communicator, it may pay to help him or her out in such discussions by asking questions about your performance and any concerns you may have. It is better to know than to be unexpectedly dismissed for failing your probationary period.

Remember, if a dispute arises and you do not agree with the assessment provided by your boss, you can use the grievance procedure to raise your concerns.

 Key Questions

How long do I have to decide whether to accept a job offer?
There are no set rules, although a couple of weeks is generally reasonable. In some cases the employer may have special reasons for needing a quick decision but, usually, if an employer is keen to employ you they will be prepared to be flexible.

What if I change my mind and decide not to accept?

If you change your mind, there is usually little that a prospective employer can do. If you have accepted a job offer and then change your mind, there is a potential breach of contract but it is extremely unlikely that the employer has suffered any loss by your subsequent change of heart. Remember your own reputation though – people gossip about such things.

What if the offer is subject to certain conditions, such as references, exam results or passing a medical?

As long as the offer is not conditional on something unlawful or discriminatory, it can be made subject to particular conditions such as satisfactory references or particular exam results.

Can the offer be withdrawn because of a bad reference?

Yes, but you may have a claim if this happens (*see* Chapter 6).

Do I need proof of the right to work in the UK, such as work permits, etc.?

All employers are required to carry out certain checks as part of the recruitment process. This usually consists of obtaining a document with your national insurance number on it in order to verify your status. If you are from overseas, your offer may be subject to proof of your right to work in the UK.

What are my rights to negotiate the terms of the offer?

You are fully entitled to try to negotiate better terms, although the terms of many jobs will be largely non-negotiable and you may be graded by the prospective employer in accordance with the amount of experience you have. In other cases negotiation over salary, bonus, hours or holiday may be expected.

How should I accept a job offer – in writing?

There are no set rules, you can accept on the phone, in person or in writing. Confirmation in writing is more certain and professional and serves as a record of when you formally accepted and what you accepted.

Should I be offered a contract or a written statement of my employment terms?

You will normally be sent an offer letter setting out some of the main terms and conditions, although some organizations do also send out the contract of employment at this stage. There is no requirement for you to be shown the full contract although you have the right to ask about the terms and conditions that apply if you accept the offer. Many companies provide you with an offer letter and contract to sign at the same time.

What if I need adjustments because I'm disabled?

This is likely to have been raised and discussed at the application and interview stage if your condition affects your job. If adjustments are needed, details of them may be discussed and agreed at the interview and offer stage of the recruitment process. Again, however, there are no rules and much will depend on the nature of your disability, and it may be that an offer is made on the condition that the necessary adjustments can be made and are reasonable (*see* Chapter 14: Disability discrimination).

What if I'm bound by a restrictive covenant?

If you are bound by a restrictive covenant from working for the organization that has offered you the job for a set period you may be in breach of contract if you take up the job. This means your old employer could take you to court and get an injunction to stop you from working for the competitor, in addition to claiming damages from you. But before you get to this stage check that the covenant is well drafted and legally enforceable. Such litigation is expensive and uncertain, and your employer would not take such action unless there was a real chance of winning.

If you are facing this situation, remember that you can always negotiate with your current employer.

Does the disciplinary procedure apply during the probationary period?

Some organizations do not exclude contractual disciplinary procedures during the probationary period. If they apply but your employer does not use them, you could have an automatic unfair dismissal claim if you have more than one year's service. It could also increase your claim for damages as you could argue that if the procedure had been followed it would have taken at least that long to run its course. This is a claim that can be added to any dismissal where the stages of a contractual disciplinary or capability procedure are not followed.

What if I already work for the company?

A similar process may apply to you as applies to external candidates. But internal offers are different as you may have a number of employment rights with the organization already. This means that the clock does not start from zero in your new job within the same company – on day one of the new job you may have two years continuous service, for example.

As a number of employment rights are linked to your length of service, and some contractual benefits may also be, this often puts you in a stronger position than if you change employers.

 ## Your Rights

1 Not to be denied an offer of employment on grounds of sex, race, religion, sexual orientation, marital status or disability.
2 To take action if an offer is retracted.
3 To the benefit of the terms and conditions contained in the contract of employment if the offer has been made and accepted.

 ## Tactics and Tips

Get the offer in writing
This is key and you should always try to do this.

Verbal offers
If the offer was made verbally note down the details and ask for it to be confirmed in writing as soon as possible. If you get nothing in writing consider writing a letter setting out your understanding of the position, as this will be evidence of what was agreed if you do enter into a dispute.

Take time
Take time to make up your mind. Changing jobs is a big step and when an employer wants you they generally want you to sign up and start straight away. There is no need to succumb to artificial pressure to accept before you are sure.

Get legal advice if you are unsure
If you are unsure about your rights or the terms of your contract get legal advice before signing up. Remember it is too late if you leave it until after you sign up as you will have lost your negotiating position.

Negotiate if appropriate

You can negotiate your terms and conditions. Try and establish what others doing the same job are paid, and what their other terms and conditions are.

Queries and your negotiating position

Raise any queries or doubts at the outset before you sign a contract – or it may be too late and you could be stuck with unattractive terms. For example, it may be that you are being asked to sign a restrictive covenant that is too extreme in your view. At the point of you being offered a job, your prospective employer often holds the balance of power in any negotiation. For this reason it is often at this stage that employers will try to get the best deal for themselves and, for example, get you to agree restrictive terms. If you think your prospective employer is 'trying it on', now is the time to raise queries and stand your ground – otherwise you'll be stuck with the terms you agreed.

Making a claim if your offer is retracted

Remember, you may have only three months from the date of your dismissal in which to lodge a claim at employment tribunal for wrongful dismissal or breach of contract although this deadline may be extended in certain situations. You have longer if you bring the claim at the High Court or county court but, in most cases, the tribunal is the preferable venue. However, you should always consider negotiating with the company first. This may help resolve the problem – and the chances are the organization will be prepared to pay up for messing you around.

→ **What next . . .**

If you need advice on job offers, the first thing you should do is ensure that you understand work–life realities and are aware of the tactics and tips every worker and employer should know in Chapter 2. If you need to take further action *see* Part 5: Taking things further. Details of organizations that can assist you and further information are in Appendix B: Contact points.

6

References

A reference can make or break your career

Your career may depend upon them, you may lose your job because they are inaccurate, or you may have to be someone else's referee, yet despite years of reference writing there is no set way in which references should be compiled.

A reference is a means of getting evidence from an employer, school or college about your character, as well as an opinion about your capability to do a job. Employers often request a reference before taking on an employee, and job offers are usually on condition that satisfactory references are supplied. In an increasingly competitive job market a good reference can make all the difference between getting a job and losing it.

Legally employers do not have to provide a reference but there are possible risks if an employer refuses to provide one. Where a reference is provided then it must be true, accurate and fair and not misleading. Failure to take reasonable care in writing a reference could lead to loss of a job and an employer being sued for damages. In practice almost all employers provide references, and most will even write a basic factual reference for those employees dismissed for under-performance or misconduct.

In terms of format references can go from being basic factual statements listing start and end dates and job titles to glorious paeans of praise.

...? What if . . .

- An estate agent that also sells financial products (e.g. mortgages) is asked to provide a reference in relation to one of their sales managers. The reference, which was based on written statements by various people in his former company, said he was seen by some of the sales staff as a person who consistently kept the best leads for himself, and that he had little regard for the team that he was meant to manage. It also said that he was a man of little or no integrity and could not be regarded as honest. The sales manager is not hired and he also then fails to secure appointments with two other companies as a result of the reference. He brings a claim for negligence and loss of earnings.

Outcome: In a case along the same lines, parts of the reference were found to have been prepared negligently. Some of the comments had not been substantiated and, when analysed in further detail by the court, were found to be without foundation. The sales manager was entitled to a careful and accurate assessment of his qualities; his reference simply repeated comments made by colleagues without checking that they could be substantiated. It may well have been the case that the employer honestly believed what the other workers said, but there was very little to justify some of the comments. An employer who provides a reference owes a duty of care to the employee in the preparation of the reference, and may be liable for damages for loss suffered as a result of negligence. In this case the sales manager won damages for the losses he had suffered.

- A bank receives a number of complaints from customers about a savings and investments advisor, alleging she had given misleading or inadequate information. During internal bank investigations some of these complaints are upheld and others rejected. It was the practice of the bank not to inform employees of all complaints or ask for comments in all cases, and except in two instances, she was unaware that such complaints had ever been made against her. When the advisor gets another job her prospective employers approach the bank for a reference. The reference provided contained no assessment of her character or ability but was confined to a factual statement that 17 complaints had been made against her. When the prospective employer decides not to employ her she becomes aware of the other complaints and is shocked that she had never been notified of them. She sues them for constructive dismissal.

Outcome: In a similar case an employee won such a claim. The bank was in breach of trust and confidence in providing the reference because it mentioned complaints that she was unaware of, and because it was misleading and potentially destructive to her career in the financial services industry.

- A woman brings a sex discrimination claim against her employer alleging that she has been dismissed because she was pregnant. This complaint was settled out of court. Her employer then fails to provide a reference for her when requested by an employment agency. She brings a claim on the basis that withholding a reference amounts to her being victimized because of her previous complaint.

Outcome: In a similar case the employee won her claim. Her former employer's failure to provide a reference was a retaliatory measure because of her complaint of sex discrimination and was a form of victimization. But beware, in a recent case, the former employer was able to prove that the discrimination complaint was not the reason for failing to provide a reference. The employee in that case had not been victimized.

 ## Key Questions

Do I have the right to see my reference?

You have the right to make a 'subject access request' under the Data Protection Act for a reference held by your current employer but supplied by a third party. You cannot however get a copy of a reference produced by your current employer – although there is nothing to stop you requesting it from your new employer after you have left. The Human Rights Act also has some bearing on this area; while an employer has the right to compile professional and personal data on employees, any unreasonable disclosure of personal information in a reference could amount to interfering with an employee's right to respect for private life.

What if my employer refuses to provide a reference?

While there is no general legal obligation to provide a reference, if an employer fails to do so because you have brought, or could have brought, a discrimination claim, then the failure may entitle you to a victimization claim (*see* Chapter 14: Discrimination and the case study above).

What points should a reference cover?

A detailed reference should cover your length of service, the position you held, your ability and competence, honesty, timekeeping, the reason for your leaving, and any other achievements or problems specific to you.

What format should a reference take?

There is no legally prescribed format for a reference. Some regulatory bodies do however require a certain format – particularly in the financial services industry.

Can my prospective employer insist on a reference?

Yes, they can. In some cases a job offer is conditional on the provision of satisfactory references.

What if my boss gives me a really bad reference and, as a result, my job offer is retracted?

If you suffer a loss as a result of an inaccurate, untruthful or unfair reference you may be in a position to bring a claim against your employer (*see* case studies above).

What if an employer gives an unrealistically good reference to get rid of an employee?

Unrealistically good references rarely pose any problems for an employer. However, if the reference is misleading then the prospective employer may have a claim against the provider of the reference. For example, if a reference says that an employee is honest and trustworthy, but in fact the employee was dismissed for theft, then the new employer could bring a claim for any losses arising from the negligent reference.

Are there any rules about who I can choose as a referee?

No, although your prospective employer may specify who your referee should be, or what sort of position the referee should hold.

 Your Rights

1 Your reference should be true, accurate, fair and not misleading.
2 You should not be denied a reference as a retaliatory measure because of a discrimination complaint or claim against your employer.

Tactics and Tips

Who you ask for a reference
Remember you can usually ask who you like within your organization for a reference. You may wish to ask a manager who you get on particularly well with rather than your actual line manager, although there may be company rules specifying the internal procedure for providing references. You may also need a personal referee. Many people just put 'references provided on request' on the bottom of their CVs rather than giving the names of referees when they first apply.

Agree wording
It is possible to agree the wording of a reference with an employer in certain circumstances. Depending on the circumstances, including the reason for leaving, it may be better to agree the wording of the reference before you leave.

Factual reference
In some cases an employer is only prepared to provide a basic factual reference (i.e. start date, leave date and job title). If you are concerned about the kind of reference you may get, you could actually ask your employer for this type of basic reference rather than a more detailed one.

Compromise agreements and settlements
A reference is sometimes agreed as part of a settlement and can be an important part of a deal. Employees who bring a claim at employment tribunal may also be prepared to settle by agreeing the wording of a reference as part of the settlement deal.

What next . . .

If you need advice on references, the first thing you should do is get ahead of the game and take advantage of the tactics and tips every employer and worker should know in Chapter 2. If you need to take things further *see* Part 5: Taking things further. Details of organizations that can assist you and further information are in Appendix B: Contact points.

Your contract

This contract is so one-sided that I am surprised to find it written on both sides of the paper
Lord Evershed, quoted in Lord Denning, *Closing Chapter*

As probably the most important document in your working life, it is essential that you know at least the basics about your contract of employment and what it means.

A contract sets out the terms and conditions upon which you are employed, listing the majority of obligations and rights of both employee and employer. These terms are often negotiable but, once agreed and accepted, the contract is binding on both parties. In some cases, such as if an agreement is based on a verbal exchange, the very act of starting work signals that you accept the terms and conditions offered, and a contract is effectively entered into.

Employers are not actually required to issue a written contract, and many people still do not have one.

Employers must, however, provide some details in writing within two months of an employee starting work. This statement of particulars is commonly referred to as a 'Section 1' statement – after section 1 of the Employment Rights Act, which includes this right. (*See* below for a detailed summary.)

It is particularly important to be aware of this as hundreds of thousands of people report serious problems with employers over their contracts, terms and conditions at work each year. Over 40 per cent of all employment problems reported to Citizens Advice Bureaux in a particular year were to do with poor terms and conditions, with some employees even having problems getting any sort of proper statement from their employers.

Your status

The phrase *contract of employment* describes your status as an employee, as opposed to that of being self-employed, or any other type of worker. This distinction is important, as only employees are entitled to certain protection and rights – such as maternity rights and compensation in the event of an unfair dismissal.

For more on the vexed issue of how to define your status see Chapter 3.

How a contract works

An employer is free to employ whoever it wants, as long as that person has not been hired as a result of an unlawful discriminatory recruitment decision or process, and the employer abides by the legal obligations relating to taking on overseas workers.

A valid contract that is legally enforceable requires an offer of employment, acceptance of that offer, an intention to enter a legal relationship and something of value to pass between the parties (called consideration). In the case of an employment contract, wages pass from an employer to an employee in exchange for the employee carrying out the work, making the contract legally binding.

Employees are entitled to a raft of rights that derive from two main sources: their contract, although not all the rights may be actually set out in writing in the contract, and the statutory rights laid down by the law.

In some instances there is a more complicated interplay between the two. For example, your employer may decide at what level to set your pay and this may be set out in your contract. But the law, through the National Minimum Wage Act says that your pay cannot be set below a minimum level. If your contract sets your wages at less than the minimum level this part of your contract will automatically become void (*see* Chapter 13). You would then have a claim against your employer for the difference between the legal minimum and your contractual wage. In the same way the law gives you the right to a legal minimum notice period – the notice in your contract must either be equal to or greater than this legal minimum (*see* Chapter 22: Notice periods).

Terms and conditions

As confusing as it may sound there are some terms in a contract that apply whether you are aware of them or not, and irrespective of whether they are actually written into the contract.

The main categories of contract terms are:

1 *Express terms*: those specifically agreed between employer and employee. If a contract is in writing, express terms are generally the written terms.

2 *Implied terms*: these are not specifically stated but are, nevertheless, deemed to be part of the contract. They include an obligation on employers to provide a safe working environment, and on you to *serve your employer faithfully* and not act against the interest of your employer's business – like competing with them in your own time. Both employer and employee are also bound by a duty of *mutual trust and confidence*, which means that neither must do anything that would destroy the trust or confidence of the other. This could happen if your boss was very abusive towards you, for example. Implied terms also commonly arise from *custom and practice*, whereby if a practice has been consistently adopted it may be regarded as a legal right. For example, if everybody in your firm gets a Christmas bonus of £500, and this has been the case for years, this has probably become a right by custom and practice.

3 *Incorporated terms*: those that are referred to in the contract but can be found in more detail in another document – such as the staff handbook. So, for example, there may be a company redundancy policy within your company that is set out in the staff handbook. Your contract may say that further terms relating to your employment are contained in the staff handbook. In stating this the redundancy policy is incorporated into your contract of employment.

4 *Statutory terms*: those that derive from the law. For example, as a result of the Equal Pay Act, a term specifying equality of pay for men and women for doing the same work exists in every contract of employment.

Section 1 statements

Your employer must give you a written statement containing the following details, within two months of your starting work:

• the *name* of your employer – your name should also be on the document;

- the *date* when your employment began;
- any period of previous employment which is regarded as *continuous* with your present employment. This applies if you have, for example, taken a new job internally within your company – the time you spent in your old job counts towards your length of service;
- your *pay* and the intervals at which it is to be paid;
- your *hours* of work;
- your *holiday* entitlement;
- your entitlement to *sick leave* and *sick pay*;
- any *pension* schemes that you can join and to which you can contribute;
- your entitlement to *notice* of termination, and the notice you must give if you leave;
- your job *title*;
- if your employment is not permanent, the *period of your employment* or, if it is for a fixed term, *the date when it is to end*;
- either the *place of work* or, if you are required or allowed to work in more than one location, this should be stated as well as the employer's address;
- details of the existence of any relevant *collective agreements* which directly affect your terms and conditions.

If you normally work in the UK but are required to work abroad for more than one month at any time, this fact should be stated and other relevant particulars relating to working abroad such as:

- the *period* for which your employment abroad is to last;
- the *currency* in which you are to be paid;
- any *additional pay* or *benefits* you may get;
- terms relating to your *return to the UK*.

If there are no relevant particulars under the above categories, this should be stated – so, for example, your statement may say there is no pension entitlement applicable to your employment.

The Section 1 statement must also say where you can get hold of your employer's *disciplinary procedures*, who to turn to if you are unhappy with a disciplinary decision (which should be in the procedure), and also details of the company's grievance procedure.

You have the right to take action at employment tribunal if your employer does not provide you with a statement listing the above and the remedy is a declaration of what your particulars of employment are and may also include an award of two or four weeks' pay.

...? What if . . .

- A company changed its sickness policy without consultation and one of its employees has challenged it as a breach of contract.

  Outcome: In a similar case the policy could be varied without the consent of the employees, because it was only a statement of practice, not a contractual term.

- A waiter is dismissed and paid one month's notice by the restaurant he works for. He is told by the manager that he is getting what he is legally entitled to, and it satisfies the statutory minimum. However, his contract says he is entitled to two months' notice pay and so he brings a wrongful dismissal claim for the outstanding month's pay.

  Outcome: He will be entitled to the outstanding one month's pay.

- A secretary had worked for her employer for over 10 years. In that time she was aware that every time someone was made redundant they would be paid two months' salary on top of the normal statutory redundancy entitlement. In fact she even had to write some of the letters, all of which stated the usual practice of paying two months' extra money. When the secretary was told she was to be made redundant as her department was closing down she learnt that she would get statutory redundancy with no mention of any other payment.

  Outcome: As it has been normal company practice over a number of years to pay an extra two months' pay to staff being made redundant, this is likely to have become a term implied into her contract by custom and practice. She should therefore raise her entitlement with her employer and if they do not agree to pay, she could bring a claim of breach of contract against her employer at employment tribunal. As part of her claim she will have to prove that there has been an established practice of making this payment on redundancy over the years.

- A banker was generating so much money (say over £23 million in the relevant timeframe) for his bank that he was referred to as a profit machine. However, he was dismissed for reasons including erratic timekeeping and inappropriate dress. He was denied a significant bonus as his employer said that the bonus was payable at their discretion under his contract. Previously, bonus payments were not discretionary and were calculated by reference to a formula. This change took place after he joined but verbal assurances were given that the change would not impact on the bonuses and that the formula that had been previously applied would be used. The employee brings a breach of contract claim against his employer.

Outcome: In a similar case, the bonus was stated to be discretionary under the employee's contract of employment, but calculations were also based on a formula for which performance was a criterion. The court held that a reasonable employer would not have exercised their discretion so as to deprive the employee of a bonus. It was irrational and perverse that he did not get a bonus and the bank clearly abused the exercise of its discretion. The employee was awarded £1.35 million.

Changes to your contract

Your contract is legally binding and there should be agreement between you and your employer before any changes are made. However, in practice changes are often made. Some contract changes occur without being thought of as changes generally because they are positive – such as, for example, when we get a pay rise.

Agreed changes

If your employer wishes to change your contract the best way is to get your consent. Sometimes changes may take place through a union or collective agreement. But what if you cannot reach agreement?

There are two main ways in which your contract may be changed without your agreement and are detailed below.

Changes imposed on you

Your employer may simply impose significant changes upon you without warning or reason. The action you can then take depends in part on the changes being imposed. You are likely to have a number of claims against your employer including breach of contract and unfair dismissal but, beware, in most cases if you do not take action against your employer quite quickly and continue to work under the changed terms, the court may deem you to have accepted the changes by your actions or lack of objection.

Fired and hired: lawful changes – like it or not

Alternatively, your employer could consult with you and if you refuse to accept the changes they could terminate your contract (by serving the required notice as set out in your contract) and then offer you a new contract with the changed terms. There is no breach of contract here but there is a dismissal – and re-engagement. The dismissal could give you the right to claim unfair dismissal but the employer may be able to show it was a fair dismissal if they had good sound business reasons for the changes to your terms and followed a fair procedure. The example below illustrates this legal approach to changing your terms and conditions.

 Mini Case Study

A company had to change employee terms and conditions due to financial problems. The company followed a fair procedure consulting with the affected employees and explaining the business reasons behind the changes. It offered the employees a new contract with the changed terms. Some agreed to the new contracts but others objected and refused. Those who did not agree to the changes had their old contracts terminated with notice and were formally offered the new contracts. Their failure to accept meant that they were dismissed. They claimed unfair dismissal against their employer at employment tribunal. The tribunal held that the dismissals were unfair as the company's financial difficulties were not so severe that they were about to go under. The company appealed.

Outcome

The decision was reversed on appeal and the court found the dismissals to be fair. It emphasized that there had been consultation and a fair procedure. The court also remarked that the motives of the employer should be considered to establish whether it has sound business reasons for making the changes – a fundamental requirement. The ruling also stated that a company could fairly dismiss employees for good business reasons if the employees refuse to accept new terms even if the new terms are not vital to the survival of the business. In addition, the union had recommended the proposed changes and most of the employees had accepted them.

Key Questions

Should I get a written contract before I start work?
There is no requirement in law for you to get a written contract before you start work, or ever. There is an obligation for your employer to provide you with a Section 1 statement within two months of you starting work. This applies no matter what sort of employee you are – whether fixed-term worker, agency worker or any other category. This is not a contract of employment, but a statement of particulars of your contractual rights.

What if my employer refuses to give me a Section 1 statement of particulars?
You can make a complaint to employment tribunal if your employer does not give you a statement of particulars. The tribunal will make a declaration as to the terms that should have been given and you may be entitled to compensation. You have to have been employed for more than two months before you can make this claim.

If I am not given a contract what should I do?
First of all you can simply request one. It may just be an administrative slip-up. If you still do not receive one – you can make a written request for a statement of particulars, which sets out details of your contractual rights. If this is not provided to you within two months of starting work, you can make a claim to tribunal to receive this statement and compensation, and your employer would then be obliged to provide you with it.

What if my employer has reneged on what we verbally agreed?
If a term has been agreed between you and your employer, but your employer reneges, you can take legal action. However, you should explore all possible alternative routes to resolve your differences before going to court. Ultimately, it is likely to be a question of who is believed and that will depend on who has the best evidence. So you should always document and date what you understood to have been agreed, preferably as close as possible to the time the agreement is reached, and also confirm your understanding of such verbal agreements in writing.

What if there is a dispute about what is 'custom and practice'?

It all depends on the evidence available. It is not uncommon for a dispute to arise based on whether a certain custom and practice exists and whether it has been consistently applied over a long period so as to become a contractual term. If no agreement can be reached as to whether a term does exist, then the matter would need to be tested in court.

What about changes to my contract – can they be made without my consent?

An employer may impose significant changes upon you and if you do not take action against the changes you may find that you are deemed to have accepted the changes by your lack of action. In addition to this, it is possible for an employer to make changes to your contract by dismissing you and re-engaging you, offering the new terms within the new contract of employment. *See* the mini case study above.

What are my rights to negotiate changes to my contract?

You are always able to attempt to negotiate your terms and conditions, though it can be a case of who has the best bargaining position. Remember that agreement needs to be reached, and if it isn't then there is little you can do about it.

What if my contract entitles me to four weeks' notice of dismissal but I am dismissed without receiving it or getting the opportunity to work the four-week period?

Every employee has the right to be given notice of the fact they are being dismissed or, alternatively, paid in lieu of the notice they should have got (*see* Chapter 22: Notice periods). As it is a contractual right, being dismissed without notice can be a breach of contract. A dismissal without being paid or being allowed to work your notice is called a *wrongful* dismissal. You can bring a wrongful dismissal claim (which effectively means you are claiming notice pay due to you) at employment tribunal but be aware that the maximum amount that you can claim at employment tribunal is £25,000. So if your claim exceeds this you will need to bring your claim at the county court or High Court. You are not entitled to notice pay if you are dismissed for gross misconduct (*see* Chapter 22: Misconduct).

Can my contract still have any bearing on me even after I have left?
Yes, terms such as restrictive covenants and confidentiality continue to have an effect (*see* pp. 261–3).

Illegal contracts and unenforceable terms

Did you know that a contract which is tainted with illegality cannot be relied upon for wrongful or unfair dismissal claims? Put simply, the law will not help if you are yourself flouting it. In the same way if a contract is for an illegal purpose it is unenforceable and you cannot therefore bring a claim to employment tribunal. And the same applies if you are a foreign employee working illegally because you do not have a work permit. So if you have agreed to take cash wages so as not to pay tax, you are defrauding the Inland Revenue and, unless you were unaware of the illegality or were not in a position to do anything about it (in which case your employer is at fault), you would have no rights for the protection of your employment at employment tribunal. This may mean you cannot claim unfair dismissal.

There are also terms that may not be enforceable – not because they are illegal but because they are contrary to the law. An example would be a term which is contrary to the sex or race discrimination legislation, such as one, for example, that says women are entitled to 25 days' holiday but men to only 20 days.

 Your Rights

1 To receive a Section 1 statement within two months of starting work.
2 To assume you have a legal contract based on a verbal agreement if there is nothing in writing.
3 To regard contract terms as void if they deny you the minimum legal rights to which you are entitled.
4 To take your employer to court for breach of contract or wrongfully dismissing you.
5 To take your employer to court if your contract is changed without good business reasons and/or in the absence of a fair procedure.

Tactics and Tips

Negotiations
Remember that it is possible for the terms of your contract to be negotiated as it is essentially an agreement between you and your employer.

Missing terms or entitlements less than legal minimums
If a term such as your right to holiday is not in the contract, you are still by law entitled to the legal minimum of 20 days per year. If there is no term – verbal or in writing – in relation to something you regularly do, remember it may become a contractual entitlement through custom and practice. So, for example, if you always take Friday afternoons off and there is nothing in writing or orally agreed to say that you shouldn't, then that practice would become a term of your contract.

Written records
You should keep a written record of all the discussions you have with your employer concerning your contract, particularly if you are not given a written contract. It would be even better if you write a letter to your employer confirming what you understand to have been agreed. This will improve your position if it becomes necessary to take the matter to employment tribunal for a statement of particulars or breach of an entitlement.

Seeking information
Be prepared to ask relevant questions and seek information about the terms of your employment. For example, you should ask for details of all the terms that apply to your employment including the disciplinary, grievance, or any other relevant procedures – if you have not already been provided with these details. If there is nothing available in writing, ask if there are any established procedures: when the same process is used over time it may become a contractual right to which you are entitled. This is known as custom and practice.

Contract changes
Remember that if a contract change is simply imposed on you without any reason being given and without consultation or proper procedure, you may have both a breach of contract and unfair dismissal claim against your employer. If you do not take any immediate action, a useful tip is to

make sure that you write to your employer objecting to the changes and reserving your rights. This is important because it could keep the avenue of legal action open to you where the courts would otherwise deem that you have accepted the changes.

Third party
In certain circumstances, a third party who gets a benefit from your employment such as your husband or wife may develop rights arising from your contract. These rights can be limited or denied if the contract is drafted to exclude them. Check the clauses of your contract if this is a concern for you.

 What next ...

If you need advice on your contract of employment or changes to it, the first thing you should do is get ahead of the game and take advantage of the tactics and tips every worker and employer should know in Chapter 2. If you need to take further steps *see* Part 5: Taking things further. Details of organizations that can assist you and further information are in Appendix B: Contact points.

Part 3: Your rights at work

8

Hours and holidays

Work expands so as to fill the time available for its completion
Parkinson's Law

Introduction

We work longer hours, an average of 43 hours a week, and have fewer holiday entitlements than many of our continental neighbours. Unlike a number of our European neighbours, we don't work a strict 35-hour week, take afternoon siestas and are, apparently, some of the last people to leave the office at night.

Still, the situation has changed for the better in the last few years, and we have Europe to thank. Before the Working Time Regulations came into force in 1998, the UK was the only country in the EU which did not give workers the right to paid holiday.

Today, along with other rights, workers have the right to four weeks' (20 working days') paid annual leave, and cannot be forced to work more than an average 48-hour working week. The main objective of this working time law is to ensure the health and safety of workers.

Although your rights look good in theory, in practice there are a large number of regional variations across Europe. Many industries and professions have secured exemptions from the legislation, and some employers simply run roughshod over this law. The National Association of Citizens Advice Bureaux emphasized this in a recent study on paid holidays, *Wish you were here*, reporting:

Thousands of working people are getting no paid holiday at all as employers use various devices and excuses to evade their legal responsibilities. Many workers face a stark choice between accepting the illegal conditions or being sacked. In most cases they are too badly paid to be able to afford to take unpaid leave and may end up working for years without a proper break.

The UK government admitted at the end of 2000 that it was disappointed the introduction of the EU working time directive had not had more of an impact on the hours many work.

However, spare a thought for workers in Japan, who, for many employers, define the work ethic – there people are known to literally work themselves to death. The term for those who do this is *karoshi*. In 2000 Japan's Supreme Court found that a company was liable for working a young employee so hard he killed himself. After 80-hour weeks and little sleep the advertising worker hanged himself. The company was found to have failed to prevent his death, and paid almost a million pounds in compensation to his family.

In the UK, the rules on working time are overly complex in some respects, with large sectors of the working population excluded. This section begins by highlighting just who is entitled to these working time rights, what they are and how you enforce them.

Workers protected

All workers (*see* Chapter 2) including freelance and agency workers are protected by the working time provisions.

However, there are a number of variations to, and exclusions from, the regulations, including those cases where workers enter individual workplace or collective agreements.

Exclusions

The main exclusions are:
- those who fall into what is known as the *unmeasured or partly unmeasured working time exemption*; this means those who decide for themselves how many hours they work (*see* Working hours below);
- *special cases* – this category includes situations where there is a need arising from a *foreseeable* surge of activity, like seasonal work, and also emergencies, or where there is a need for consistent continuity of activity. Examples of the latter include those involved with the media, agriculture, docks and airports;
- domestic workers in private households; although they are covered by the right to rest periods, breaks and annual leave;
- the genuinely self-employed;

- seafarers, those using inland waterways, and the aviation sector are covered by separate regulations;
- certain exclusions apply to mobile workers which are defined as 'any worker employed as a member of travelling or flying personnel by an undertaking which operates transport services for passengers or goods by road or air'.

Enforcement

A breach of your rights to daily and weekly time off, rest breaks and paid annual leave is a matter you could take directly to employment tribunal. Breach of working time limits is a criminal offence for which an organization can be fined. Employment tribunals, the Health and Safety Executive and local authorities enforce the regulations.

 Your Rights

1 *Weekly hours*: to work no more than 48 hours on average a week. But note this is complicated by the exact period over which your hours are averaged.
2 *Night workers*: to work no more than an average of eight hours night work in a 24-hour period. You are also entitled to free health assessments.
3 *Weekly time off*: one 24-hour period off each seven-day week.
4 *Daily time-off*: at least 11 hours off each day.
5 *Daily rest breaks*: 20 minutes off as a break if you work for six consecutive hours.
6 *Holiday*: you are entitled to four weeks' (20 working days') paid holiday per year.

Working hours

Most memorable . . . was the discovery made by all the rich men in England at once that women and children could work twenty-five hours a day without many of them dying or becoming excessively deformed. This was known as the Industrial Revelation.

W. C. Sellar and R. J. Yeatman, *1066 and all that*

Workplace conditions and the number of hours we work have long been a cause for concern and debate. In fact it was the Victorians who really began the process of tackling welfare reform, giving many workers protection and rights for the first time.

A series of Factory Acts in the nineteenth century laid down minimum acceptable working conditions in the huge textile mills, created as a result of the Industrial Revolution and, by 1850, work in these mills was limited to 10 hours a day. Other new laws targeted individual industries – the Shop Act of 1911, for example, introduced half-day early closing to protect shop assistants from exploitation.

Today, we still work the longest hours in Europe, with male full-time employees toiling an average of 45.7 hours a week and women 40.7 hours. Despite the Working Time Regulations, the long-hours culture is still very much alive. In a recent survey by the Institute of Personnel and Development many people regularly working over 48 hours a week reported mistakes at work, stress and a detrimental effect on their home lives as a result.

In comparison the French have implemented a 35-hour working week (*see* below) and many other European countries work around 40 hours a week.

At first glance your legal position is quite straightforward. All workers are entitled to limit their working hours to no more than an average of 48 hours a week, although there are some exemptions (*see* above).

What counts as working time

One of the most important questions is how working time is calculated, and what is included and excluded from the calculation. Generally, working time is taken to mean time when you are at your employer's disposal. It includes overtime, travelling time if you need to travel as part of your job, as well as training. Working lunches are included, as is any time that you spend working abroad if your employer's business is based in the UK.

If you think your working time is too high remember travel time between home and work does not count. Also excluded are lunch breaks, rest breaks, travel time outside normal working time, and non-work-related evening classes or day release courses. Any time spent on holiday, maternity leave or sick is excluded from the calculation of your working time. If a worker does not need to be present at the workplace when 'on-call' but needs to be contactable, then on-call time does not count as 'working time'.

Exemptions

There is a special category of workers who operate under an exemption called 'unmeasured or partly unmeasured working time'.

If you are a senior worker and can independently decide on your own level of working time, or alternatively an element of your working time is predetermined but you choose to work longer hours, then you may fall into this exemption.

One useful hint here – the Department of Trade and Industry have produced useful guidance on the Regulations. Although they are not required to do so, employment tribunals are likely to take account of this guidance when dealing with claims and issues.

Opting out

If you want to opt out of the Working Time Regulations, or your employer requests that you do, there is a fairly simple procedure for you to follow. This involves you signing a simple opt-out form that states that you agree to work in excess of the working time limits. Alternatively this may be included in your contract of employment.

An example of the wording of an opt-out agreement:

I agree to work any additional hours as may be necessary in order to properly carry out my duties and I agree that the limit in the Working Time Regulations shall not apply to me, and therefore my work time may exceed 48 hours on average per week.

 What if . . .

- A builder generally works a 39-hour week. His colleagues sign opt-outs so that they can work more than 48 hours on average per week. When an opportunity to do overtime arises, he is refused the chance to do it on the basis that he wasn't working the same hours as his colleagues.

He brought a claim of having suffered unfair treatment (a detriment) as he was being unfairly refused overtime.

Outcome: A claim along these lines in a similar case succeeded. This is because denying the employee the right to overtime specifically related to the fact he would not sign an opt-out. This amounts to a detriment.

• A sales representative chose to work beyond a weekly average of 48 hours per week as she wanted to earn extra commission. In such a case the Working Time Regulations do not cover her as her work pattern falls into the category known as partly unmeasured working time. She was able to independently decide how much work she was going to do and she was therefore excluded from the right to have her working hours limited.

• An employee working as a sales representative claims that she was made to work more than 48 hours on average per week. Her employers claim that she fell within the unmeasured working time exemption. She brought a claim to employment tribunal.

Outcome: In a similar case an employee succeeded as the court decided that her employer did control her work as she was required to visit a certain number of clients a day. On winning her claim she will be entitled to require her working time to be limited to 48 hours on average per week.

 Mini Case Study

France's 35-hour week

France's controversial 35-hour working week became law in 2001. Controversial, because it means employers with a workforce of over 20 have to reduce weekly hours to an average of 35. However, as with most employment law, there are exemptions and opt-outs for many industries and professions.

The Bank of France and Medef, the French employers federation, have both warned of the inflationary burden of these measures on the economy and of rising labour costs. The French government credits measures such as this one with creating hundreds of thousands of new jobs.

Many employees are unhappy about the arrangements too as, in practice, it often means that they have to take long enforced holidays when many would prefer to have salary rises and paid overtime instead.

Many use their overtime days to *faire le pont* or 'bridge the gap' by adding days off in a week containing a national holiday to make long weekends.

Key Questions

Does the 48-hour maximum apply to me?
The regulation of working hours applies to all workers, including freelance and agency workers. However, there are a number of exemptions, which are set out on page 62. These workers may be protected by different regulations.

What if I want to work longer hours?
All workers are entitled to opt out of the working time limit. Opting out will mean you can work unlimited hours. All you need to do is to sign an opt-out form. An important point to bear in mind is that if you change your mind you can opt back in again, but you may need to give your employer up to three months' notice.

How are averages calculated?
All the laws and regulations refer to not working more than 48 hours *on average*. In most cases the average is taken over a 17-week period. This period is known technically as the 'reference period', and it can be extended in some circumstances. Any period of sickness, maternity or paternity leave or holiday is excluded from the reference period, and the time and hours lost this way are made up by adding in the working days from the start of the next reference period.

So, for example, if you worked the following hours:

Week 1–10	49 hours each week
Week 11	Holiday
Week 12–15	40 hours each week
Week 16–17	38 hours each week
Week 1 of next 17-week period	52 hours

- The total hours you worked in the 17 weeks reference period would be 726.
- However, as you missed one week the first week of the next reference period is used to fill the gap. This means adding the 52 hours (which were done in the first week of the next reference period) into the equation.
- Total hours 778, divided by 17 weeks = 45.76 hours on average per week.
- This means that you would not be exceeding the legal limit of 48 hours on average per week.

Who logs the hours I work?

Your employer is required to record your hours of work to ensure that they do not exceed 48 hours per week on average. Your employer does not need to keep records of the hours you work if you have signed an opt-out, but it does need to retain records for two years for those who have not opted out.

What about collective or workforce agreements in my organization?

The reference period (*see* above) can be extended through a collective or workforce agreement.

Collective agreements are between the employer and trade union, while workforce agreements are between the employer and workforce representatives. In themselves these are rarely legally binding although their terms are often incorporated into employee contracts. They deal with issues like pay, holidays and hours.

If I work longer hours can I take some off in lieu?

Whether you can take time off in lieu is a question of the contract between you and your employer.

I feel forced to work longer hours to keep my job. What are my rights?

If your employer is forcing you to forgo a right or you are subjected to any other loss or unfairness (a detriment) relating to your rights, you have the right to bring a claim against your employer. A detriment could include a failure to gain promotion, a reduction in pay, or unjustified disciplinary action. The amount a tribunal could award you is unlimited.

There is no right to bring a direct claim at tribunal in relation to your employer's breach of the weekly hours limit as this is enforced as detailed above. However, case law has clarified that there is an automatic contractual obligation on employers not to require an employee to work in excess of 48 hours on average per week. This is a claim you can take to employment tribunal.

I was dismissed for not agreeing to sign an opt-out – what are my rights?

You have the right to bring an automatic unfair dismissal claim if you are dismissed in connection with the regulations or for asserting your rights under the regulations. Automatic unfairness in this context means that the case is proved if you can show that the reason for your dismissal was connected to these rights. Also there is no qualifying period of employment or upper age limit for such claims (*see* Chapter 22: Being dismissed).

I'm a younger worker under 16/18 years – do I have the same rights?
Yes. For younger workers there is a maximum working day of eight hours and a maximum working week of 40 hours. Young workers are also prohibited from being employed during the 'restricted period' which is normally between 10 p.m. and 6 a.m. Additional provisions apply to children under 16.

Is there an automatic right to overtime payment?
There is no automatic right to overtime payment. There is also no legal control over the rate of overtime pay as long as it does not fall below statutory minimum wage rates (*see* Chapter 13). All provisions relating to overtime, including benefits such as food allowance, must be contractually agreed between you and your employer.

What about work involving heavy physical or mental strain – are there any special provisions?
There are special provisions on hours of work, but only if you are a night worker. If you fall into this category you can only work eight actual (not average) hours per night.

 Mini Case Study

Sunday workers
The Sunday trading laws were relaxed in 1994 and now shopping, as well as other leisure activities, are fully established as part of the British way of life. Despite reservations, including those of the Church, Sunday has effectively become just another working day.

A government survey in 2000 found one in eight full-time employees regularly worked both Saturdays and Sundays.

In England and Wales, there are special rules that apply if you are a shop worker or betting worker which relate to working on Sundays. They do not apply to you if you only work on Sundays. If you fall into this category you have the right not to be dismissed for refusing to work on Sunday, and the right not to be subjected to any other unfairness for refusing to work on Sunday such as being denied promotion or training. You have the right to object to working on Sundays. If you have contractually agreed to work on Sunday, you need to give your employer notice that you are opting out of working on Sunday. You must then serve a three-month notice period during which time you will still be required to work on Sundays. If you have not agreed to work on Sundays and are being asked to, you have the right to refuse. You can take your employer to tribunal if your rights are denied.

 ## Your Rights

1 To work no more than an average 48 hours per week.
2 To opt out and work as many hours as you wish.
3 To opt back in and limit your working time to an average of 48 hours per week.
4 To work a limit of an average of eight hours in a 24-hour period if you fit the definition of a night worker (*see* Chapter 10).
5 To work no more than eight actual (not average) hours per night if your work involves special hazards or heavy physical or mental strain.
6 To bring a claim at employment tribunal.
7 To bring an automatic unfair dismissal claim if you are dismissed in connection with these rights (*see* below).

 ## Tactics and Tips

Opting back into the Regulations
A useful tip is that if you change your mind about having opted out of the Regulations, in other words you have decided you would like to limit your working hours to 48 on average per week, you can opt back into the working time restriction. You may need to give your employer up to three months' notice, depending on the terms and conditions your employer has adopted relating to working time; it may be just one week's notice.

The Department of Trade and Industry (DTI) guidance
The DTI produce useful guidance on the Regulations and tribunal may take their guidance into account although they are not required to do so. It may therefore be useful to get hold of a copy if you need to consider your rights further.

What next . . .

If you need advice on your working hours, the first thing you should do is get ahead of the game and take advantage of the tactics and tips every employer and worker should know in Chapter 2. If you need to take things further *see* Part 5: Taking things further. Details of organizations that can assist you and further information are in Appendix B: Contact points.

Rest breaks and time off

You are entitled to at least 11 hours off between each working day.

Many people simply do not take the time off to which they are entitled. Sometimes this may be because they prefer not to, but more often this is because they feel they are unable to do so because of their workload. Although different companies have different approaches all too often they frown on breaks, or routinely schedule meetings in meal breaks.

The law lays down detailed entitlements to breaks and time off; entitlements that you can enforce at employment tribunal if you are denied them. You are allowed three types of time off: *rest breaks*, *daily rest* and *weekly rest*.

Rest breaks
You are entitled to a 20-minute break if you work more than six consecutive hours – in practice this is the lunch break for many of us. Employers are not required to make sure you take this time off, just to see that you are not prevented from doing so. Rest breaks should not be taken at the start or end of a working period, as they would not really then be classified as a break.

Daily rest
You are entitled to a minimum of 11 hours rest in between each working day.

Weekly rest

Weekly rest means the right to one day off a week, amounting to a minimum of 24 consecutive hours off.

The majority of us are used to taking weekends off and the weekend period satisfies this right to weekly rest. The time can be averaged over a two-week period, so the minimum entitlement is a weekend off every two weeks.

 What if . . .

- A store manager works without any days off or breaks for over a month. He works 11- to 12-hour days and complains about his excessive hours. He then resigns without notice and brings a claim for constructive dismissal, and automatic unfair dismissal under the Regulations.
  Outcome: In a similar case an employee's claim succeeded and the dismissal was unfair as it was in breach of his entitlement to breaks under the Regulations.
- A trainee accountant feels obliged to work through his breaks in order to get through his workload. He becomes ill with stress as a result and brings a claim for breach of his entitlement to rest breaks.
  Outcome: As long as he was not prevented from taking rest breaks he would not have a claim against his employer. However he may have had a claim arising out of his illness (*see* Chapter 18).

Exemptions and exclusions

The Working Time Regulations apply to all workers, including freelance and agency workers. However, there are a number of exemptions, which are referred to earlier.

 Key Questions

What about part-time, agency, freelance and contract workers, etc.?
All of the above qualify for these entitlements if they do not fall within the excluded categories and, in the case of rest breaks, work for at least six hours at a stretch. These regulations apply to workers, not just

employees. A worker includes an individual who works under a contract of employment, or is generally under the control of another. If there are questions over status, the key is when and how the work is done, who provides equipment and tools, and who takes care of the financial administration, like paying the tax.

The genuinely self-employed, such as those running their own businesses and those who work for a variety of different organizations, are excluded.

Are days off in addition to annual leave?
Yes.

Am I paid during my breaks?
Daily and weekly rest breaks are not paid as they are not part of your working time. Rest breaks during the working day do not have to be paid but they are mostly built into the working day and form part of the lunch break.

Do I get more breaks if my work is monotonous?
You are entitled to 'adequate rest breaks', which means that your employer may need to consider giving you shorter breaks more frequently. Monotonous work could be doing the same task on a continuous production line.

Are rest breaks in addition to meal breaks?
No, they can overlap so your lunch hour will include your right to a 20-minute break.

Can my boss force me to give up my breaks or time off?
You have the right to take the breaks and if you are denied the right you can bring a claim at employment tribunal. The tribunal has the right to award compensation.

If I don't take my breaks can I go home earlier/get overtime/take time off in lieu?
There is no provision in the regulations that allows you to do that. However, a variation such as this may be agreed through a collective or workforce agreement as the time off may be seen as compensatory rest.

Should access to any facilities be provided (for example, food and hot drinks in the middle of the night)?

There are no specific provisions relating to this but you are entitled to take the break away from your workstation if you have one.

Do I have to take my break?

You do not have to take a break and your employer is not required to monitor whether you have. If your employer insists on you taking a break it is likely that he or she is being responsible and looking out for your health and safety.

What records does my employer need to make?

Your employer does not need to keep records of your rest breaks, days off and annual leave although it would be prudent to do so in the case of days off and annual leave.

Do I have the right to the same day off each week?

Not necessarily, it will depend on your contract of employment and working arrangements.

Do younger workers (below the age of 18 years and over the minimum school leaving age) have additional protection?

Yes, they do. With regard to rest breaks, if a young worker is required to work more than four and a half hours in one go then he or she is entitled to a rest break of 30 instead of 20 minutes. Only in exceptional circumstances can a young worker's entitlement to rest breaks be changed. And if they are then the young worker must get his or her compensatory rest within three weeks.

A young worker is entitled to a 12-hour uninterrupted period off (instead of 11 hours) in each day and is entitled to weekly time off of two days each week. Unlike for adult workers, the two days off cannot be averaged over two weeks. There are exceptions and possible variations to this basic entitlement that apply in limited circumstances.

 Your Rights

1 A break of at least 20 minutes if working more than six hours.
2 Eleven hours' uninterrupted break between each working day.
3 Weekly rest of at least 24 hours a week.

What next . . .

If you need advice on your entitlements to rest the first thing you should do is get ahead of the game and take advantage of the tactics and tips every worker and employer should know in Chapter 2. If you need to take things further see Part 5: Taking things further. Details of organizations that can assist you and further information are in Appendix B: Contact points.

Night working

You should not work more than an average of eight hours in every 24 at night if you are classified as a night worker.

According to the Office for National Statistics, around 1 million people are working at 11 p.m. each night, with at least 300,000 working between 2 and 5 a.m. However, these figures could seriously underestimate the true number as we increasingly become a 24-hour society.

More and more shops are opening overnight, in addition to more services, call centres and transport facilities. While many of us may have to work some nights as part of a shift pattern others prefer to work at night because there is less interference from management, and fewer distractions.

If you work nights regularly and satisfy the definition of a night worker then you qualify for extra rights over day workers, including a limit on your daily average hours and free health assessments, as well as the right to be transferred to day work if working at nights is making you unwell.

The law defines night time as between 11 p.m. and 6 a.m. To be classed as a night worker you have to work more than three of these hours as part of your normal work pattern, although this can be varied if you and your employer agree to the variation. If it is varied, the shift must be at least seven hours long and include the period from midnight to 5 a.m.

If your shifts vary and your working time regularly includes at least three hours of night time on most days, or on a regular basis, then it is also likely you are classed as a night worker. The position is likely to be clarified further through the European Court of Justice, but it is clear that working nights occasionally does not automatically qualify you as a night worker.

What if . . .

- A shop assistant works until 1 a.m. in the morning as he is on what his company calls the night shift.
  Outcome: Since his regular work pattern does not mean that he worked three hours during the period between 11 p.m. and 6 a.m. his work is not classified as night work.
- A machine operator is asked to work nights, three hours of which fall into the period 11 p.m. to 6 a.m. She starts to feel ill and her doctor said that she should not work nights. The doctor gives her a medical certificate to show that her illness was related to her working nights. Her employers refused to transfer her to a day shift.
  Outcome: The HSE and local authorities are responsible for enforcing this provision of the Regulations. An employer who fails to comply with the obligation to transfer employees in these circumstances to suitable day work is guilty of a criminal offence and will be liable to pay a fine. She should report the matter to the relevant authority.

 Key Questions

Are there different rights for those who work occasional night shifts and dedicated night workers?
Yes. You may not be defined as a night worker if you only occasionally work night shifts, in which case you will not qualify for the rights in this section.

So what are my rights if I do some night shifts, say one week in three?
You should work night shifts as a normal course, which generally means that you work those hours on the majority of your working days. Other work patterns can also qualify as long as night work is a regular feature of your work. One week in three spent working during the night time was held to be night work.

But what if I regularly finish work at 1 a.m.?
The number of hours you need to work at night to qualify as a night worker can be specified in a workforce or collective agreement. So even though you do not work three hours between 11 p.m. and 6 a.m., you may still qualify as a night worker.

How are averages of night hours worked out?
Averages are calculated in just the same way as for other hours of work.

I must work no more than eight actual hours if my work involves a special hazard – what is a special hazard?
Either you can agree with your employer that a particular kind of work involves a special hazard as part of a workforce or collective agreement, or a risk assessment process may establish that the work poses a significant risk. If special hazards do apply, then you must not work more than eight actual hours – as opposed to on average per night.

Must my employer take into account my health in asking me to work nights?
Your employer must offer you regular health assessments if you are a night worker and before you start night work. They should keep a record of your name, when you had the assessment and the result of the assessment.

How much time off a week am I allowed?
You are entitled to all the normal rest breaks and time off (*see* pp. 71–5).

Should I be paid more for working nights?
There is no provision for extra pay for night work in the Regulations.

Does my employer have to provide transport to and from work?
No, any such arrangements would be a matter of what is contractually agreed between you and your employer.

 Your Rights

1 To work no more than eight hours per day on average doing night work. The same averaging process over a 17-week period applies as for other working time (*see* p. 67).
2 Free health assessments before you start working nights and on a regular basis thereafter.
3 To be transferred to suitable day work if you are suffering from health problems caused or made worse by working nights.
4 To work a limit of no more than eight hours (without averaging) if

your night work involves special hazards or heavy physical or mental strain.

 What next . . .

If you need advice on night work the first thing you should do is get ahead of the game and take advantage of the tactics and tips every worker should know in Chapter 2. If you need to take things further *see* Part 5: Taking things further. Details of organizations that can assist you and further information are in Appendix B: Contact points.

Holidays

One of the symptoms of approaching nervous breakdown is the belief that one's work is terribly important. If I were a medical man, I should prescribe holiday to any patient who considered his work important.
Bertrand Russell

The idea of *paid* holiday is a relatively modern one. Today, many of us take four weeks' paid leave a year for granted, but it only became a legal right for many in 1998, with the UK being the last country in the EU at the time to pass such legislation.

In fact, the very notion of holiday is a relatively modern one too. The Factory Acts of the nineteenth century introduced working time regulation with half days on Saturdays, in addition to Sundays off and, in 1871, the Bank Holidays Act added a few days of public holidays too. But it wasn't until the twentieth century that holidays really took hold, as few could really afford to take them.

Most employers now acknowledge that holidays are vital to the health and well-being of their staff and that they are likely to work more productively and feel more motivated if they have time off. There is a growing realization that holiday and time off are vital to achieving a reasonable work–life balance too (*see* Chapter 9).

However, despite this the National Association of Citizens Advice Bureaux says many employers, especially smaller ones, continue to dodge the law. It says employees are deprived of holiday by being told they have no rights or that the employer cannot afford to let them take a break.

In the UK employees have a basic legal right to 20 days' paid leave each year. In Europe there are widely differing holiday entitlements, from around 20 days in Belgium and Italy (excluding bank or public holidays) to 30 in Germany and Austria.

All of these are far more generous than countries outside Europe: many Americans get only two weeks' paid holiday a year.

 What if . . .

- Staff in a painting and decorating service firm had their pay reduced without their consent. This is done by their employer in order to finance rights to holiday pay arising from the Regulations. The employees complained to an employment tribunal.
  Outcome: In a similar case it was held to be unlawful to reduce the employees' hourly rates to fund holiday pay. The employees' claim would succeed.
- A mini cab driver took 10 days' holiday approved by her employers but they only paid her for seven days, telling her that she had not accrued the rest of her entitlement yet. They said they would pay her later when she had accrued the entitlement to the other three days. She takes her firm to tribunal to claim the holiday pay she is owed.
  Outcome: She is entitled to payment for the three days' holiday pay she was denied and is likely to win her claim. If her employer had not approved the extra three days' holiday the position would be different but as they had, she is entitled to have her holiday leave paid.
- A manufacturing firm decided to increase the hourly rate of their part-time workers, the extra payment representing their holiday pay. When workers then took holiday they were not paid anything further.
  Outcome: In a similar case this was held to be lawful, but certain requirements must be satisfied. Fundamentally, there must be mutual agreement for the payment of holiday pay in this way, and the payment must represent a true addition to the contractual rate of pay. Whether such a scheme is lawful depends on exactly how it works. If you are concerned about this you should seek advice.

Bank holidays

Bank holidays can be included as part of your entitlement to 20 days' paid holiday although some employers allow you to take them on top of annual leave entitlement.

Up to a third of all employees regularly work bank holidays. As with paid annual leave, the number of bank holidays varies widely across Europe, with national days off, and regional holidays too. The Netherlands has six, the UK nine, Ireland 10, Belgium and Luxembourg 11, Spain 14 and Portugal 14.

Sometimes there are extra public holidays to mark special occasions, for example, the extra day granted in June 2002 to celebrate the Queen's Golden Jubilee.

 Key Questions

Who qualifies for four weeks' paid holiday?
You qualify if you are a worker, as opposed to self-employed, and do not fall into the excluded sectors (*see* pp. 61–3).

What about agency/contract/part-time workers, etc.?
Yes, such workers are entitled to holiday, although in the case of part-timers and short-term workers, the entitlement may be pro rata. Their entitlement is also 20 days per annum and their employer pays them. In the case of agency workers, who pays the holiday pay depends on the commercial arrangements between the agency and company in question.

Is there a minimum qualifying period of employment before I can take holiday?
There is no qualifying period for this right, so you should be able to take holiday straightaway, although your employer can prevent you taking it at a particular time if it is inconvenient for business reasons.

How much notice do I have to give my employer before taking holiday?
You can agree with your employer how much notice needs to be given. The amount may be set out in your contract of employment, but in the absence of agreement, you need to give your employer notice of at least twice the length of the holiday you wish to take.

Can I be refused holiday?

Your employer cannot deny you the right to holiday altogether. If this happens you have the right to bring a claim at employment tribunal. But your employer can refuse to let you take holiday at a particular time. Given the notice period mentioned above, your employer needs to tell you that your request for holiday has been denied at a point equivalent to the length of time you want to take off before the start date of the holiday. So, if you want to take a week off, you should have requested this two weeks before you go and the employer must refuse you a week before you go – no later.

Can an employer rule out me taking my holiday during some periods and insist that I take it during other periods?

Yes, very typically, employers often provide for a Christmas shutdown period and this is lawful. Alternatively, if your employer's business is seasonal or has predictable busy periods, your employer can rule out any holiday leave during that period.

What about religious festivals?

Although your employer may have the right to stop you taking holiday at a particular time, if the reason for the time off is due to a religious commitment, you may have a religious discrimination, race discrimination or human rights supported claim (*see* Chapter 14).

What if I don't think my employer is being fair?

You have the right to take your employer to employment tribunal if they subject you to unfairness because of your wish to take annual leave or if you are denied leave. You should raise a grievance first, though.

What about bereavement, maternity, parental emergencies?

Specific separate rights to leave exist in relation to parental, maternity and emergency leave in relation to dependants. In all other cases, although agreement to your leave is subject to your employer, most employers are likely to be reasonable in the event of an emergency.

How is my holiday pay calculated?

If your pay and hours are not variable then your entitlement is to your normal basic pay. You will only get overtime pay as part of your holiday pay if your overtime is guaranteed (which is not the case for most people). If your hours and pay vary then your holiday pay will be the average pay you received in the last 12 weeks. To calculate this you need to add up the pay you received in the last 12 weeks before your holiday and divide the figure by 12. Bonuses and commission can also be included in this way.

Can my employers insist that I take my leave?
Prudent employers may encourage you or insist on you taking leave, but there is no obligation for them to do so.

Can I carry holiday over to next year?
No, there is no legal right to do this, but you may be able to carry over the contractual part of your entitlement to the next holiday year. So, for example, if you have the right to 25 days a year, you may be able to carry over five days, as the 20 are statutory holidays under the regulations as opposed to contractual holidays.

If I don't take my holiday entitlement can I be paid instead?
No, that is not legal, except on leaving.

What about my holiday entitlement if I am leaving work?
You are entitled to pay in lieu of holiday on leaving your job, and your entitlement is pro-rated in accordance with your leaving date.

Can I still get holiday pay if I am off work due to sickness throughout the whole holiday year?
No, you will not be entitled to holiday pay in such circumstances.

 Your Rights

You have the right to 20 days' paid holiday per year. You get the same entitlement (pro rata) if you work part-time or are engaged for a fixed term of less than a year.

 What next . . .

If you need advice on your right to holidays, the first thing you should do is get ahead of the game and take advantage of the tactics and tips every worker and employer should know in Chapter 2. If you need to take things further *see* Part 5. Details of organizations that can assist you and further information are in Appendix B: Contact points.

9

Family-friendly rights

67 per cent of working women are back at work within nine months of giving birth

The work–life balance

Perhaps the most significant change in the workplace in recent years is the underlying change in our own attitude to work. We recognize work patterns need to be more flexible to adapt to the way we live and work nowadays. The need to balance work life with home life is a live issue both in the UK and across Europe, driven in part by growing demands on us, especially with the rise in the service sector, which now employs by far and away the greatest number of workers. This sector often demands staff to be on duty round the clock as we move more and more to a 24-7 culture which leads to irregular and anti-social working patterns that simply erode family life.

The charity Parents at Work say many of the problems parents face are obvious; the majority of working mothers do not see enough of their children, 40 per cent of fathers who work do so for more than 50 hours a week, registered childcare is only available to one in nine children under age eight years, and employers are given little incentive to introduce family-friendly policies.

But things are changing. With more mothers working than ever before and the majority of working women back in their job within nine months, compared to 45 per cent in 1988, and just nine per cent in 1971, women are clearly central to the issue of work–life balance. This rise in working mothers and the decline in the proportion of men working has forced the issue of the work–life balance onto the political agenda.

In 2000 the government launched its work–life balance campaign with a study of the work–life balance, which acknowledged that while there is substantial demand for flexible working, other than part-time working only a few employers operated flexible arrangements. This new politics of time challenges the rigid 9 a.m.–5 p.m. work pattern and takes an innovative look at the management of our time. Since then a number of new rights have been put into place to enhance the balance between work and family life. At the extreme, trade unions at the European level are even debating the idea of lifetime working hours, so that we all work a certain number of hours during the course of our lives which can be increased or decreased to cater for changes in the demands of our personal life. But whatever the extent of flexibility, employers generally agree that people work best when they can strike a balance between work and home life and the main advantages of work–life balance include happier staff, improved commitment and, in some instances, an increase in productivity.

But what does work–life balance actually mean in practical terms? A couple of examples are illustrated below.

 Mini Case Study

Bristol City Council
As part of the 'Time of our lives in Bristol' flexible working project, a pilot scheme for the opening of the library on Sunday was implemented. Participation in the scheme was voluntary and staff could choose how often they wanted to work on Sunday. Full-time staff exchanged their Sunday hours for hours they would have worked during the week and part-time staff could increase their weekly hours. The extended opening was very popular with the public and the project was an overall success. The change in work pattern not only resulted in an improved service to the public, but was coupled with an increase in flexibility and employees' choices available to achieve work–life balance.

 Mini Case Study

Co-operative Bank
A division of this bank that employs 200 staff, most of whom are women, sought to improve staff retention. A pilot project was started to explore the benefits of teleworking to both employees and the business. The combination of the union, IT specialists and staff eventually signed up to an agreement for home-working and teleworking. The bank, as a result,

did retain skilled staff but also benefited from the cost of setting up employees with home workstations being lower than buying extra office space. The employees achieve a better balance between work and home but also say they are more productive and efficient, and can concentrate better.

Among the recent initiatives are substantial changes to maternity leave and pay (*see* Becoming a Parent below), which includes revised maternity rights, the rights to parental leave, the right to flexible working, the right to adoption leave and pay, the right to take time off for dependants, the right to two weeks' paid paternity leave for men, as well as protection for part-time and fixed-term workers (*see* Chapter 10).

Becoming a parent

Every year around 730,000 babies are born in the UK

Each year over 400,000 working women have babies. The latest statistics show that the majority of women are back at work within nine months of giving birth. This represents one of the biggest changes in the workplace in the last 30 years. As late as the early 1970s just nine per cent of women returned to work within nine months. Mothers are now undoubtedly a vital resource for employers. This makes the legal issues around parenthood some of the most difficult in law.

We've all heard about the director, manager or co-worker who believes women should stay at home with the baby, and about cases where a job disappears when an employee is on maternity leave. The law has recognized for a long time the vulnerability of working mothers and mothers-to-be; but the complexity of the law has often left both employer and employee equally mystified. One senior judge, Judge Brown-Wilkinson, was driven to remark that 'these statutory provisions are of inordinate complexity exceeding the worst excesses of a taxing statute'.

In December 1999, long-awaited changes to the law were introduced which significantly simplify the situation. New rights were established to protect women against being subjected to unfairness or dismissal as a result of their pregnancy or motherhood.

In addition, women have for some time had the right not to suffer sex discrimination and as women alone have babies, unfairness because of pregnancy or childbirth inevitably amounts to sex discrimination.

Employers likewise have to take extra care to protect women's health and safety when pregnant or breastfeeding.

Other key rights include the right to maternity leave and pay. Women also have the right to take time off for antenatal care to attend appointments.

It should be stressed that only employees are entitled to these rights. There are some exclusions as well: members of the police force, for example.

What follows sets out the minimum that an employee is entitled to. In practice, many companies offer extra benefits over and above the statutory minimum.

Maternity leave

There are three types of leave women are entitled to:

1 **ordinary maternity leave** – 26 weeks;
2 **additional maternity leave** – this is added on to ordinary maternity leave and runs to a maximum of 26 weeks;
3 **compulsory maternity leave** – two weeks from the birth of the child or four weeks if you work in a factory. It is unlawful for you to work during compulsory maternity leave and your employer may be criminally liable if you are made to work during this leave period.

One thing to be clear about is that the right to ordinary maternity leave is applicable from day one so you do not need to have worked for an employer for any length of time. You qualify for additional maternity leave when you have been working for 26 weeks for your employer by the time that you are 14 weeks away from the due date of your baby's birth.

You must give your employer notice that you intend to take maternity leave no later than the end of the 15th week before childbirth, but there is no need to give notice of your return as it is assumed unless you say otherwise. The notice does not need to be in writing but you must give your employer a medical certificate confirming the week of childbirth. The Mat B1 maternity certificate (automatically provided by your GP at the beginning of your antenatal care) is adequate for this purpose.

Maternity pay

The two main forms of benefit are *statutory maternity pay* and *maternity allowance*. Statutory maternity pay covers 26 weeks in total and only six of those weeks are close in value (currently 90 per cent) to the employee's normal pay at work. If the employee does not qualify for statutory maternity pay then she will usually receive maternity allowance.

Qualifying
To be entitled to maternity pay the employee needs to have worked for the employer for 26 weeks before she reaches the fourteenth week before the birth due date. She must also be earning at a level equal to the lower earnings limit for national insurance contributions (you can find out the current lower earnings limit from the contacts listed below). The employee's 21 days' notice of her intention to take time off for maternity leave also serves as notice for statutory maternity pay purposes. This does not need to be in writing, although you do need to give your employer a certificate stating the expected week of childbirth (like the Mat B1).

The payment
The first 6 weeks of maternity pay are at 90 per cent of the employee's pay. Thereafter the statutory minimum rate is £106 (April 2005).

Employers' relief
Employers get reimbursement for 92 per cent of the statutory maternity payments they make. Small employers get 100 per cent reimbursement for statutory maternity payments made. To qualify as a small employer they have to have a national insurance liability of £45,000 (April 2005).

Maternity allowance
The employee is entitled to this if she is employed, but does not qualify for statutory maternity pay, or has been recently employed or self-employed for 26 out of 66 weeks by the time she reaches the week before her child's birth due date. The allowance is for 18 weeks and is claimed from the Benefits Agency on form MA1.

Antenatal care

If you are pregnant, you are entitled to paid time off for antenatal care. To be paid you may be required to produce a certificate confirming your pregnancy and (after your first appointment) an appointment card. Your employer should ask you for these documents but if you are not asked then there is no need to produce them.

If you are refused time off or not paid for the time off, then you can take your employer to employment tribunal and you may get awarded pay for the time you should have been allowed off, or for the period of time you took off unpaid.

An employer would be most unwise to refuse you time off for antenatal care as you may be able to bring a number of potential claims as a result. These include the possible right to claim automatic unfair constructive dismissal, unlawful detriment and sex discrimination.

Paternity leave

Fathers are entitled to two weeks' paid paternity leave around the time of the birth of their child if they have 26 weeks' service. It is paid at statutory maternity pay levels (£106 (April 2005)).

Adoption

Employees are entitled to paid adoptive leave. One adoptive parent can elect to take up to 26 weeks of leave to be paid at the lower rate of statutory maternity pay – £106 per week (April 2005). The adoptive parent should be employed for at least 26 weeks. Remember that employees will also have the right to parental leave on adoption (*see* above).

Returning on a part-time basis

It is now quite common for an employee on maternity leave to wish to return on a part-time basis at least for a while, if not permanently. But do you have a right to this? The short answer is that there is no direct legal right to return on a part-time basis. Your right is to return to the same job on the same terms and conditions.

However, this is complicated by the fact that a refusal to allow you to return on a part-time basis after maternity leave may mean you have an indirect sex discrimination claim against your employer (*see* Chapter 14 for a fuller explanation of indirect discrimination). This is because it is generally women who have primary childcare responsibility and a refusal to adjust hours impacts on more women than men. But it is lawful if your employer can objectively justify the denial. So your employer should consider your request and have good business reasons if it decides not to grant your request. Such an employee can also make a request to work flexibly (*see* Chapter 10). Employers have to be careful in dealing with this, as one employer from Birmingham discovered. They decided to implement a policy letting all women returning from maternity leave work part-time. When a new father's request to work part-time after the birth of his child was denied he claimed direct sex discrimination and won the right at employment tribunal.

 Maternity step-by-step guide

Event/decision	*Action checklist*
You find out you are pregnant	• nothing to do straightaway • date of baby's birth obtained • tell your employer about pregnancy in order to take time off for antenatal care
What sort of leave do you qualify for?	• ordinary maternity leave, and • additional maternity leave if you have been working for your employer for 26 weeks by the time you reach 14 weeks before the due date
You need to plan your leave	• leave can start any time after the eleventh week before the due date
When do you tell your employer?	• employer to be notified at the latest during the 15th week before childbirth is expected
What if you are ill before your leave starts?	• treated as normal sick leave, unless it is pregnancy-related

	and occurs any time 4 weeks before leave due to start, in which case it may trigger start of maternity leave
What if you are sick at the end of maternity leave?	• normal sickness provisions of employer apply, unless sickness is related to maternity
What if you want to return from maternity leave early?	• Must give employer 28 days' notice
What do I need to do to prepare my employer for my return on the date planned?	• Nothing – it is assumed that you will return
	• Employer can make enquiries to those entitled to additional maternity leave (*see* Key Questions)
When does my additional maternity leave end?	• 26 weeks from the end of ordinary maternity leave
What if I decide not to return?	• Give notice of your decision in accordance with your contract or statutory minimum
	• In practice you may agree with your employer to waive this requirement

 What if . . .

• A woman was not consulted about her impending redundancy as she was on maternity leave.
  Outcome: This is unlawful direct discrimination and unfair dismissal. The employee would be entitled to bring these claims at employment tribunal. In a similar case an employee won £5,000 for injury to feelings.
• A woman was on maternity leave and as a result was not given training offered to others in her department.
  Outcome: This is unlawful discrimination and unlawful detriment and the employee would be entitled to bring these claims at employment tribunal.
• A request to return on a part-time basis following maternity leave is refused. It is refused without being given any consideration.
  Outcome: The employee can claim indirect sex discrimination and her

claim is likely to succeed unless the employer is able to justify the decision on the grounds of the business needs of the organization in question. So if a business can show that it needs continuity throughout the whole working week, for example, then there may be strong arguments to back their decision. If that is not the case then the refusal indirectly discriminates against women as women usually have primary childcare responsibilities.

- A male employee requests paid time off to attend antenatal classes with his wife.

Outcome: There is no right to paid time off for antenatal care for partners of pregnant women. His employers have the right to refuse his request and require that he takes the leave from his holiday entitlement or takes it unpaid.

 Key Questions

What notice must I give for maternity leave? And what about paternity leave?

For both maternity leave entitlements you must give your employer notice of the date you intend to start your leave in or before the 15th week before childbirth. It must state the fact of your pregnancy, the expected due date of your child's birth, and when you intend to start your leave. For paternity leave, *see* above.

What if I am sick as a result of my pregnancy before my leave is due to start?

If your sickness happens within four weeks before your due date and is related to your pregnancy then your maternity leave will automatically start. If the sickness is unrelated to the pregnancy, then it would be normal sick leave.

Sickness before this period should be treated as ordinary sick leave although if your sickness is maternity-related, employers should beware as any negative treatment could amount to an unlawful detriment or discrimination.

What if the environment in which I work could be dangerous for my unborn child?

Your employer is obliged to look after your health and safety at work. If there is a risk to you or your unborn child or even a risk when breastfeeding then you have the right to be offered suitable alternative employment if any is available. If there is none then you have the right to be suspended from work. Maternity suspension is on full pay and lasts as long as the risk lasts. You cannot be dismissed for this reason and there is no length of time that you need to be employed for before you get the benefit of this right – it applies from day one.

Similarly, if you work nights and have a certificate from your doctor saying that your health could be adversely affected by working nights, you cannot be made to work nights.

What about my pay and benefits on maternity leave?

Your contract of employment continues during your *ordinary leave period* and, therefore, your continuity of employment continues to accrue, so you are entitled to have the time off count towards calculating any redundancy or holiday entitlement. You also have the right to benefit from all the terms and conditions of employment you enjoyed previously, apart from your wages and salary. So you should continue to receive all perks for private use, such as mobile phones, health club and professional subscriptions, company car and share option schemes.

Your contract also continues during your *additional leave period*, but in the same way as in the ordinary leave period, you do not have any right to salary or wages. Remember that some employers pay over and above statutory minimum levels and so you may be paid for more than this and for longer.

During additional maternity leave you continue to have the same rights in relation to notice, redundancy and other entitlements, but the time spent on additional maternity leave is not counted when calculating your length of service.

However, unlike the ordinary leave period, all your other terms and conditions become dormant. Assuming you have not agreed otherwise, the only terms and conditions that apply to you are:

- your employer's obligation of trust and confidence. This means they will be breaking your contract if anything is done to breach the trust and confidence of the relationship, such as telling your clients that you have left the organization;
- you are bound by your obligation of good faith to your employer. So

you will, for example, be breaking the contract if you commercially damage the company's reputation while on maternity leave;

- you are entitled to notice of termination if you are dismissed and must give notice if you terminate the relationship. This will be at statutory minimum levels unless your contract specifies a longer period of notice (*see* Chapter 22: Notice periods);
- you are entitled to redundancy benefits if you are made redundant;
- any terms and conditions on disciplinary and grievance procedures will continue to apply;
- you are bound by any terms in your contract of employment relating to confidential information, acceptance of gifts and/or other benefits, and participation in any other business, all of which relate to some extent to your obligation of good faith to your employer.

On your return you should also be entitled to benefit from any pay rises granted while you were away whether on ordinary or additional leave.

What about my pension?
There is a distinction between paid and unpaid maternity leave (ordinary or additional). If you are on paid leave, whether on statutory pay or enhanced levels, your pension contribution is calculated as if you are working in the usual way. If you make a contribution, your contribution is based on the amount you are being paid.

Your pension rights will continue to accrue during your ordinary maternity leave period.

Your pension rights during unpaid additional maternity leave will depend on the rules of the scheme.

How much notice do I need to give of my return?
There is no need to give your employer notice of your intention to return to work at the end of ordinary or additional maternity leave as it is assumed that you will take your full entitlement. If you want to return early then you need to give your employer 28 days' notice.

Do I have the right to return to my same job?
Yes, you do after ordinary maternity leave – the same job on the same terms and conditions. After additional maternity leave the same right exists, however, if there are unforeseen circumstances (other than redundancy) which mean that it is not reasonably practicable to return to the

same job, then you are entitled to suitable alternative work on terms that are no less favourable than your former job.

Can I add holiday to my maternity leave?
There is no reason why you cannot do this although it will be subject to the approval of your employer.

What if I am made redundant during maternity leave?
You have a legal right to be offered alternative employment before the end of your leave if a suitable vacancy exists. It should be suitable, appropriate and on terms that are not less favourable than those that you were on before.

You will have priority over other employees if an available vacancy exists. What is more, even though you are on maternity leave and away from the office, you have a right to be consulted regarding the redundancy situation. Failing to do so may give rise to sex discrimination, unlawful detriment and/or automatic unfair dismissal claims.

You are also entitled to receive a statement from your employer in writing giving the reason for your dismissal, whether or not you have requested one. If you do not receive one, you can make a claim to the employment tribunal to get one.

What about men going with their partners to scans and other antenatal appointments – are they entitled to any statutory time off?
No, there is no legal entitlement to time off in such circumstances but employers may provide additional contractual rights allowing you time off for such matters or may be willing to come to an agreement with you.

Do gay or lesbian couples have any rights?
Every woman, irrespective of whether they are lesbian, is entitled to the above maternity rights. A new raft of anti-discrimination measures from Europe, including new rights preventing discrimination against homosexuals will soon be put into place (*see* Chapter 14).

Tactics and Tips

Parental leave
Remember that on top of all these rights you also have the right to take parental leave of 13 weeks within the first five years of your child's life. This right is unrelated and unaffected by any maternity leave that you may take.

Returning part-time and flexible working
If your request to work flexibly or to return on a part-time basis is refused, the time limit in which you must lodge a claim may roll forward from the date of the refusal – as it may be seen as a continuing act of discrimination so there is in effect no three-month deadline for lodging a claim as there is for other acts of discrimination. You should take early advice if this applies to you.

Benefits
There are tax credits and other benefits that working parents may be entitled to. It is worth checking your entitlements.

 Your Rights

1 Care for your health and safety while pregnant at work and breast-feeding.
2 Not to suffer unfairness (a detriment) or dismissal connected to pregnancy or childbirth.
3 Not to be discriminated against in relation to pregnancy or childbirth.
4 Time off for ante-natal care.
5 Maternity leave.
6 To receive at least statutory maternity pay or maternity allowance.
7 To return to your job after maternity leave.
8 To be offered a suitable vacancy in the event of redundancy.
9 To tax credits and grants in certain situations.
10 Rights to paternity and adoptive leave for fathers.

Parental leave

If you are a mother or father – either natural or adoptive – you have the right to 13 weeks' unpaid parental leave per child. The leave can be taken up to the child's fifth birthday. In order to qualify for this right you will need to have worked for at least one year with your employer. The leave must be taken in blocks of at least one week and up to four weeks can be taken in any year, although the parental leave provisions may be varied to suit you and your employer better through a collective or workforce agreement.

You remain employed during your leave and will have the right to return to your job unless the time taken off is more than four weeks, in which case, if it is not feasible to give you your old job back your employer must allow you to return to a suitable alternative job with terms not less favourable that those you had before.

 What if . . .

• An employee works for a large retailer and decides to take four weeks' parental leave in December although he knows it is the busiest month of the year for his company. He gives his employer notice in early November.
  Outcome: The employer can give the employee a notice of postponement after consulting with the employee and explaining that taking leave at the busiest time of the year will unduly disrupt the business. The postponement is legally valid if the employer consults with the employee and explains the problem, gives him notice of the postponement within seven days of the employee's request for leave, and postpones the parental leave for no more than six months.

 Key Questions

Do I qualify for parental leave?
There are some excluded categories, including the police and armed forces. As noted above, you also need to have one year's service and to be a parent to qualify for this right.

Is there anything that my employer needs from me before I can take parental leave?

If requested you may be required to produce evidence that you are responsible for a child, as well as evidence of your child's date of birth or adoption.

Do both men and women have the right to this leave?

Yes.

I am due to go on maternity leave – can I add my parental leave entitlement to the end of my maternity leave period?

Yes, there is nothing to stop you from doing this, although if you take this leave after additional maternity leave you may not be given your old job back if it is not feasible to do so. Your employer must however allow you to return to a suitable alternative job with terms not less favourable that those you had before.

How much notice do I need to give to my employer that I wish to take leave?

You must give at least 21 days' notice to your employer, although a different notice period may apply as this provision can be varied through a collective or workforce agreement. If you fail to give the appropriate period of notice you will be entitled to parental leave.

Can my employer postpone my planned parental leave?

Yes, if the operation of your employer's business would be unduly disrupted by the leave then your employer can delay your leave by up to six months (*see* 'What if . . .' above). Your employer should consult with you about rescheduling the leave and you should receive notice of the postponement, in writing, stating the reason and when you will be able to take the leave. You should receive this notice no later than seven days after giving your employer notice of your wish to take parental leave.

This right to postpone does not apply if your leave is booked to correspond with the birth of your child or the adoption date of your child.

What if my child is disabled?

Your entitlements are more flexible if your child is disabled. For example, you can take the leave in blocks of less than a week. Also the entitlement to leave is 18 weeks and can be taken at any time up to the child's eighteenth birthday. Your employer may ask you to provide evidence that your child is receiving disability living allowance.

My child was injured at school – can I take parental leave?

If it is to deal with such urgent, but short-term, matters then time off for dependants is more likely be appropriate (*see* below). If the time off is for more medium- or long-term periods, such as looking after your child during recovery, then it will depend on the scheme your employer has in place, which may account for such problems. Generally, there is a notice period that applies but you could negotiate the position with your employer.

Can the right to time off be carried over from one year to the next?

Unless your employer varies the position, you have the right to take up to four weeks per year until your child's fifth birthday. This means that, as long as you have not used your leave up, you can take the leave in the next year but, if you do not take it in the first few years – as you are restricted to four weeks a year – you may miss out on being able to take all of the leave.

I only work three days a week, what is a week's parental leave for me?

It is your normal working week so, for you, it would be that three-day period.

I am self-employed – do I have the right to parental leave?

No, only employees have this right – but remember that you may, in fact, be an employee even though you think you are self-employed (*see* Chapter 3).

I have been denied promotion and I think it is because I took parental leave this year – is there anything I can do?

If you are subjected to unfairness (a detriment) then you are entitled to take your employer to employment tribunal. The hurdle you need to overcome is proving that the unfairness is connected to you having taken parental leave. If you are considering taking things further *see* Part 5: Taking things further.

Do my pensions and benefits continue during parental leave?

Your pension rights will accrue in relation to work done and, therefore, occupational pension rights that have accrued prior to you taking parental leave are frozen until you return to work. Your leave will not affect your right to your 20 days of statutory holiday under the working time regulations, although any holiday above this amount should be dealt with by your contract of employment.

Bonus entitlements are not straightforward and much will depend on your entitlements in your contract. It is unlikely that you will be entitled to a bonus if it relates to performance during the period of your absence on leave.

Parental leave does not affect your ability to accrue continuous employment for rights such as redundancy.

What if I want to take the leave – but to travel as opposed to spending time with my children?
The right is to spend time with your children, and so your employer could take disciplinary action if they discover that is not the reason for your leave. In reality, it is improbable that it will be possible to monitor your activities during your leave.

Does my employer need to keep records of my leave?
There is no formal obligation to do so although an employer would be wise to keep such records.

 Your Rights

1 To 13 weeks' unpaid parental leave in relation to each child.
2 For your employment to continue throughout your parental leave.
3 For your terms and conditions of employment to be preserved throughout parental leave.
4 To bring a claim at employment tribunal if you are dismissed, made redundant or treated unfairly because you took or wanted to take parental leave.
5 To bring a claim at employment tribunal if your employer prevents, or tries to prevent, you from taking the leave or unreasonably postpones your leave.

Time off work for dependants

Your childminder calls you at 8 a.m. on Monday morning to say she is unavailable for work because she is sick; your child's school calls to say your daughter has broken her arm falling off the climbing frame – these are the sorts of situations we have all come across at work. Sometimes there is no alternative but to take time off work, and while the majority of employers are understanding in such circumstances, some are more difficult, often leaving a desperate employee with no choice but to telephone in sick. Until recently the law did not provide you with any legal right to time off. All employees now have the right to take a reasonable period of time off work for a dependant in certain circumstances. Inevitably, the length of time you are permitted will depend on the incident that has arisen and any arrangements your employer is able to put into place to cover for your absence.

Who is classed as a dependant and what circumstances are covered? A dependant is a partner (who may be your husband or wife), your child or your parents. Also included is someone who lives within your household, such as an elderly relative. Excluded are live-in employees such as a nanny, as well as lodgers.

Many of us have at one time 'adopted' an elderly neighbour – if they rely upon you to assist if they are hurt or become ill they may also be classed as a dependant.

You are able to take time of in the following circumstances:
- to help if a dependant falls ill or gets hurt (this includes mental injury or illness);
- if your dependant is giving birth;
- in order to make arrangements for longer-term care for a dependant who is ill or injured;
- if your dependant dies;
- to deal with unexpected breakdowns in the arrangements that you have in place for the care of a dependant (for example, your nanny is unwell and unable take care of the children);
- to deal with an incident involving your child at school.

 ## What if . . .

- You have just started a new job and get a call from school to say that your child has been injured.
  Outcome: Even though you have not worked there long, you will have the right to take time off to sort the matter out and arrange for the appropriate care of your child.
- Your childminder calls, without notice, to say that she is too ill to look after the children today.
  Outcome: You will have a reasonable amount of time to arrange alternative childcare.

- You receive a call from an elderly neighbour whom you often help out. He says that he feels unwell and thinks he needs to get to a hospital. **Outcome:** You can take time off to make arrangements for him to receive medical assistance.

 Key Questions

Are there any other requirements that need to be satisfied for this right?
Yes. It is essential for you to tell your employer the reason for your absence as soon as you can and, where possible, how long you expect to be absent. There is no qualifying period that you need to have worked for your employer before you can take this time off work.

How much time can I take off?
There is no rule as to how much time off you are allowed – it depends on the situation that you face. It may be hours in some cases to a few days in others. It should be reasonable and you should be able to justify it. If the time you take off does not appear to your employer to be reasonable, you may be called to account.

Is the time off paid?
You have no right to the time being paid although this may depend on your contractual terms and the normal practice of your employer. Some employers will pay employees during this time off as such occurrences are out of the employee's control and rarely happen. It can also be an administrative burden on the employer to dock your wages.

My daughter broke her leg at school, but my employer refused to let me have time off – what can I do?
You can make a complaint to an employment tribunal against your employer and your employer may be ordered to pay compensation. Note that you will only have three months from the date of the refusal in which to lodge the complaint at employment tribunal (*see* Part 5: Taking things further).

My son is going into hospital in three weeks' time. Do I have the right to take time off for my child?

If a problem is not an emergency in that it is not unforeseen or sudden then this right does not apply. You have the right to take time off as holiday (*see* Chapter 8) or alternatively as parental leave (see above).

 Your Rights

- The right to take time off in the event of an emergency or if something unexpected or sudden happens affecting a dependant of yours.
- The right to bring a claim at tribunal if you are unreasonably refused the time off.
- The right to request flexible working. Also aimed at assisting workers balance their work and family life is the introduction of the right to request flexible working. This is covered in Chapter 10.

 Contact Points

Parents at Work – charity with objective of promoting change in the workplace
Address: Fifth Floor, 45 Beech Street, London EC2Y 8AD.
Telephone: 020 7628 3565
Website: www.parentsatwork.org.uk

Maternity Alliance
Address: Unit 1.3, 2–6 Northburgh Street, London EC1V 0AY.
Information Line: 020 7588 8582
E-mail: info@maternityalliance.org.uk

TIGER (tailored interactive guidance on employment rights) – Website at DTI, which helps with your maternity pay entitlement
Website: www.tiger.gov.uk

Social Security Office and Job Centres – for info on children's and working families' tax credits and maternity grants for mothers on low incomes – 0845 609 5000

What next . . .

If you need advice on your rights on becoming a parent, the first thing you should do is get ahead of the game and take advantage of the tactics and tips every worker should know in Chapter 2. If you need to take things further *see* Part 5: Taking things further. Details of organizations that can assist you and further information are in Appendix B: Contact points.

10

Flexible working

Introduction

We are no longer a nation of nine-to-fivers, working Monday to Friday and enjoying all our evenings and weekends in front of the home hearth

Employers and the government have begun to recognize that more flexible working patterns that fit our individual needs are vital if working parents and other workers are to achieve some balance between the competing demands of work and life, the so-called work–life balance (*see* Chapter 9).

Changes to our patterns of work have come about as a result of a number of factors, including the huge rise in the number of working mothers, the 24-hour nature of an increasingly service-orientated economy, and technological changes that mean more of us can work from home, or at great distances from our customers and employers.

The trouble with the law is that for many years it continued to assume we were all working full-time – five days a week on permanent contracts which left all those on different work patterns in something of a legal vacuum. So for many the key qualifying factors for employment protection (like the right to a fair dismissal), employment status and continuous employment were either unclear or unachievable.

In this section we examine the right to request a flexible working arrangement from your employer as well as the rights of those working under various work patterns. We look at those benefiting from legal protection especially designed for their pattern of work (like part-time workers) and those who have a limited amount or no special protection due to their work patterns. Employees, workers and the self-employed (such as freelancers and consultants) work under various different work patterns and the possible combinations are endless, such as a freelancer working from home on an ad hoc basis. Whatever your work pattern, employment status is important, and has a major impact on the degree to which you are protected by the law (*see* Chapter 3).

The right to flexible working

One of the most far-reaching recent changes to the law is the introduction of the right to request flexible working. The new right is for working parents to request flexible working to assist them in balancing parental and work commitments. This means if you qualify, you have the right to request your employer to consider a proposal to change your working arrangements to help you accommodate family responsibilities. Your employer is then obliged to give consideration to your request and follow certain procedures. The only problem is that your employer is entitled to reject your request for a number of reasons that are considered further below.

Attempts to make work life more flexible is a repeated theme in the workplace. Commonly requests for flexibility or part-time work arise on returning to work after a period of maternity leave. There have been a number of highly publicized cases in this area which have highlighted that an outright refusal of an employee's request for the adjustment can expose the company to an indirect sex discrimination claim. Due consideration should be given to the nature of the employee's request and the business case for and against the implementation of the change requested. There is no absolute obligation for the employer to accept the employee's request, but in order to avoid the risk of a successful indirect discrimination claim the employer must demonstrate that the request was given careful consideration and that there was a sound and justifiable business case against introduction of the change. In other words an employer would need to *justify objectively* the rejection of such a request.

The fundamental lesson is that an employer must be unbiased and keep an open mind when considering the commercial feasibility of allowing an employee to return on a part-time basis following maternity leave. As ever, a careful and well-documented paper trail should be created in the event that a claim does arise. Similar considerations apply in relation to flexible working.

If the change is agreed to, a permanent change in your contract is put into place.

The changes that you may request could for example include a change in your hours of work, the days when you are required to work or a request to work from home. You do need to have responsibility for a child who has a specific relationship to you, which is detailed below. Remember, there is no general right to have your contract varied. The change must be specifically in order to assist you in caring for a child.

What if . . .

- An employee who has three years' service wishes to start work an hour later to enable her to drop her baby off at nursery before starting work. Although she deals with clients, the busy time of day is after lunch so she believes the request is reasonable and will not have any negative impact.
  Outcome: In such a case the employer should grant her request.
- An employee is a foster parent and wishes to work four days a week rather than five to assist her in meeting family commitments.
  Outcome: a foster parent is entitled to make a claim for this variation as long as they have been working at the company for at least 26 weeks and the foster child is under the age of six or disabled.

 Key Questions

Do I qualify for the right to request flexible working?
There are qualification requirements that need to be satisfied in order for you to be entitled to make a request for flexible working.
- you must have continuous employment for a period of not less than twenty-six weeks;
- you must be either a mother, father, adopter, guardian or foster parent of the child or be married to or the partner of the child's mother, father, adopter, guardian or foster parent;
- you must expect to have responsibility for the upbringing of the child;
- the child must be under the age of six (unless disabled, see later) although the request can be made at any time up to two weeks before the child's sixth birthday.

What if I am in a homosexual relationship?
A partner means a person whether of the opposite sex or of the same sex who lives with the child and mother, father, adopter, guardian or foster parent, in an enduring family relationship but is not a relative of the mother, father, adopter, guardian or foster parent. So as long as you satisfy these criteria you will qualify.

What information is needed to make a request?

Requirements for an application for flexible working include that it must be made in writing, be dated, state whether a previous application has been made by you, and if so, when that application was made. You must explain as part of the application how the requested change could be put into place and what you believe the effect of the change would be. You should also be able to show that the relationship condition is satisfied and possibly certify the fact on the relevant form. Note that the DTI have helpfully drafted forms that can be adapted by companies. These can be found at http://www.dti.gov.uk/er/flexible.htm which is the link for the flexible working page, from which links to the different guidance documents can be located.

If my request is rejected can I make another one in a few months?

No, only one request per year is permitted.

On what basis can my employer reject my request?

There are only certain reasons that an employer can use as a basis to refuse your request. A wise employer would clearly ensure that they can demonstrate the veracity of such claims. The grounds for rejecting your claim are:

- the burden of additional costs;
- detrimental effect on ability to meet customer demand;
- inability to reorganize work amongst existing staff;
- inability to recruit additional staff;
- detrimental impact on quality;
- detrimental impact on performance;
- insufficiency of work during periods when the employee proposes to work;
- planned structural changes.

How do I go about applying?

The law sets out a prescribed procedure for the making of an application.
  Steps in the process are:

- You make the request for change.
- Your employer must hold a meeting to discuss the application with you within twenty-eight days of the application.
- Your employer may instead agree the contract variation within the twenty-eight-day period, but they must issue a notice to this effect (stating the agreed contract variation and the date from which it is to take effect).

- If a meeting is held, your employer must give notice of the decision in writing within fourteen days of the meeting.
- If agreed, the contractual variation must be stated along with the date from which it is to take effect.
- If the contractual variation is not agreed, the grounds on which the application is refused must be stated. It must be one of the statutory grounds noted above. Your employer should also set out the basis on which reliance is being placed upon the ground in question.
- You are entitled to appeal by notice in writing within 14 days of the decision, setting out the grounds of your appeal. Your appeal should be dated.
- Your employer must then hold an appeal meeting within 14 days unless on receipt of the appeal they change their mind and agree the variation. If the variation is agreed at this stage then you should be notified of agreement to the variation and the date on which it is to take effect should be confirmed.
- If an appeal meeting occurs, a decision must be given within 14 days of the meeting. The same information should be given, that is, confirmation of the contractual variation and the date from which it is to take effect.
- You and your employer may agree in writing to an extension of time for any of the above periods, but any agreement to change time limits must specify what the adjustment is and the new time limit. This written agreed variation to the time limits must also be dated and a copy should be sent to you.
- If the person who would normally consider your application is on holiday or sick on the day when the application is made, the 28-day time period starts when that person returns to the office.
- The time and place of any meeting under the above procedure should be convenient to both you and your employer.

What if I don't want to attend the meeting alone?

You are entitled to have a companion present at the meeting, however, the companion must be a worker employed by your employer. The companion may address the meeting and confer, but does not have the right to answer questions on your behalf. If the companion is unavailable for a meeting you can request a postponement, and your employer must agree provided it is convenient for all and the postponement is no more than seven days after the date of the original date of the proposed meeting.

What if I make an application then change my mind about varying my contract?

The application for flexible working is treated as withdrawn where you:

- give notification orally or in writing; or,
- without reasonable cause, fail to attend a meeting; or,
- without reasonable cause, fail to provide your employer with information they require to assess your application.

Your employer must confirm any withdrawal in writing.

Can I make the application by e-mail?

Yes, you can. If an application is made by e-mail or other electronic communication, it is treated as made on the day on which it was transmitted.

What if my application is in relation to my disabled child?

If you have a disabled child, you can make an application for flexible working any time up to the child's eighteenth birthday.

What if my employer refuses to hold a meeting with me?

An employer will be in breach of the law by virtue of any of the following:

- failure to hold a meeting;
- failure to notify you of a decision;
- refusal for a reason that is not one of the statutory reasons detailed above, i.e.: burden of additional costs, detrimental effect on ability to meet customer demand, inability to reorganize work among existing staff, detrimental impact on quality or performance, insufficiency of work during the periods the employee proposes to work, planned structural changes.

What claims can I make if I think my employer is in breach?

You can make an application to Employment Tribunal on one of two grounds:

    (a) your employer got the facts wrong; and/or

    (b) your employer failed to comply with the specified statutory procedure.

The maximum penalty which the employment tribunal can apply is eight weeks' pay capped at £280 (2005) per week. There is also a potential award of two weeks' pay for failure to allow the employee to be accompanied by a colleague. Furthermore if you are dismissed for making this request you would also have an unfair dismissal claim.

Your Rights

1 To make a claim for flexible working if you qualify.
2 To have your employer follow the statutory procedure.
3 To make a claim at employment tribunal if your employer gets their facts wrong or fails to follow the procedure.

Part-time workers

In 2000, part-time workers were finally granted the right to equal treatment (on a pro-rata basis) with their full-time colleagues employed under the same kind of contract. The Part-Time Workers (Prevention of Less Favourable Treatment) Regulations 2000 put this protection in place. For over seven million part-time workers in the UK, this law arrived not a day too soon.

Previously, fairly complex and sophisticated cases had shown that denying part-timers pro-rata terms and conditions was a form of indirect sex discrimination as the part-timers were predominantly women (44 per cent of all women who work are employed part-time, compared to just nine per cent of men).

Such claims were perhaps symbolized by the thousands of part-time workers who were denied pension rights and brought claims that were finally decided in their favour by the European Court of Justice. As a result of these and other such discrimination cases, only a foolhardy employer would deny pro-rata terms and conditions to their part-time workers.

So part-time workers have the right not to be treated less favourably than comparable full-time workers unless their employer can justify their decision. This means part-time employees should have pro-rata terms and conditions, must not be excluded from training and should not be selected for redundancy on the grounds that they work fewer hours than their full-time working colleagues.

In addition, if a part-time worker does decide to bring a claim for discrimination there is no qualifying period or upper age limit for doing so.

What if . . .

- An accountant wants to transfer from full- to part-time work. Her employer refuses to allow her.
  Outcome: There is no strict legal right to transfer from full-time to part-time work. However, if the request is related to childcare responsibilities then a possible indirect sex discrimination claim may exist (*see* Chapter 14).

- A transport company changed the rostering system for their train drivers. All 2023 male drivers were able to comply with the changes. Twenty of 21 females could also comply. One female could not comply because of her childcare arrangements. She was a single parent. She claimed indirect sex discrimination.
  Outcome: In a similar case an employee won her claim. Even though the majority of the female drivers could comply, only a small percentage of all the drivers were women (21 out of 2023) and the statistics on women that could comply could not be taken to indicate whether women in general would be affected by such a requirement. The court was entitled to take on board the fact that most single parents are likely to be women in reaching the decision that the requirement indirectly discriminated against women.

- A teacher wished to return on a part-time basis after maternity leave and put forward proposals. This was denied even though her employer did not make any enquiries or consult with her about some of the difficulties of her situation, and how to overcome them. Her employer did not provide objective justification for the decision and the teacher brought a claim of indirect sex discrimination.
  Outcome: It is likely to be discriminatory (on the basis most part-timers are women). This is especially so as the teacher's proposals were not taken into account and she was not consulted about her wishes and the possible problems that may arise.

- A part-time worker was paid at a lower hourly rate than his male colleagues who worked full-time. He brought a claim under the new part-time workers regulations.
  Outcome: Under the Regulations the part-time worker would be likely to succeed unless his employer can objectively justify the difference in his pay as compared to his full-time colleagues.

Key Questions

What is a part-time worker?

Most workplaces have established patterns of work that are referred to as full-time, as opposed to part-time. A part-time worker is a worker who is paid partly or wholly according to the hours worked and is not a full-time worker by reference to the custom and practice of the employer in question. In other words, the assessment is by reference to the normal working patterns of the workplace in question. In assessing if a part-timer is being treated fairly, the terms and conditions of a part-time worker are compared to a full-time worker on the same type of contract doing the same, or broadly similar, work.

What if there is no one in the organization with whom the part-time worker's job can be compared?

A worker employed at another workplace of the same employer ('a comparator') can be used for comparison if they satisfy the above conditions. However, the comparison must be made with a 'real' as opposed to hypothetical employee. There is no provision in the law for comparison to be made with a hypothetical worker.

Who do the Regulations apply to?

The Regulations apply to all workers although employees have additional protection as certain elements of this law apply only to employees. The Regulations effectively apply to all except the genuinely self-employed.

Do I have the right to work part-time?

No, the Regulations do not give you this right although any prudent employer would give due consideration to such a request. But remember in certain situations – such as on return to work on a part-time basis following maternity leave, refusal of such a request can amount to discrimination (*see* Chapter 14).

How does overtime work?

A part-time worker is entitled to overtime at the same rate as a full-time worker but only once he or she has worked more than the hours a full-timer in the organization would normally work.

When is an employer justified in denying benefits to a part-time worker on a pro-rata basis?

There is little guidance in the Regulations on this point, but the DTI guidance states that less favourable treatment can only be justified if it aims to achieve a legitimate business objective, is necessary to achieve that objective and is an appropriate way of achieving that objective.

 Your Rights

1 Not to be treated less favourably than an equivalent full-time worker unless your employer can objectively justify its action.

2 Not to be subjected to any unfairness (detriment) by any act or failure to act.

3 To obtain a written statement from your employer within 21 days of your request if you feel you are being treated less favourably than a full-time worker.

4 As an employee, to claim automatic unfair dismissal (*see* Chapter 22: Being dismissed) if you are dismissed for asserting any of your rights under these Regulations.

5 To bring a complaint to employment tribunal if you are subjected to a detriment for asserting your rights under these Regulations.

Fixed-term workers

Fixed-term work is where a person is engaged to work for a set period of time, with a definite start and end date. For example, when he is engaged to complete a specific task or when he is engaged until the occurrence of a particular event like the completion of a building project. Around 800,000 people are on fixed-term or contract work and this number is likely to increase with the increasing popularity of flexible working.

Fixed term workers are protected by special regulations which give them similar protection to part-time workers. A fixed-term worker should not be subjected to unfairness as compared to their permanent counterparts. They are protected against victimization and can bring a complaint to an employment tribunal for a declaration or compensation to remedy any such unfairness.

Agency temps

Workers placed by agencies are commonly referred to as 'temps'. Temporary workers can also include people engaged directly by organizations on temporary employment contracts. One of the biggest areas of change has been the growth in the number of agency temps. There are many differing estimates, but around 9,000 agencies provide both permanent and temporary staff. Currently there are thought to be at least 500,000 agency temps in employment.

Until recently this was an area that was not properly regulated and there was much opportunity for abuse such as the charging of excessively high fees if the temp is taken on as a permanent member of staff, or the imposition of lockout or quarantine periods during which the temp cannot work for the organization at which the agency placed him or her. Often the status of a temp placed by an agency was tested in the courts and in some instances workers were held to be employees of the agency that placed them, and in other cases held to be employees of the organization at which they were placed. The position was far from clear. Regulations to control and govern agency workers as well as make their employment status clearer are now in place.

Other flexible work patterns

Casual workers

A casual worker is not just one that is a little more laid back! It is a term used to describe workers who tend to be assigned on demand in an ad hoc fashion. For example, an energy plant could have an intermittent need to show around groups of visitors. The plant may keep a list of people to contact who are able to show the visitors around as and when necessary instead of using their staff.

A casual worker may not be an employee if the fundamental obligation to be provided with work and the requirement to do the work ('mutuality of obligation') is missing from the equation. The question is: does the organization have to provide the casual worker with work and does the casual worker have to do the work or can they pass it by? If they can pass it by, the worker is unlikely to be an employee.

Casual workers tend to fall outside the definition of an employee as the essential and necessary component of 'mutuality of obligation' is often missing.

If such workers can point to an 'umbrella' contract or agreement governing all their assignments they are more likely to establish employment status. In theory, an employee may have employment status during a short-term assignment, but it is unlikely that adequate continuous employment can be accrued during the course of such assignment and a certain amount of continuous employment is required for the majority of employment rights.

Seasonal workers

Seasonal workers are taken on to accommodate seasonal demand or other surges in demand. They are considered to be employees and enjoy normal employment protection if they qualify by having any necessary continuous employment. If a seasonal worker is habitually re-engaged, and the periods of unemployment between engagements are short, then the employee may gain continuous service rights during the absences.

Home workers

Home working used to be associated with the piece worker – stuffing envelopes, or making decorative covers for coathangers – but technological advances mean home workers can be anybody from the local craftsman working from home to the young executive who works part-time from home.

According to a recent survey around one in eight workplaces allow some of their staff to work at home. And the latest estimate of the national Labour Force Survey says around a third of a million teleworkers (the word used to describe working from home while communicating with your office by phone, fax or computer) work from home. A great number of workers, however, work in call centres remote from the people they talk to. In some cases this can be in a different country and – as part of the sophisticated 'virtual' systems – reports of the weather at their customers' locality automatically appear on screen so that the worker can lend a little more authenticity to the friendly conversation.

Shift workers

Shift workers work shifts that between them are usually designed to cover up to 24 hours in the day, for example, in a production plant or retail outlet which never shuts down. As we move more and more towards a service economy the demand for shift workers is growing.

Shift working is an extremely stressful mode of working and reports show that such workers can suffer more from certain ill-health conditions. For this reason, nightshift working qualifies for free health assessments (*see* Chapter 8: Night working). Shiftworking is protected in the normal way as there is usually no question as to whether you are classed as an employee.

Job sharers

Job sharing is most common among women returning to work on a part-time basis after maternity leave. Some jobs require full-time input and the only way they can be done part-time is if two people literally share the job. Studies by New Ways to Work, a charity supporting flexible working have established that in certain cases it is possible for even the most senior jobs to be shared.

Understandably, job sharing is far easier if you work for a larger company. A survey by the DTI showed that it was only available to 17 per cent in companies that employed fewer than 10 workers while it was available to over 65 per cent in companies that had 250 workers.

Annual hours contracts

Annual hours describes a system where an employee is required to do a certain number of hours on an annual basis, rather than under the more commonplace weekly pattern. This can be useful if work is seasonal. Such workers are likely to have no problem in establishing employment status (*see* Chapter 7).

Zero hours contracts

A zero hours contract is a contract where an employer is not obliged to provide a minimum number of hours' work. There is a question mark over whether the worker is actually an employee under such an arrangement. This is because the essential requirement of 'mutuality of obligations' – that is the employer should be required to provide work and the employee should be required to do it – may be missing. Such contracts were historically used to abuse the position of the workers subjecting them to unpaid time if there was no work available. With the Working Time Regulations and the National Minimum Wage Act, such abuse is not now possible.

 Key Questions

Do I have the same rights as other workers?
Anyone on one of the above work patterns will either be an employee or worker unless they are genuinely self-employed. Rights as an employee should be unaffected by the above work patterns provided adequate continuous employment can be accumulated and there is mutuality of obligations (*see* Chapter 3).

What about pay benefits and overtime?
All arrangements will depend on the contractual arrangement between you and the organization at which you are engaged, but will be subject to statutory minimum entitlements, such as the right to no less than a minimum wage.

If I'm working from home do I have the same rights as at work?
Yes, although the way in which you are managed and your performance is assessed would of course need to be altered to reflect your place of work. Your employer would need to make sure that your home environment satisfies health and safety standards and ensure that your equipment is safely set up.

Can I be forced to become a shift worker?
Your consent would normally be needed as such a change in hours would mean a change to your contract of employment. However, if your employer has good sound business reasons for making the change and carries out a proper process in implementing the change including consulting with you then you may lose your job if you refuse to agree to become a shift worker (*see* Chapter 7: Changes to your contract).

What sort of recovery time is allowed between day/night shifts, etc. – if I'm changing shifts continually?
See Chapter 8.

What about nights – do I have extra rights?
See Chapter 8: Night working.

What are my rights to share my job?
There is no right to a job share. The consent of your employer is needed. If your reasons are your child care responsibilities then a refusal to allow you to job share or return part-time without clear and objective justification by an employer could give rise to an indirect sex discrimination claim (*see* Chapter 9: Becoming a parent).

Can I be forced into job-sharing?
No. Being forced is likely to be a breach of contract and give you the right to claim constructive dismissal (*see* Chapter 23).

Am I liable for my job-sharer's mistakes?
If you are sharing a job you may have joint responsibility to carry out the duties. It is possible depending on the nature of the job that you could be equally responsible for the mistakes of your sharer.

 What next . . .

If you need advice on flexible working, the first thing you should do is get ahead of the game and take advantage of the tactic and tips every worker should know at Chapter 2. If you need to take things further *see* Part 5: Taking things further. Details of organizations that can assist you and further information are in Appendix B: Contact Points.

11

Public and other duties

At some stage we all need time off work, whether to attend to jury service, trade union duties or for study. Balancing the requirements of work with the inevitable demands on our time that daily life can throw in our path can be a struggle. But take comfort in the fact you have the legal right to take time off work in the circumstances detailed in this chapter although you are not entitled to be paid in all cases.

Public duties

Perhaps one of the best-known forms of public duty is that of a Justice of the Peace. These are lay magistrates appointed by the Lord Chancellor to magistrates' courts to hear criminal cases. There are many other forms of public duty that people can undertake. Although unpaid, you are allowed reasonable time off work to perform these duties. Whether the time required is reasonable will depend on several factors such as the nature of your public duties, the time you have already taken off and your employer's circumstances. The key question asked is what effect your absence will have on the business.

Remember, your contract of employment (some terms of which may be in your staff handbook) may entitle you to paid time off work.

Jury service is also a common reason for taking time off work. There is no legal right to take time off work for jury service although, paradoxically, if your employer prevented you from performing jury service they may be in contempt of court.

If you are denied time off for public duties you can go to employment tribunal and if your claim succeeds you will be entitled to such compensation as the tribunal considers fair and that reflects your losses.

Occupational pension scheme trustees

If you are an employee and also a trustee of an occupational pension scheme, you have the right to take a reasonable amount of paid time off during working hours to perform your duties and to take any necessary training. You do not need any length of employment with your employer to qualify for this right.

You can take your employer to employment tribunal if you are denied this right.

Employee representatives

If you have been elected as an employee representative for the purposes of a redundancy exercise or a transfer of your employers' business, you have the right to paid time off in order to perform these functions and to undergo any necessary training. You do not need any length of employment with your employer to qualify for this right.

You can take your employer to employment tribunal if you are denied this right.

Study/training for young workers

This applies if you have left school but are under the age of 18 years and have not achieved the standard of achievement set by the Secretary of State for Education and Employment. This standard is set out in the Right to Time Off for Study or Training Regulations 1999 and sets down a list of standards which should be achieved by all school leavers, for example, five GCSEs grade A–C, or one NVQ or SVQ at level 2. If this applies, you have the right to take reasonable paid time off work for study or training to achieve certain specified qualifications that would contribute to your attaining the standard or help improve your employment prospects.

You can take your employer to employment tribunal if you are denied this right.

Trade union duties

You are entitled to paid time off work to carry out your various duties and undergo training if you are a trade union official. Your trade union must be recognized by your employer for this right to apply.

You can take your employer to employment tribunal if you are denied this right.

Safety representatives

Safety representatives are entitled to paid time off to perform their duties and get training in health and safety matters.

You can take your employer to employment tribunal if you are denied this right.

Sabbaticals and career breaks

There is no legal entitlement to a career break or sabbatical, although some employers do grant a contractual entitlement to such leave to their workers. The terms governing such absence may be set out in your contract or staff handbook. If employers offer this leave, the entitlement usually arises after employees have completed a number of years' service with the organization and is seen as a reward for loyalty.

Surveys show that employees increasingly value benefits of this kind as the need and desire for flexible working patterns grow. Changes to parental leave (*see* Chapter 9) highlight the increasing awareness of politicians that the commercial objectives of the workplace need to be balanced with our home lives.

 What next . . .

If you need advice on taking time off work for public duties or other reasons, the first thing you should do is get ahead of the game and take advantage of the tactics and tips every worker should know in Chapter 2.

If you need to take things further *see* Part 5: Taking things further. Details of organizations that can assist you and further information are in Appendix B: Contact points.

Sickness

Employees take over eight sick days off a year on average
Institute of Personnel and Development

Perhaps you have the flu, or are off again with backache. Or you may be worried about what your employer may do about the days you have taken off genuinely sick. Or perhaps you are taking a 'sickie' because you just can't face your boss, or want a day off.

Although surveys of sickness leave can be inaccurate, as people do not tend always to tell the full story when asked, employers manage to build up a far more accurate picture. The Institute of Personnel and Development, who surveyed employers, say workers help themselves to an average of three 'sickie' days a year. The most common reason given was minor illnesses such as colds and flu.

In a bid to tackle this some employers have now introduced so called 'duvet days', a day or two extra annual holiday that can be taken at short notice when staff don't feel like coming into work.

Whatever the reasons you have certain rights but there are also certain measures your employer can take. The first thing to do is establish the reason for your absence and the type of sickness that you are suffering from, as these affect what rights you will have.

Genuine frequent short-term sickness

This includes flu, stomach upsets, sports injuries, general sickness, head-aches and so on. It does not include symptoms of major illnesses or an indication that you suffer from a serious underlying condition such as ME or AIDS. In such cases your employer needs to examine the level of your absences and the associated reasons. We all suffer from the odd bout of flu, etc. and it would be unreasonable for an employer to take action against you for such absences. It is when such absences become too frequent or amount to an unacceptable amount of total time off work that action can be taken by an employer.

If you have had persistent absences your employer may choose to follow their special absence procedure or the disciplinary procedure and warn you if your absence levels are unacceptable. Ultimately, you may be dismissed because your employer does have the right to say enough is enough. Make no mistake, your employer is entitled to make the point that the level of your attendance is inadequate for the needs of the business even when there is no question as to the authenticity of your sickness.

Long-term illnesses

Long-term illnesses include ones that are serious, that may require ongoing treatment (such as back problems) and those that may even be terminal. These sorts of conditions may qualify as a disability under the Disability Discrimination Act giving you various rights as detailed in Chapter 14.

If your illness is serious or long-term your employer is likely to handle your absenteeism in a completely different way to absenteeism arising from those frequently absent for minor ailments. Ultimately, you could be dismissed because of your illness but it may be unfair and/or discriminatory unless your employer goes about it in the correct way. Your employer should establish the exact medical position as far as possible, consult with you and look at alternative employment and reasonable adjustments where appropriate. Your employer should also check any eligibility for permanent health insurance, if such a scheme is available to you. If all that is done and no solution is found, then you could lawfully lose your job.

Malingerers

There are also so-called 'malingerers', those who are not ill at all but pretend to be to get a day off work. Some even push it as far as habitually taking Mondays or Fridays off so they can have a nice long weekend. If your employer suspects you of malingering, you may be disciplined and even dismissed. The main hurdle for your employer is gathering enough evidence to formulate the necessary reasonable belief that you are deceiving them. But be warned by the example of the construction company who, after a tip-off, sent a personal investigator around to check on one of their builders off sick with a bad back only to discover that he was working on a competitor's building site, while claiming sick pay. He was dismissed for gross misconduct (*see* Chapter 22: Misconduct).

If you are dismissed for any of the above you have certain rights – *see* below for details.

 What if . . .

- An employee was frequently off sick and was dismissed for persistent absenteeism. In her last 18 months she was absent about 25 per cent of the time (eight per cent absence was agreed as acceptable with the union – as a general guide). Her absences were often covered by medical certificates, which referred to conditions such as 'dizzy spells, anxiety and nerves, bronchitis, virus infection, cystitis, althruigra of the left knee, and dyspepsia and flatulence'. The employee had received warnings and it was clear that she was not suffering from any long-term illness. The employment tribunal found the dismissal unfair, but the employers appealed to the Employment Appeal Tribunal.
  Outcome: The dismissal in a similar case was fair. In cases of intermittent absences due to minor ailments your employer should undertake a fair review of your attendance record and the reasons for absences. You should be warned in accordance with the company's disciplinary procedure after you have had the opportunity to put forward any comments about your absences. If your attendance does not improve your employer will be justified in dismissing you.
- An employee is off sick frequently with fatigue and receives a warning for the high level of her absences. She is then off for three months although her diagnosis is clear. Her employer dismisses her without taking any further action saying her absences are having too much of a detrimental impact on the business.
  Outcome: This is likely to be an unfair dismissal if she has more than one year's service. Her condition is clearly potentially serious and her employer should have discovered her true medical position and consulted with her before taking any action. It may transpire that she has a condition that qualifies as a disability in which case she may have

a claim for disability discrimination irrespective of how long she has been at the company.

- James often takes time off sick when he is really quite well. Sometimes he goes to a local sports centre to play football when he is off work and at the weekends. He went to the sports centre after calling in sick for the third day in a row. A colleague, John, who has taken a week's parental leave attends the same sports centre to teach his daughter to play football and spots James. James is playing football and looks well. The next day John reports seeing James to human resources and James is called into an investigatory meeting. James admits to being there but says that he started to feel better at about lunchtime and thought the fresh air would do him good.

Outcome: After investigating the matter further by taking a statement from John, James is called to a disciplinary hearing. James' employer wants to dismiss him, but decides to give him the benefit of the doubt this time as his story sounded plausible. They decided to give him a final written warning and confirm orally and in writing that any further breach of discipline could result in his dismissal.

 Key Questions

Am I entitled to any sick leave?
You should be entitled to sick leave from your employer but if you are, for example, dismissed for taking sick leave, you will only be able to claim that you have been unfairly dismissed if you have enough continuous service of one year. Otherwise you cannot do anything about it unless you qualify as disabled under the Disability Discrimination Act (*see* Chapter 14), in which case you may have a claim for disability discrimination. The level of pay you will be entitled to is at least statutory sick pay level (*see* below). You may be entitled to a higher level of sick pay if you are entitled to it under your contract of employment.

I am frequently off work for a couple of days just due to being sickly – what is my position?
Case law points to a number of factors that should be taken into account in this situation. These include the nature of your illnesses, whether illnesses will recur, how long you are absent on each occasion, your employer's need to get the work done, and how your absences impact on

your colleagues. Your employer should explain the situation to you and follow disciplinary procedures before reaching any decision.

Do I have to get a doctor's report if I am frequently off sick for short periods?

No. By the very nature of short-term illnesses, it is unlikely to make any difference because the absences are owing to non-serious short-term ailments from which you would have recovered before a doctor could report on it. If the short-term illnesses point to an underlying condition then a doctor's report may be relevant. If you are disciplined or dismissed it is not really because of the illnesses you suffer from, but because they are too frequent and disruptive to the business.

What if it is alcohol related?

If your sickness absences are self-induced because of alcoholism then, as long as there is evidence verifying that as the reason, you can be dismissed in the same way as someone persistently off work for short periods. If it affects your concentration at work or your ability to do the job, you could be dismissed for misconduct (*see* Chapter 22). Although alcoholism may be recognized as an addiction it is specifically excluded as a disability under the Disability Discrimination Act so there is no added protection from that law. Employers must, however, beware as if the alcohol exacerbates an existing illness or causes a more serious condition – such as liver damage – then it may be inappropriate to deal with the issue as a matter of conduct.

How much paid sick leave am I entitled to?

The amount of sick leave you are entitled to depends on the terms of your employment and the nature of your illness. You are entitled to statutory sick pay as a minimum entitlement (*see* below), but often employers increase your sickness entitlement beyond the minimum and grant you a period of full pay.

Am I entitled to more paid sick leave if I have a serious illness or need an operation?

Again, this is a matter of your contract, but your employer would be foolish to deny you the right to more time off if you have a serious condition as they may be falling foul of the law on disability discrimination law. As for pay, again it is a matter of the contract, but remember anything in the contract can be negotiated.

Does my employer need to get a doctor's report if I am off sick with a serious condition?

Yes. They will not be in a position to consult or take any action if they do not. They may also need to get an expert's report.

Statutory sick pay

The bare minimum

Many employers have a contractual scheme set up to deal with sickness and sick pay, but there are legal minimums to which you are entitled. The rules of the national scheme are fairly complicated but, essentially, it consists of the following provisions.

You need to be an employee and be aged between 16 and 65 years with earnings high enough to pay national insurance contributions. You are entitled to up to 28 weeks' pay although you are not paid for the first three days. Your employer is allowed to request evidence of your sickness, such as self-certification for the first seven days, and a doctor's certificate for any longer periods. It is paid at a flat rate of £68.20 (2005) a week.

 Key Questions

Will I still be paid if I am seriously ill?

Whether you are paid depends on the contractual terms on sick pay either in your contract or handbook. You are entitled to at least statutory sick pay (*see* above). Some employers operate a discretionary sick pay scheme so, in the case of a serious illness, they can opt to extend pay at their discretion. A recent case has established that workers on long-term sick leave whose contractual and statutory sick pay may have expired are entitled to be paid for holiday taken while absent from work.

Whatever my illness, will my company help with the costs of treatment?

Unless there is a right to private medical insurance or any other benefit entitling you to such costs, there is no right to get help from your employer towards the cost of any treatment.

What if I am sick and it is related to my disability?

If you qualify as disabled under the Disability Discrimination Act, you are entitled to special rights and protection (*see* Chapter 14: Disability discrimination).

What if my sickness is related to my pregnancy?

If your sickness is related to your pregnancy, any adverse treatment against you by your employer could give you the right to a sex discrimination claim against your employer. This is an area in which there has been a lot of litigation and you should take advice if this applies to you.

What if my GP's report and the company doctor's report conflict?

The law allows an employer to prioritize the report of the company doctor, as it is likely that he or she will have a better understanding of their business and the roles to be performed.

Do I have a right to see the medical report?

You do not have the right to see the company doctor's medical report but you do have the right to see, and even withhold part or all of, the report provided by your GP – or the doctor who is responsible for your clinical care. This is under the Access to Medical Reports Act. Your consent is also required before your doctor can be approached for a report.

If I get caught out pulling a 'sickie' what can I do?

You have the right to the procedures set out in your disciplinary policy and it is a useful tip to ensure that your employer follows them. They do promote a fair and unbiased approach to matters of discipline. If you are guilty, you can expect to be disciplined and even potentially dismissed if your cheating amounted to a serious breach of contract.

Am I entitled to permanent health insurance?

Your contract may entitle you to this right in the case of serious illness. There is no general law entitling you to this right, which can be very generous and cover a proportion of your salary until retirement or death.

Your Rights

1 Not to be unfairly dismissed.
2 Procedural fairness in how your absence is handled.
3 Protection against disability discrimination.

 Tactics and Tips

Permanent health insurance

If you do have this right, you will need to satisfy the scheme rules to qualify. Sometimes contracts are badly drafted and do not state that the benefit is subject to qualifying under the scheme rules. If that is the case, you may be able to claim that you are entitled to the right from your employers even if the insurer turns you down. If you are dismissed before you get a chance to establish whether you are entitled to permanent health insurance provided by your employer, you may again have a claim against your company.

Grievance procedure

If you are not satisfied with the way in which sickness matters are being handled you could raise a 'grievance' against your employer. Raising a grievance is a way of making a formal complaint within your company, and the process, which is now statutory, is often set down in your contract or staff handbook, although you can still raise a grievance even if there is no procedure in writing. In most cases this merely means writing a letter to your boss raising the complaint.

Notice entitlements

Remember that if you are dismissed for any reason except gross misconduct you are entitled to a minimum of one week's notice for each year of service, up to a maximum of 12 weeks. If your contract specifies shorter periods than this, it is incorrect and you can rely on the legal minimum periods. If your contract provides for longer periods than the legal minimum, you are entitled to the longer period.

References

The whole business of getting a helpful reference is obviously a particular worry for those facing dismissal for sickness absence. If you are in this position it is a good idea to ask your current employer to agree the wording of your reference before you leave. Often an employer will agree to provide just a basic factual reference stating start and end dates and the duties you undertook. Remember they are under an obligation to be honest and may be contacted for further information.

 What next . . .

If you need advice on sickness absence, the first thing you should do is get ahead of the game and take advantage of the tactics and tips every worker should know in Chapter 2. If you need to take things further *see* Part 5: Taking things further. Details of organizations that can assist you and further information are in Appendix B: Contact points.

13

Pay

The average pay of full-time employees was around £25,000 in 2003

Let's face it – most of us work for the money! And, sadly, money is as likely to be the root of as many problems in the workplace as it is in other walks of life. In fact, over a quarter of those looking for a new job claim the main reason for moving was because their pay was unsatisfactory.

The law regulates pay in some detail. Not only does it set a minimum level at which you are entitled to be paid, but you are also protected against money being taken by your employer from your pay without your consent. Your employer must also provide details of your pay in your contract or statement of particulars of employment (*see* Chapter 7) and provide you with a pay statement.

Until a few years ago the only law governing your pay was the agreement between you and your employer – your contract. But the National Minimum Wage Act now sets a minimum hourly rate (*see* below).

If you are paid above the national minimum wage, it is your contract of employment that regulates your pay. So all terms and conditions relating to pay, such as overtime, bonuses, and weekend rates are controlled by the contractual arrangement you have agreed to.

In employment law pay is one of your most important statutory entitlements, so denial of pay or deductions from pay without your consent will entitle you to bring a claim against your employer.

The national minimum wage

The government introduced a national minimum wage in April 1999 for all workers. Your employer must not pay you less than this minimum wage. If you are under the age of 18 years you do not qualify and the rate varies depending on your age (those under the age of 22 years are entitled to less) and the nature of your engagement, such as whether it can be defined as accredited training or an apprenticeship.

The independent Low Pay Commission charged with monitoring and evaluating the impact of the national minimum wage concluded that the minimum wage has been a success, and there has not been any adverse impact on employment or UK business. The vast majority (over 70 per cent) of those benefiting are women.

National minimum wage is currently set at £5.05 (October 2005). A lower rate of £4.25 (October 2005) applies to younger workers aged 18–22 years.

These rates apply to all workers whether part-time, full-time workers, agency or home workers, irrespective of the size of the organization. Only those genuinely self-employed are excluded (*see* Chapter 3).

If you are not paid the national minimum wage you can bring a claim at employment tribunal or county court to recover the money you should have been paid. If you are dismissed for asserting your right to the minimum wage, you will have the right to bring an automatic unfair dismissal claim. You can also complain to an employment tribunal if you have been subjected to unfairness (a detriment) for claiming the national minimum wage.

Your employer will be guilty of a criminal offence if it takes certain unlawful actions such as refusing to pay you national minimum wage or failing to keep records or keeping false records.

 Key Questions

Who is eligible for the minimum wage?
All workers except certain categories, including the genuinely self-employed, volunteers, members of the armed forces, those under 18 years, and people living and working as part of a family, such as au pairs.

How are 'hours' and 'pay' defined?
To calculate if you are being paid at national minimum pay levels, you need to calculate your average hourly rate. So you need to know the pay received in the pay reference period as well as the hours worked. There are detailed rules on how certain payments are to be treated, but you first need to establish the gross pay. Broadly, in addition to basic pay the following are examples of payment that are included in the calculation of gross pay:

- incentive payments;
- commission payments;
- bonuses;
- tips;
- accommodation, subject to a financial limit, although the general rule is that benefits in kind do not count.

Payments out of your salary such as tax and national insurance contributions reduce your pay in the calculation of gross pay. And allowances, which are payments not consolidated into your normal pay, are also excluded. An example of an allowance is a daily attendance fee.

How are the hours calculated?

The hours you work depend on the type of work that you do. You either do salaried work, output work, timework or unmeasured work – which applies when work doesn't fall into the category of salaried, output or time work but the worker is required to work when needed or when work is available. There are also special rules on the treatment of travel time, on-call time, etc.

What if my employer doesn't comply?

You have the right to claim for lost wages and automatic unfair dismissal if your employer dismisses you as a result of your claim for the minimum wage. You also have the right not to be subjected to unfairness (a detriment) because you wish to claim minimum wage. You can make a written request to inspect your employer's records to establish if you are being paid the minimum wage and your employer must produce the records within 14 days. Remember, it is a serious matter for your employer – they can be subjected to criminal liability for failing to comply with this law.

...? What if . . .

- An employee received training that cost her company £3,000 and then immediately decided to resign to join a competing company. However, her contract states that if she leaves within a year of the training she would have to repay the costs of training. She therefore owed £3,000 to her employer, but the company owed the employee a week's worth of accrued but untaken holiday pay and wished to set this money off against the £3,000.

Outcome: There is no term in the employee's contract of employment entitling her employer to deduct money from her pay. So if they do this, the employee could bring an unlawful deduction claim against her employer. The only lawful way to recover the money from her is for her employer to pay her the money she is due and then request repayment of the £3,000 she owes them. If she refuses to pay they will need to take her to court to recover the money. This is likely to be a costly exercise and defeating the object of recovering the £3,000.

- A worker's wages included a 50 per cent uplift because he worked in London. There was another uplift arising from his pay grade under the salary scale system used at his work. The employee brought a claim at tribunal on the basis these payments should be disregarded in accounting for the calculation of national minimum wage in his case as they were allowances. (As noted above allowances are excluded from the calculation of national minimum wage and they are payments which are not consolidated into normal pay. An example of an allowance is a daily attendance fee.)

  Outcome: In a similar case, the sums were taken into account in calculating the minimum wage, as they were not allowances.

- A community care assistant travelled from one house to the next to carry out her duties. She was a time worker, which means she was paid with reference to the time she worked and was not contracted to do a certain number of salaried hours. She claimed that her travelling time should also be paid at national minimum wage level.

  Outcome: A recent amendment to the law means that travel between assignments at premises that your employer does not occupy should be treated as work. She is therefore likely to be entitled to the extra pay.

 Key Questions

What if I'm having difficulty in getting paid?
You have the right to take your employer to employment tribunal as this may amount to an unlawful deduction from your salary and you could also claim constructive unfair dismissal if you have one year's service (*see* Chapter 23).

Do I have the right to a written pay statement?
Yes. It should contain the gross amount of your wages, deductions and the net amount of your wages.

What if I don't get a pay statement?
You can refer the matter to employment tribunal. If you have not received one or you have one but deductions have been made without you being notified, the tribunal may award you a sum equal to the deductions which were made in the last 13 weeks without you being notified. In practice, a tribunal will only make a token award if it was a technical slip up by your employer.

Do I have the right to see my employer's pay records for me?
You have a specific right to see records in order to establish if you are being paid the national minimum wage. You must make the request in writing and the organization must supply the records within 14 days.

How is pay for weekend work, night work, commission, public holidays, overtime work, and bonus payments calculated?
If these are contractual items then payment for all of these is dependent on the terms of your contract of employment, or custom and practice, and subject to national minimum wage levels. Employers use many different approaches to payment for the above. There are, for example, numerous bonus schemes, and many different systems for paying overtime.

What about any expenses I incur in the course of my work?
You have the right to recover expenses incurred during the course of work performed for the company. This is usually an express term in your contract or, if there is none, then it will be what's called an implied term of your contract (*see* Chapter 7).

Do I have the right to equal pay with male/female colleagues?
Yes. Men and women have the right to be paid equally for equal work. This right is rooted in European legislation and is covered further in Chapter 14: Sex discrimination and equal pay.

What about holiday pay – how does that work?
You are entitled to be paid holiday leave for 20 days a year under the Working Time Regulations. This is covered in Chapter 8: Holidays.

Can my employer make deductions from my pay?
Not without your written consent or the contractual right (*see* above).

Can my employer change my pay without telling me?
Any change to your contractual provisions should be made with your consent. In very particular circumstances changes may be possible if your employer has good business reasons and follows a careful procedure (*see* Chapter 7).

My company's gone bust. What are my rights?
There are funds set aside by the government to pay you to a limited extent for your entitlements (*see* Chapter 22: Insolvency).

If I'm sick what happens to my pay?
If you are sick you are entitled as a minimum to statutory sick pay. Your contract of employment may provide you with additional sick pay entitlements (*see* Chapter 12).

What about if I need time off?
You have the right to time off in certain circumstances. How your pay is dealt with depends on the circumstances and your reasons (*see* Chapter 8: Holidays; Chapter 9; or Chapter 11).

What are my rights to maternity pay?
Rights to statutory maternity pay or maternity allowance as a minimum are detailed in Chapter 9: Becoming a parent.

What about pay during parental leave?
Parental leave is unpaid (*see* Chapter 9).

 Your Rights

1 To have details of your pay in writing in a statement of particulars of your employment (*see* Chapter 7).
2 To receive an itemized pay statement.
3 Not to have any money deducted from your pay without your consent.
4 To be paid at least the national minimum wage.
5 To claim your losses if you are not paid the national minimum wage.

6 Not to be subjected to any unfairness (detriment) for claiming the national minimum wage.

 Tactics and Tips

Records
Remember that you can request to see records of your pay entitlement if necessary.

Confirmation in writing
You should request that everything discussed regarding your pay or changes to it are confirmed in writing. This prevents misunderstandings and ensures that everyone clearly understands the position.

 What next . . .

If you need advice on your pay, the first thing you should do is get ahead of the game and take advantage of the tactics and tips every worker should know in Chapter 2. If you need to take things further *see* Part 5: Taking things further. Details of organizations that can assist you and further information are in Appendix B: Contact points.

14

Discrimination

There is no limit to how much you could be awarded if you are
discriminated against

Introduction

Thirty years after the first legislation to outlaw discrimination in this country, there is now a welter of European and domestic legislation, coupled with case law, that is altering this area of the law more quickly than almost any other. In particular, the Human Rights Act is likely to have a significant impact, bringing far more people under the protective umbrella of the law.

The current law protects you from various specific forms of discrimination through Acts and Regulations passed by Parliament over the last 30 years. These are:

1 the Sex Discrimination Act 1975 (SDA);
2 the Race Relations Act 1975 (RRA);
3 the Equal Pay Act 1970 (EPA);
4 the Disability Discrimination Act 1995 (DDA);
5 the Employment Equality (Sexual Orientation) Regulations 2003 (SOR);
6 the Employment Equality (Religion or Belief) Regulations 2003 (RBR).

These acts protect you from being discriminated against at work on the grounds of your sex, marital status, race, religion, sexual orientation or disability, and make it unlawful to offer different pay and conditions to men and women doing the same job.

Transsexuals are recognized and protected under existing law on sex discrimination, and regulations exist specifically setting out their rights.

There is currently no law preventing age discrimination either, with just a recommended code of practice on age discrimination in place, which has no actual force of law. Protection against age discrimination will be put into place in 2006.

Europe's changing laws

The anti-discrimination proposals on the way from Europe are based on Article 13 of the Treaty of Amsterdam, agreed at the 1997 summit. This makes anti-discrimination a basic principle, outlawing discrimination on the grounds of racial and ethnic origin, religion, belief, disability, age and sexual orientation.

Before the Treaty of Amsterdam there were only provisions on equal pay and discrimination on the grounds of nationality.

Types of discrimination

Currently there are three basic types of discrimination.

Direct
This is where, for reasons based on your sex, race, disability, marital status, or the fact you are a transsexual, you are treated less favourably. In practice this can mean failing to get a job, denial of a promotion or other opportunities, or being harassed or dismissed for these reasons.

Indirect
Indirect sex discrimination takes place when an employer imposes a requirement or condition, such that it would be to the detriment of a considerably larger proportion of people of a particular sex, and the employer cannot justify it. In the case of race discrimination the require-ment or condition must be such that the proportion of people in a particular racial group who can comply with it is considerably smaller than the proportion of people outside of that racial group. As with indirect sex discrimination, the employer must be unable to justify it.

To be classed as discrimination the condition must be shown to be detrimental to those concerned. For example, an employer could say that only people of a certain height should apply for a job. As men are generally taller than women, such a requirement is likely to be discriminatory. However, an employer does have a get-out clause: if it is able to justify imposing the condition. Another example, an organization imposed a requirement that its Customer Care Manager, responsible for its five most important customers, work full-time rather than part-time after returning from maternity leave. The company justified this on the grounds that an experienced well-informed full-time Customer Care Manager was essential to foster continuity and familiarity with these important customers.

Victimization

This is perhaps one of the most misunderstood forms of discrimination, perhaps because it is often taken to mean unfair treatment, or being picked on. In legal terms victimization occurs when your employer treats you less favourably because you threatened, or actually brought a discrimination claim, or helped another to do so.

 Mini Case Study

- A woman brought a sex discrimination claim against her employer alleging that she had been dismissed because she was pregnant. The complaint was settled out of court. Her employer then failed to provide a reference for her when requested by an employment agency. She brought a claim on the basis that withholding a reference was unlawful, and that she was being victimized because of her previous complaint.

Outcome
Her former employer's failure to provide a reference may be viewed by a tribunal as a retaliatory measure because of her discrimination complaint, and may amount to victimization.

Discrimination law is different

There are a number of important differences between discrimination law and other employment law.

No upper limit

Unlike the law on unfair dismissal, if there is a finding of discrimination, there is no maximum amount that you can be awarded. The amount you are awarded is calculated by reference to the position you would have been in had you not been dismissed. So, if you were a city high-flier on course for earnings and bonuses worth a total of £2,000,000 had you not been dismissed, the tribunal could award you that much money.

Injury to feelings
There is an additional award in discrimination cases of injury to feelings.

No qualifying period
You do not need to have served a qualifying period of service in order to lodge a discrimination claim. You could lodge proceedings on your first day in a job; in fact even job applicants can bring a claim.

Not just employees
The law doesn't just protect employees. It also includes job applicants, consultants, agency workers and the self-employed. For example, a contract cleaner working at the offices of a client company can take not only her employer but also the client company to employment tribunal for discrimination. In certain circumstances even former employees are protected.

Not just dismissal
Unlike the law on unfair dismissal, discrimination claims can be brought where no dismissal has taken place. So a claim can proceed while you are working for the organization.

Late employment tribunal applications
For claims of unfair dismissal and discrimination the time limit for submitting a claim to an employment tribunal is three months from the moment of dismissal or the act complained of. If an unfair dismissal claim is submitted late then the tribunal will need to determine whether or not it was reasonably practicable for the claim to be submitted in time. However, if a discrimination claim is submitted to employment tribunal after the expiry of the three-month deadline, then a tribunal can hear the case if it decides it is 'just and equitable' for them to do so. You should take legal advice in these circumstances.

Questionnaires
Discrimination claims involve the use of detailed questionnaires, enabling you to find out more evidence and information relating to your complaint. A tribunal will take an organization's failure to reply to such a questionnaire as an inference against the organization. Quite often questionnaires are also used tactically. An enormous number of questions are sometimes asked, and data and statistics requested, and these can be costly or difficult to obtain. In some instances the submission of the questionnaire can encourage an organization to settle a claim.

Who is liable?

You may wonder who is actually responsible for an act of discrimination, the organization or the individual? A manager may refuse to promote someone because of his or her sex, or an employee may racially harass fellow employees. The employee guilty of discrimination can be taken to tribunal but the law also says that the employer can be held responsible for the acts of its employees, which is what happens in practice in the majority of cases.

Burden of proof

The burden of proof in discrimination claims used to be on the job applicant or employee. In other words, it was up to the employee to prove that he or she had been discriminated against. It is now in part up to the employer to prove that it has not been guilty of discrimination.

The three commissions

There are three commissions that work to support the main areas of anti-discrimination legislation. These are the *Equal Opportunities Commission*, the *Commission for Racial Equality* and the *Disability Rights Commission*. They have the power to conduct formal investigations, issue non-discrimination notices and assist individual claims of unlawful discrimination. Contacts for them can be found in Appendix B: Contact points. There are plans to have a single equality commission in the future.

Sex discrimination and equal pay

On average women earn 18 per cent less than men per hour

How many female secretaries are there in your office? How many female engineers? The questions may sound facile, but stereotyping such as this is just part and parcel of the prejudice women can still face at work.

The organization charged with tackling sex discrimination, the Equal Opportunities Commission, says:

25 years after the Sex Discrimination Act, and 30 after the Equal Pay Act was introduced, women are still sacked because they are pregnant, paid less for equal work, and earn less over a lifetime than men, even if they never have children.

Some progress has been made with the national minimum wage, the focus on the work–life balance (*see* Chapter 9), and the Human Rights Act. And of course, women are doing it for themselves. As more and more women come into the workplace, the inequalities are being eroded. There are over 12.6 million women and 15.5 million men in employment in the UK and the gap is closing. In 1971, 56 per cent of women in the UK were classed as economically active (in work, or seeking work). By the turn of the century that had risen to 72 per cent, while the number of economically active men had gone down from 91 per cent to 84 per cent.

The basic objective of the Sex Discrimination law is to ensure that men and women are treated equally and that there is no difference in the treatment of workers just because of their sex. The protection applies to all stages of the employment process from advertisements and the process of getting a job, through to promotion and dismissal.

The law in this area works on the basis of a comparison between the sexes, so a woman should not be treated less favourably than a man would be. For example, if a man is promoted after achieving certain targets, but a woman is not, then the woman may have a discrimination claim by comparing her position with that of the man. It is also unlawful to aid, instruct, pressure or induce others to discriminate.

Equal pay

This is one of the most problematic issues in the UK today. Scores of studies have revealed that even though the law in this area has been in force for decades, there are still significant and unacceptable differences in the pay of men and women. The discrepancy may in part be sustained as a result of a general reluctance on the part of UK workers to disclose information about their pay. Another reason is that the law on equal pay used to be very complex and that makes taking your employer to court expensive. This has now changed and the new rules should go some way to ensure parity in the pay of men and women.

Legislation on equal pay is designed to ensure that men and women are paid at the same level to do 'like work'. This means they either do the same work or it is deemed to be equivalent or of 'equal value' under a job evaluation study.

Alternatively, an independent expert can be asked to undertake the assessment. The comparison is of more than just pay – it covers the terms of a contract generally.

Recent changes in this law aimed at simplying it should help to tackle the differences in pay between men and women.

 What if . . .

- A woman went to a men's clothing store, which already employed seven men, to ask whether there were any jobs going. First she was told there were no vacancies; then she was told that the job was not suitable for a woman as it involved taking the inside leg measurement of male customers. The applicant had a lot of experience in men's tailoring and had taken such measurements many times before. She was not offered the position and claimed sex discrimination.
  Outcome: In a similar case the store was found to have unlawfully discriminated and the woman won her claim.
- A female train operator was notified of changes to staff rosters and alleged that the changes indirectly discriminated against women with childcare responsibilities. Indirect discrimination is based on the statistical comparison of the number of men and women who can comply with a particular requirement.
  Outcome: An employee in a similar case was one of only 21 females out of 2,044 train operators. All other employees, both male and female, were able to comply with the changes. However, given there were so many more men than women, and the fact it was common knowledge that single parents primarily responsible for childcare are more likely to be women, the court decided that the employee had been discriminated against.

 Key Questions

What is sex discrimination?
Sex discrimination takes place when you are treated less favourably than a colleague of the opposite sex. Your employer might offer you less favourable terms and conditions, or there might be fewer opportunities for promotion, transfer, training, benefits, facilities or other services. Discrimination can also occur if you have been dismissed on discriminatory grounds, subjected to abuse, or put at some disadvantage compared to employees of the opposite sex.

Who does the Sex Discrimination Act cover?

The Act gives protection to job applicants, contract workers, the self-employed and, in some instances, even former employees, in addition to employees. However, you may not be covered in the same way or to the same extent if you are working outside the UK, or if you are a police officer, prison officer, a minister of religion or a member of the armed forces.

Can job advertisements specify male/female applicants only?

Employers can specify male or female staff only when gender is a genuine occupational qualification necessary for that job. For example, this could apply in single sex establishments such as hospitals, prisons and old people's homes. In other cases the courts are likely to regard such ads as indicating an intention to discriminate.

The Equal Opportunities Commission is responsible for the enforcement of the provisions on advertisements. A tribunal can make a declaration that an advertisement is discriminatory.

Do I have to reveal to a prospective employer that I'm married/have children?

If asked – there is no reason why you should not as you are protected against discrimination on such grounds. If you lie on an application form, at interview or once at work, you could be disciplined or dismissed.

Can I be discriminated against because I'm pregnant?

No, this is unlawful (*see* Chapter 9: Becoming a parent).

What about positive discrimination?

Positive discrimination is against the law. Any attempt to redress an imbalance where, for example, women are under represented in an organization, is unlawful – although there are limited exceptions to this.

Positive discrimination is a risky measure to take as it means that in treating a woman more favourably her employer would be treating her male comparator less favourably. This could leave the employer open to being sued for discrimination.

Can I legally be paid less because I'm a woman?

Not if the work that you do is the same or equivalent to that of a man.

I'm not being promoted because I'm a man/woman – what are my rights?
Make sure you have good evidence to support your claim. Remember that you can find out more through the questionnaire procedure and that a tribunal will draw inferences and conclusions from the evidence supplied, or lack of it (*see* p. 142). So in this sort of situation you could seek advice on commencing discrimination proceedings against your employer. It may be advisable, in any event, to raise an internal grievance first as this may result in a resolution of the matter.

What about clothing? Can a woman be forced to wear trousers, a uniform, etc?
If certain clothing or uniform is required for the job that you do (to present a professional image, for example), then it is reasonable for your employer to require you to comply with its dress code. However, the Human Rights Act gives us the right to freedom of expression, which could include clothing. Case law will soon determine the situation.

Is it discriminatory if my employer doesn't make allowances for the fact I have family commitments?
Yes, it can be, depending on the circumstances. See above and Chapter 9.

 Your Rights

1 Not to be treated less favourably because of your sex, marital status, pregnancy or childbirth, or because you are a transsexual.
2 Not to be victimized if you have brought a claim, or helped someone bring a claim.
3 To bring discrimination proceedings if unlawful discrimination has occurred.

 What next . . .

If you need advice on sex discrimination, the first thing you should do is get ahead of the game and take advantage of the tactics and tips every worker and employer should know in Chapter 2. If you need to take things further *see* Part 5: Taking things further. Details of organizations that can assist you and further information are in Appendix B: Contact points.

Race discrimination

Race discrimination is discrimination on the grounds of colour, race, nationality or ethnic origins

The impact of the Stephen Lawrence inquiry report brought a new impetus to efforts to improve race relations, and raised questions about the extent of institutionalized racism. The Commission for Racial Equality saw this report as a watershed for UK race relations.

The fundamental objective of the Race Relations Act (RRA) is to ensure that workers are not discriminated against because of their race. The Act defines racial discrimination as discrimination on the grounds of colour, race, nationality or ethnic origins. You are protected at all stages of the employment process; from the job advertisement, to appointment, promotion and dismissal. The law in this area works on the basis of a comparison between the races. So, if someone of one race feels they have been discriminated against, the question asked is whether someone of a different race would have been treated in the same way.

It is also unlawful to aid, instruct, pressure or induce others to discriminate.

Changes in the law now mean that it is partly your employer's responsibility to prove that they did not discriminate against you. The burden of proving discrimination no longer rests solely on the employee.

There are some exemptions to the law. For example, it may be most effective to have a Bengali social worker working within the Bengali community. In this case the law would regard a person's race to be a genuinely necessary requirement to the job.

There are around 1.4 million members of ethnic minority groups over the age of 16 years and in employment in the UK, according to the Labour Force Survey. Of these, 450,000 are black workers, 440,000 Indian, 230,000 Pakistani or Bangladeshi, and 58,000 Chinese.

The Commission for Racial Equality stated that during 2000 around 11,000 people sought advice on their racial discrimination complaints. In 2000/01 the Employment Tribunal Service registered almost 3,500 cases, a rise of almost 25 per cent in two years.

What if . . .

- A black man who worked in a fast food chain complained that he was given a greater proportion of menial tasks than his white colleagues, and as a result he was not able to qualify for promotion. The tribunal considered the system of allocating menial tasks and the basis of promotion.
  Outcome: In a similar case an employee was denied the opportunity of promotion, as his duties were restricted. The system of promotion and allocation of tasks was entirely at the discretion of management and both systems were abused. The employee's claim of race discrimination succeeded.
- An Asian employee was passed over for promotion. A white candidate got the job even though he had fewer qualifications and less experience. There was no convincing evidence to rebut the charge of discrimination.
  Outcome: The employee in a similar case won his claim because the employer failed to supply any evidence supporting the promotion of the less-qualified candidate.
- A West Indian applied in person for a job at a hotel and was told that the job was taken but when she telephoned later she was told the job was available. She brought a claim of race discrimination.
  Outcome: In the absence of a reasonable explanation from the hotel, an applicant's claim in a similar situation succeeded.

 Key Questions

What is race discrimination?
Race discrimination takes place when you are treated less favourably than another on the grounds of your race.

Your employer might offer you less favourable terms and conditions, or there might be fewer opportunities for promotion, transfer, training, benefits, facilities or other services. Discrimination can also occur if you have been dismissed on discriminatory grounds, subjected to abuse, or put at some disadvantage compared to employees of another race.

Does the Race Relations Act cover me?

The Act covers more than just employees. Job applicants, contract workers, the self-employed and, in some instances, even former employees are all afforded protection.

I'm being insulted and given racist names. Is that discrimination?

Depending on the nature of the insults this could be racial harassment (*see* Chapter 15).

Who is exempt from the RRA?

There are some professions and types of worker excluded from the RRA including overseas employees, seafarers, certain crown employees and, in some cases, where national security is involved.

Are there any circumstances under which race discrimination is allowed?

Yes, but only if it is a genuine occupational requirement in order to perform the job, such as the Bengali social worker cited above, or where, for example, a Chinese waiter is employed in a Chinese restaurant for reasons of authenticity.

Can job advertisements specify a preference for a particular colour, race, nationality or religion?

Yes, but only if it is a genuine occupational requirement in order to perform the job, such as the Chinese waiter mentioned above. Otherwise it would be discriminatory.

The Commission for Racial Equality is responsible for the enforcement of the provisions on advertisements. A tribunal can make a declaration that an advertisement is discriminatory.

One of the conditions of the job is good written English – is that discrimination?

Yes, unless the requirement is necessary to the job. For example, a recruitment manager for a manufacturing company needs to recruit 20 new staff to work as machine operators. As part of the recruitment process he asks the candidates, who are from a number of different ethnic groupings, to perform a written test. This is likely to be discriminatory as it favours people brought up in the UK, and writing skills are not necessary for the work to be performed.

What about positive discrimination?
Positive discrimination is against the law. Any attempt to redress an imbalance because ethnic minorities are under represented in an organization is unlawful.

What about clothing – do I have the right to wear what I want, especially if it is part of my faith/heritage?
There is a possibility that an item of dress, which relates to religion, could be protected by the RRA. For example, to stop a Sikh wearing a turban could have a disproportionate impact on Indians, as most Sikhs are Indian. This would be indirect discrimination, and unless it can be objectively justified, it would be unlawful. The Human Rights Act and new European directives may soon give you new rights.

What if I've been discriminated against but my boss says it wasn't intentional?
It makes no difference what your boss says after the event. Intention is not relevant in discrimination matters.

I'm being paid less because of my race – what are my rights?
You have the right to bring a race discrimination claim. You should be as certain as possible that the reason you are being paid less is your race. Remember, you can use the discrimination questionnaire procedure to assist in gathering evidence.

I'm being denied promotion because I complained about race discrimination – what are my rights?
You have the right to bring a separate claim for victimization (*see* p. 141).

 Your Rights

1 Not to be treated less favourably because of your race, colour, nationality, or ethnic or national origin.
2 Not to be victimized if you have a complaint, bring a claim or help someone bring a claim of race discrimination.
3 To bring discrimination proceedings if unlawful discrimination has occurred.

What next . . .

If you need advice on race discrimination, the first thing you should do is get ahead of the game and take advantage of the tactics and tips every worker and employer should know in Chapter 2. If you need to take things further *see* Part 5: Taking things further. Details of organizations that can assist you and further information are in Appendix B: Contact points.

Disability discrimination

Although relatively new, the Disability Discrimination Act (DDA) is full of conditions, difficult definitions and adjustments that have to be 'reasonably made' by an employer. And then, like snakes and ladders, when conditions are satisfied and reasonable adjustments have been made, you suddenly discover that whole categories of disability and worker are excluded from legal protection – that employers are allowed to discriminate against the disabled in some cases. Confused? This chapter will guide you through the maze.

Under a broad definition of disability (*see* below) millions are working. However, the reality is that disabled people are much more likely to be unemployed than the non-disabled, and that prejudice and ignorance are still rife in the workplace in the UK.

The DDA has gone some way to tackling this situation. It gives people with disabilities new rights when they access goods, services and facilities, and some new employment rights, and public bodies now have a positive duty to promote equality of opportunity.

So who does the DDA cover? The Act defines a disabled person quite specifically (*see* below) and there are a large number of conditions and illnesses within its scope.

To bring a claim for disability discrimination there are three main questions that are considered:

1 Are you disabled as defined by the DDA?
2 Has your employer treated you less favourably for a reason relating to your disability, without any justification for doing so?
3 Has your employer satisfied its duty to make 'reasonable adjustments'?

A reasonable adjustment is a positive obligation imposed on employers requiring them to consider making changes to the premises and/or working practices in order to accommodate the needs of the disabled worker. This is discussed further below.

Defining disability

In legal terminology disability has a very specific definition, and in order to qualify for protection you must satisfy the definition completely. In practice this is a complex and contentious area because there are so many different conditions and impairments that are potentially covered by the law. The Act defines disability as:

a physical or mental impairment which has a substantial and long-term adverse effect on his (or her) ability to carry out normal day-to-day activities

To understand exactly what this means it is easiest to break it down into its component parts.

Physical or mental impairment
A physical impairment can be almost any condition that satisfies the rest of the definition – it is not necessary to have a clear diagnosis.

A mental impairment no longer needs to be clinically well recognised. More conditions are covered than people are generally aware, although people who have psychiatric conditions can be reluctant to admit to them, and often refuse to make use of the protection the law offers.

Substantial
This means that the condition has to be more than just minor or trivial.

Long-term
This means that your condition has lasted at least a year, is likely to last a year, or will last the rest of your life where the condition is terminal and you are not expected to survive for longer than a year. The definition of long-term also includes conditions that are in remission but are likely to recur.

Normal day-to-day activities
This means that the condition substantially affects at least one of the following:
• your mobility or ability to get around;

- your manual dexterity or how well you can use your hands;
- your physical co-ordination;
- your continence;
- your ability to lift, carry or move everyday objects;
- your speech, hearing or eyesight;
- your memory or ability to concentrate, learn or understand;
- your perception of the risk of physical danger.

Also protected

Past disabilities

People who had disabilities from which they have now recovered may also be protected by the DDA. For example, if you had a condition that lasted a year or more (and satisfied the other criteria of the definition of disability) but you have recovered then, if you are refused a new job on the grounds of your past illness, you would be protected by the DDA.

Medication and corrective measures

If you are on medication and as a result your condition is fully controlled, or you have an artificial limb and are now able to walk, you are still classified as disabled. The law ignores the impact of any corrective measures or medication although for obvious reasons an exception to this rule is the wearing of glasses or lenses for the correction of eyesight.

Progressive conditions

Conditions that are progressive are regarded as disabilities even if the conditions do not yet have a substantial effect on the ability to carry out normal day-to-day activities. If you have no symptoms at all then you are not covered by the DDA, but as soon as some symptoms occur, even if they are mild, you are protected.

HIV, Cancer and MS

You are deemed to be disabled if you suffer from any of these conditions.

Disfigurements

A severe disfigurement counts as a disability even if it does not match the definition above.

Registered disabled
You are automatically classed as disabled if you were registered disabled (under the Disabled Persons (Employment) Act 1944).

Excluded conditions
There are certain conditions that are specifically excluded from protection even though they satisfy the definition. These include addiction to alcohol, nicotine or drugs, and a tendency to arson, theft and exhibitionism.

Less favourable treatment
An employer discriminates against a disabled person if, for a reason relating to his disability, they treat him less favourably than they would treat someone to whom that reason does not or would not apply, and the employer cannot show the treatment is justified.

Reasonable adjustments

If you have a disability then your employer is required to consider making what are known as *reasonable adjustments* to its premises and working practices to accommodate you.

Reasonable adjustments are defined as steps that are reasonable for an employer to take to ensure its premises or working practices do not put a disabled worker at a disadvantage in comparison to his or her non-disabled colleagues. The objective is to remove or reduce the practical impact of their disability in the workplace. There is no general duty to make reasonable adjustments in anticipation of disabled workers – rather it arises on a case-by-case basis.

Sometimes there may not be a reasonable adjustment that can be made, and other times an adjustment may be possible – but it may not seem reasonable in the eyes of the law.

Whether or not an adjustment is reasonable depends on the factors detailed below, and reasonableness will be different depending on the nature of the work and disability, and the employer's circumstances.

The factors that are taken into account in deciding whether it is reasonable for the employer to make an adjustment are:
- the extent to which it would prevent the condition in question;
- the extent to which it is practicable for the employer to take the step;
- the financial and other costs of change, and the extent of any disruption caused;

- the extent of the employer's financial and other resources;
- the availability of financial or other assistance for taking the step.

Failing to make reasonable adjustments will mean that the employer is taken to have treated a disabled person less favourably because of his or her disability unless the employer can justify not making any adjustments, or show that undertaking adjustments would make no difference.

It would be impossible to list all the reasonable adjustments that could be made because there are so many physical and mental conditions, and so many different types of jobs. However, the DDA does include several codes of practice that set out guidance for employers. Unlike other codes employers are obliged to follow these codes.

Among the examples of reasonable adjustments the DDA code of practice cites the following:

- *Making adjustments to premises* – this could mean widening a doorway for a wheelchair, moving light switches or providing appropriate contrasts in decor to help the safe mobility of a visually impaired person. Your prospective employer should ask you about any special needs you may have.
- *Allocating some of a disabled person's duties to another person* – this may mean that if a job occasionally involves going onto the open roof of a building, an employer might have to transfer this work away from someone with severe vertigo.
- *Transferring a disabled person to fill an existing vacancy* – if an employee becomes disabled, or has a disability which worsens, to the extent that he or she cannot carry on with his or her current job, and there is no reasonable adjustment which would enable the employee from continuing to do the current job, then the disabled person might have to be considered for any suitable alternative posts which are available.
- *Altering a disabled person's working hours* – for example, allowing the disabled person to work flexible hours to enable additional breaks to overcome fatigue. As an example, a company was held to have discriminated against an employee with ME by failing to allow her to temporarily work from home in order to enable her to establish herself in employment. They found against the company on the ground that they had failed to make a reasonable adjustment.
- *Assigning a disabled person to a different place of work* – by, for example, transferring a wheelchair user's workstation to the ground floor.
- *Allowing the person to be absent during working hours for rehabilitation, assessment or treatment* – for example, to attend physiotherapy, psychoanalysis or undertake employment rehabilitation.
- *Giving the disabled person, or arranging for him or her to be given,*

training – this could be training in the use of particular pieces of equipment unique to the disabled person, or training appropriate for all employees but which needs altering because of the disability.

- *Acquiring or modifying equipment* – for example, providing a specially adapted keyboard for a visually impaired person or someone with arthritis. There is no requirement to provide or modify equipment for personal purposes unconnected with work, such as providing a wheelchair if a person needs one in any event but does not have one – the disadvantage here does not come from the employer's arrangements or premises.

- *Modifying instructions or reference manuals* – the format of instructions or manuals may need to be modified (for example, produced in braille or audio tape) and instructions for people with learning disabilities may need to be conveyed orally with individual demonstration.

- *Modifying procedures for testing or assessment* – a person with restricted manual dexterity might be disadvantaged by a written test, so an employer might have to give that person an oral test. For example, in order to qualify for promotion a manager had to complete some tests. Although not diagnosed, he has what he believes may be chronic fatigue syndrome. His employers provided a separate room with a bed for him to undertake the tests, and rather than having one hour, he was given as long as he needed.

- *Providing a reader or interpreter* – this could even mean a colleague reading mail to a visually impaired worker.

- *Providing supervision* – if, for example, a person's disability means they lack confidence, the provision of a support worker could be a reasonable adjustment.

Justification

Uniquely with disability law you can be turned down for a job, treated less favourably or even dismissed because of your disability. The law effectively allows discrimination in cases where an employer can justify its action. For example, if there is no adjustment that could be reasonably made to allow you to carry out your job, or if it would not be reasonable to make such an adjustment (based on the factors detailed above), then your employer may be justified in dismissing you. For example, an office worker who has a learning difficulty is dismissed because he cannot sort papers as quickly as his colleagues. He is dismissed even though there is little difference in productivity between him and his colleagues. There is unlikely to be 'justification' for dismissing him as there is no significant difference in productivity.

 What if . . .

- A chemist was made redundant. He suffered from a visual impairment from birth, which meant that even with powerful glasses he could not see well enough to drive. From the beginning his visual impairment had been an issue with his managers, and he had been turned down for a number of promotions because of his eyesight. He claimed that his selection for redundancy was discriminatory.

  Outcome: In a similar case the employee succeeded in his claim and was awarded over £100,000.

- A woman who applied for a job suffered from photosensitive epilepsy that was controlled by medication, and she had mentioned the disability on her CV. She was not contacted about any arrangements for the interview, but arrived at the interview with sunglasses around her neck. The room had bright fluorescent lighting and she commented on this, remarking she might be disadvantaged. During the interview she never used the sunglasses and did not tell the interviewer that she felt unwell. She did not get the job and complained that the interviewer had failed to make a reasonable adjustment because of the bright lighting in the room and was therefore in breach of the DDA.

  Outcome: In a similar case the employee's claim failed. She had not been unlawfully discriminated against on the grounds of her disability as a result of a failure to make a reasonable adjustment to the physical features of the premises. The condition was rare and no reasonable employer could be expected to know without being told that the lighting would cause her a substantial disadvantage. In any event the interviewers were led to believe that she brought her sunglasses in case she needed them.

- An information technology graduate with cerebral palsy was offered a job with the Constabulary. He needed assistance in going to the toilet which meant that someone had to accompany him. The Constabulary decided after investigating that it was not a reasonable adjustment for them to make. The offer was withdrawn and the graduate claimed disability discrimination. The grounds were the failure to comply with their duty to make a reasonable adjustment by not providing a personal carer.

Outcome: In a similar case the applicant's claim failed. A line has to be drawn and this was too much to expect of the employer. The employer's duty to make reasonable adjustments does not extend as far as to provide carers to attend to the personal need of employees.

- A diabetic applied for a job at a distribution centre, but didn't get the position on the grounds that there was no way to reduce the risk of injury to someone with his condition working in a low temperature environment.

  Outcome: The decision not to employ the diabetic is likely to be justified, as the risk could not be reduced by the modification of equipment.

- An employee was dismissed following complaints about his disturbing behaviour. He suffered from 'thought broadcasting', which meant he imagined that other people could access his thoughts. He was a paranoid schizophrenic and had been hearing voices, which interrupted his concentration. He brought a disability discrimination complaint, but the employment tribunal decided that he was not disabled, as his condition did not have a substantial effect on his normal day-to-day activities. The employee appealed to the employment appeal tribunal.

  Outcome: It was found in a similar case that the employee was disabled, as the original tribunal failed to take account of the fact he was unable to carry on a normal day-to-day conversation with work colleagues.

 ## Key Questions

Am I covered by the Disability Discrimination Act?
As with sex and race discrimination, protection extends to more than just employees. Job applicants, apprentices, agency workers and the self-employed are also protected.

Which types of employees are excluded from protection?
There are certain workers excluded from protection including those who work outside the UK, those involved in national security and certain state and crown employees, including among others, police officers, Ministry of Defence Police, British Transport Police, prison officers, fire fighters, the naval, military or air forces.

How am I protected?

If you do not get a job for a reason related to your disability and you are the best candidate for the job, then you can bring a claim against an organization unless it can justify its actions.

Once an employee you have the right to be offered the same terms and conditions as non-disabled colleagues, unless any discrepancy can be justified. You also have the right to be offered the same opportunities for promotion, transfer, training or any other benefits.

Do I have to reveal I'm disabled in my application?

Not if you are not asked, and particularly if it does not impact on your ability to do the job. However, if you lie on your application form, you would expose yourself to a disciplinary sanction or dismissal if employed. In addition, if you do need a reasonable adjustment to be made or additional help, you are unlikely to receive such assistance if your employer is unaware of your condition. In some ways you may be denying yourself valuable legal protection.

Do I have to be registered disabled to get my rights?

No, you do not have to be registered disabled to benefit from the DDA, but if you are registered disabled then you will automatically qualify as disabled under the DDA.

Do I need to be diagnosed as having a disability for my employer to recognize that I am protected?

Recent case law has made it clear that an actual diagnosis is not necessary for an employee to be protected by the DDA.

) *Mini Case Study*

An employee had a serious condition which meant that he was off work for a long time. There was no clear diagnosis and he was dismissed after being away for nearly a year, although the employee had asked his employer to wait until he had seen an immunologist before taking any action. After his dismissal, his condition was confirmed as chronic fatigue syndrome. His employer argued that they were unaware that he had the condition at the time of his dismissal.

Outcome

The employer had enough knowledge of the symptoms of the disability, and was aware of the employee's symptoms at the time of his dismissal. For this reason he had been dismissed for a reason relating to his disability, and his dismissal was therefore discriminatory. It did not matter that the condition had not been identified by name or medically confirmed.

My condition affects my ability to do my job, but I can still carry out all normal day-to-day activities. What are my rights?
Your condition does not satisfy the definition of disability and therefore, you will not be protected by the DDA.

 Mini Case Study

An employee worked for a DIY store. As a result of heart surgery he was not able to lift heavy items as this could risk his health, although his job required him to carry heavy items. When he was dismissed from his job he claimed disability discrimination.

Outcome

One part of the definition of disability is that a person's ability to carry out *normal day-to-day activities* is affected. Among other things this includes their ability to lift, carry or otherwise move everyday objects. However, further guidance from the Secretary of State for Education and Employment on the definition of disability states that this does not cover someone who is unable to carry heavy luggage without assistance. The employee was not disabled and therefore had no disability rights in this case. It is interesting to note that the employee's condition meant that he could not do his job, but despite this had no protection, as 'normal' activities were unaffected.

What if I become disabled while in my current job?
If you develop an illness or suffer from an injury then you may become disabled while in your current job. For example, if an employee has a car accident and, as a result, loses his leg, then he would qualify as disabled for the purposes of the DDA. This is because he has an impairment that has a long-term adverse effect on his ability to perform normal day-to-day activities. If his job was desk-based then there may not be any need to make any reasonable adjustment to accommodate him. Perhaps he might

take longer to get to the office, so the adjustment needed may be flexibility in the start and finish times of his working day. If his job involves walking it might be appropriate for him to be given an alternative job.

What about my special needs – what are my rights?
First, you have to show you qualify as disabled. Then you need to let your employer or prospective employer know about your special needs. If your needs arise because of your disability your employer must assess if an adjustment to accommodate your special needs is possible and reasonable, based on the factors noted above.

 Mini Case Study

An employee was left disabled because of an accident that affected his leg, and he suffered from some amount of pain. He was dismissed for unrelated reasons and claimed, among other things, that his employer had failed to make a reasonable adjustment by not providing anywhere private for him to conduct personal physiotherapy on his leg.

Outcome
His claim failed. He hadn't told his employer that he needed privacy to massage his leg, and his employers were therefore not under a duty to provide it.

Can an employer advertise a job stating that it will not accept any disabled applicants?
If this is the case and a disabled applicant does not get the job, there will be a presumption at employment tribunal that the reason relates to the person's disability. The organization that placed the advertisement will need to prove that the presumption is untrue, or be able to justify the discrimination.

What if an employer claims their lease prevents them making necessary changes to the building?
The DDA can override the lease, and alterations may well have to be made in order to comply with the duty to make reasonable adjustments.

I think I'm being discriminated against – what do I do?

You may initially wish to raise the matter informally to see if it can be resolved. You could also raise a grievance. If you are not sure whether you are being treated less favourably – you can get the position clarified by sending the organization a discrimination questionnaire, which you can obtain from the Disability Rights Commission. The Commission can also provide guidance and assist you in your claim.

Your Rights

1 Not to be discriminated against for a reason relating to your disability.
2 To have reasonable adjustments made to your place of work or working practices to ensure you are not put at a disadvantage in comparison with non-disabled colleagues.

Tactics and Tips

Codes and guidance

These are very useful and easy to understand. Do get hold of copies if you need further information. Also bear in mind that employment tribunals are required to take them into account when determining issues relating to a disability claim. Their failure to do so will be classified as an error in law.

Health and Safety Executive

This is an excellent source of guidance if you have any questions about a particular condition and whether it may amount to a disability. They also have useful information on reasonable adjustments for different impairments.

Medical evidence

It may be necessary to show medical evidence, but remember that the ultimate decision as to whether a person has a disability lies with the tribunal as it is a legal rather than a medical decision.

Contact Points

Disability Rights Commission – has offices in London, Manchester, Cardiff and Edinburgh.
Helpline: 08457 622633 **Textphone:** 08457 622 644
Address: Seventh Floor, 222 Grays Inn Road, London WC1X 8HL
Telephone: 020 7211 4110 **Minicom:** 020 7211 4037
Website: www.drc-gb.org

Royal Association for Disability and Rehabilitation (RADAR)
Address: 12 City Forum, 250 City Road, London EC1V 8AF
Telephone: 020 7250 3222
Website: www.radar.org.uk

 What next . . .

If you need advice on disability discrimination, the first thing you should do is get ahead of the game and take advantage of the tactics and tips every worker and employer should know in Chapter 2. If you need to take things further see Part 5: Taking things further. Details of organizations that can assist you and further information are in Appendix B: Contact points.

Religion and sexual orientation discrimination

Recently introduced law in these areas makes it unlawful to discriminate against or harass someone in the workplace on grounds of religion, belief or sexual orientation. They are a welcome addition to existing discrimination law, which at times was stretched to try and introduce religious discrimination through the provisions of race discrimination and protection for lesbian and gay people though sex discrimination law. The new law applies to all workplaces and both in the private and public sectors.

Protection applies where someone is discriminated against, or treated less favourably than others, because of their religion or belief or sexual orientation. An employer discriminates against someone directly, or indirectly, by victimizing or harassing them. 'Harassment' means unwanted conduct that violates people's dignity or creates an intimidating, hostile, degrading, humiliating or offensive environment.

Perception of religion or sexual orientation is also protected. So if you are mistreated because you are mistakenly thought to have a particular religion or particular sexual orientation you will be protected even if that religion or orientation does not in fact apply to you. In many ways the provisions are similar to existing discrimination law and in the same way, in limited circumstances there are exceptions where a job has to be done by a person of a particular religion or sexual orientation. The general principles of discrimination law covered earlier in this chapter apply to these categories of discrimination law as well, so there is no minimum length of employment needed to bring a claim, but you don't even have to be an employee; job applicants are also protected, and the compensation you may be awarded is unlimited.

 Mini Case Study

A Muslim employee wished to perform the religious pilgrimage known as Hajj for which he would need to travel to Makkah in Saudi Arabia. He was employed to clean buses and was on a salary of £8,000. In order to perform the pilgrimage properly he would need six weeks off work. When he requested leave from work, he did not receive a response. After putting his request in writing, his manager said if he heard nothing he could assume it was OK to take the leave he needed.

On his return from holiday he was sacked for gross misconduct on the basis that his time off work was unauthorized. He brought a claim to employment tribunal for unfair dismissal and religious discrimination.
Outcome: in a similar case the employment tribunal held that the employee had been unfairly dismissed and discriminated against on the grounds of his religion. He was awarded compensation of £10,000.

Key Questions

What is a religion or belief?

Any religion, religious belief or similar philosophical or political belief could fall within the new law. Whether the philosophical or political beliefs are similar to a religious belief is a question of fact for the employment tribunal in each case. There is no statutory definition of a religion or belief. Relevant factors could include considering whether collective worship takes place, whether there is a clear belief system or if there is a profound belief affecting behaviour or view of the world.

What is religious discrimination?

Religious discrimination could be something that happens directly to someone, such as: not getting a job because of your religion; being dismissed because of your religion; being denied training or promotion; or being subjected to harassment. You may even have a claim for harassment because of treatment you receive because of your partner's or parents' belief or because you stand up for another employee's beliefs.

Indirect discrimination could also apply. This is where a requirement or condition applies which has a detrimental effect on a particular religion. Indirect discrimination cases often feature advertisements, dress codes and working hours requirements which impact on a particular religion, such as dress codes insisting on certain headdress being worn, which may have the effect of preventing turbans or hijabs being worn.

Can my employer refuse to, for example, let me pray at work?

Each case is determined on its facts and the business environment of your employer. For example, if you need to pray at a certain time but the prayer time conflicts with a crucial aspect of your job when you need to be available then your employer may be justified in refusing to allow you to take time off to pray. Employers are not required to provide a prayer room but it would be a good idea for an appropriate location to be designated for such use.

There is a real drinking culture at my work, and often promotions are discussed at the pub, but as I don't drink alcohol, I feel that I am excluded. Is there anything I can do?

There is the possibility that you may have a claim, say for example if you discover you have been passed over for promotion because you did not take part in meetings at the pub. Your employer should take care to ensure that you and other employees are not excluded from actual benefits and promotions because you do not accompany fellow employees to the pub. One of the best ways to prevent problems is for employers to ensure that their managers and staff receive training on these issues. And as an added bonus, if a claim is brought, your employer can cite the training given as part of its defence.

What is meant by sexual orientation?
Sexual orientation can mean you are attracted to a person of the same sex, the opposite sex, or both. So it can refer to heterosexuals, homosexuals and bisexuals.

Although I am not gay, I have an effeminate manner and as a result I am constantly harassed and taunted at work. Do I have any rights?
Yes, you are protected by the law if you are perceived to be gay even if you are not. It is the impact on you which is taken into account, not the intention of the harasser, and so 'jokes' about homosexuality could mean that you have a claim. You should follow internal procedures first and raise a grievance in an attempt to stop the bad treatment. Once aware of your grievance, your employer should take immediate steps to prevent further harassment taking place. If that does not work, you could bring a claim at employment tribunal.

Is there anything my employer should do to prevent a breach of this law?
Your employer should have updated the company policies, procedures and induction process to take account of this law. They should also ensure the manager responsible for other staff understands all discrimination law and knows what steps to take if discrimination or harassment is taking place or suspected to be. Also, by taking these steps they may avoid being held responsible by a tribunal for any harassment that may take place.

 Your Rights

1 Not to be discriminated against, or treated less favourably on the grounds of your religion, belief or your sexual orientation.
2 Not to be victimized because you have brought a claim or helped someone else bring a claim.

3 To bring discrimination proceedings if unlawful discrimination has occurred.

 What next . . .

If you need advice on religion and sexual orientation discrimination, the first thing you should do is get ahead of the game and take advantage of the tactics and tips every worker should know in Chapter 2. If you need to take them further, *see* Part 5: Taking things further. Details of organizations that can assist you and further information are in Appendix B: Contact points.

Other types of discrimination

Transsexual discrimination

Gender reassignment is a medical term for the changing of a person's sex through alteration of physiological, hormonal or other characteristics. There are now specific regulations, which protect transsexuals against discrimination on the grounds of gender reassignment in employment and vocational training. The regulations say that a transsexual cannot be treated less favourably than other people on the grounds that the individual intends to undergo, is undergoing or has undergone gender reassignment.

In addition to protection against discrimination, if a person is off work to have his or her gender changed, that person must be treated as if he or she were absent due to sickness or injury.

 Mini Case Study

A technician who was born a man announced that he was undergoing a sex change and that his new name would be Niki. Because of this the technician was subjected to serious harassment from male colleagues for nearly three years. The technician then went off work due to sickness for nearly five months, and was dismissed. Niki alleged sex discrimination as her employers failed to take any action despite being aware of the harassment that she was being subjected to.

Outcome
Niki won her case. Discrimination and harassment relating to gender reassignment are forms of sex discrimination.

Age discrimination

While older workers do have the benefit of the same employment rights as their younger counterparts there is no legislation that protects them against discrimination, although if they are dismissed or made redundant because of their age, they can bring an unfair dismissal claim on that basis. The government has signed up to the European agenda and an anti-discrimination directive means there will be protection against age discrimination in this country by 2006 (*see* Chapter 25).

Illness in the family: genetic discrimination

Imagine getting the sack because your mother has a disease that you may inherit. That's exactly what happened in the USA when a woman remarked at work that her mother suffered from Huntingdon's disease and there was a 30 per cent chance that she would inherit it. Another lost her job when her employers discovered that she had a gene linked to a certain kind of cancer.

Driven by employers' healthcare costs and a desire to keep employee-absence cost to a minimum, such behaviour is a recent phenomenon arising only as a result of our increasingly sophisticated knowledge of genetics. Some employers have introduced genetic testing to determine whether their employees have any genetic diseases. Many states in the USA have introduced legal protection against discrimination arising from genetic testing, as have some European countries, where genetic tests are prohibited. There is presently no protection in the UK against 'genetic discrimination'.

Disability discrimination law (*see* pp. 152–64) specifically requires the symptoms of a genetic illness to show themselves before any protection is afforded.

If you are dismissed as a result of a genetic discrimination, then you could claim unfair dismissal although to make such a claim you would need at least one year's service. But this offers no help to job applicants and those with less than one year's service. There is also no solace for those denied promotion or subjected to unfairness as a result of genetic discrimination although the testing and use of the test results are bound to raise human rights issues.

The draft Data Protection Act Code of Practice provides guidance on genetic testing in the workplace and emphasizes that it may be undertaken if, for example, a particular genetic variation is likely to pose a serious safety risk to others. Otherwise it should be undertaken on a voluntary basis.

As genetic technology develops and dovetails with an increase in medical information employers want to know about you before taking you on, protection against genetic discrimination is likely to become a necessity.

 ## Contact Points

Discrimination Law Association – seeking improvement in law and practice for claimants
Address: PO Box 20848, London SE22 0YP
Telephone: 020 7450 3663
Website: www.discrimination-law.org.uk

Equal Opportunities Commission
Address: Arndale House, Arndale Centre, Manchester M4 3EQ
Telephone: 0161 833 9244
Scotland: St Stephens House, 279 Bath Street, Glasgow G2 4JL
Telephone: 0141 248 5833
Wales: Windsor House, Windsor Place, Cardiff CF10 3GE
Telephone: 029 2034 3552
Website: www.eoc.org.uk

Equality Commission (N Ireland)
Address: Andras House, 60 Great Victoria Street, Belfast BT2 7BB
Telephone: 028 90 500 600
Website: www.equalityni.org

Lesbian and Gay Employment Rights (LAGER)
Address: Unit 1G, Leroy House, 436 Essex Road, London N1 3QP

Telephone: Lesbian Helpline and Minicom 020 7704 8066
Gay Men's Helpline and Minicom 020 7704 6066
Website: www.lager.dircon.co.uk

Liberty – independent human rights organization
Address: 21 Tabard Street, London SE1 4LA
Telephone: 020 7403 3888
Legal advice line: 020 7378 8659
Website: www.liberty-human-rights.org.uk

Stonewall – gay rights group
Address: 46–48 Grosvenor Gardens, London SW1W 0EB
Telephone: 020 7881 9440
Website: www.stonewall.org.uk

 Tactics and Tips

Codes and guidance

There are codes of practice in all areas of discrimination, which can be obtained from the Equal Opportunities Commission, Commission for Racial Equality, and Disability Rights Commission. They are very useful sources of information and generally written in an accessible style. Do get hold of a copy if you need further information. Also bear in mind that although they are not legally binding, employment tribunals are required to take the codes into account when determining issues relating to discrimination claims.

Going to tribunal

Tribunals take a much more inquisitorial approach to discrimination cases than they would normally do. This means they will be asking questions and intervening as they see fit.

Time limits

In all matters of discrimination you have three months from the act of discrimination in which to lodge your claim although there are circumstances when this deadline is extended. The tribunal does, however, have a general discretion to consider a complaint, which is beyond the three-month time limit if it considers that it is fair to do so.

Company procedure

You should always be aware of your company's equal opportunities policies, or any other relevant procedures. Matters can be reported informally or formally, and should be reported as soon as possible.

Apologies

Organizations are often prepared to include an apology as part of a settlement. It is useful to bear this in mind, as this is often what someone bringing a claim really wants.

References

Remember that if an employee experiences any difficulties after having complained about discrimination – such as difficulty getting a reference – this could give rise to a further claim of victimization. Often employers will agree to provide just a basic factual reference stating start and end dates and the duties you undertook. An outright refusal to provide a reference can mean an employer is breaking the law.

Written records

Written records of all incidents of discrimination should be kept. These will help make the position clearer and be an extremely valuable source of evidence if the matter ends up at employment tribunal.

 ## What next . . .

If you need advice on discrimination, the first thing you should do is get ahead of the game and take advantage of the tactics and tips every worker and employer should know in Chapter 2. If you need to take things further see Part 5: Taking things further. Details of organizations that can assist you and further information are in Appendix B: Contact points.

Harassment and bullying

Insulting remarks and unwanted advances can amount to harassment

Harassment

We can all picture the scene: December, the season of office parties when employers and their staff come together to let off steam. Invariably, with the help of a few drinks, another year, perhaps another bonus, and in most cases the forthcoming holiday, is celebrated. Sometimes those office flirtations and party pranks go horribly wrong, crossing the boundary between acceptable conduct and harassment.

Christmas parties may be the most clichéd example, but harassment occurs all year long. The good news is that the law offers some protection, treating many such cases as discrimination. The bad news is that the embarrassment and anguish felt can often be exacerbated by the difficulty in establishing in law when someone's behaviour towards you becomes harassment.

A legal definition of harassment in employment law has now been introduced. Harrassment is an act of discrimination which amounts to less favourable treatment under the discrimination acts and that is the reason why it is unlawful. The definition is:

. . . unwanted conduct which has the purpose or effect of either violating another person's dignity or creating an intimidating, hostile, degrading, humiliating or offensive environment.

The main categories of harassment currently covered by the law are sexual, racial, religious, sexual orientation and disability harassment; harassment on other grounds may also be a breach of the Human Rights Act. The European Commission code of practice on sexual harassment defines it as:

. . . unwanted conduct of a sexual nature, or other conduct based on sex affecting the dignity of women and men at work. [That includes] conduct which is unwanted, unreasonable and offensive, which creates an intimidating, hostile or humiliating working environment.

In this country in 2006, harassment due to your age will also be included.

Harassment can be physical, verbal or even non-verbal conduct – the essential characteristic is that it amounts to unwanted attentions. Sexual harassment is stereotypically undertaken by a man against a woman although it can occur against men as well. Whether the conduct is unreasonable or offensive is up to the affected person. Usually, in these circumstances, it is not just a matter of assessing the nature of the behaviour but a question of the way the behaviour makes that particular person feel.

Harassment can amount to a criminal offence under circumstances such as the Protection from Harassment Act, although for this to be the case the harasser would need to have seriously harassed you on more than one occasion.

 What if . . .

- An employee is called a black bastard to his face by his superior.
  Outcome: In a similar case this amounted to discrimination.
- A West Indian employee is physically assaulted at work and called a 'coolie'. Initially the tribunal felt that while the term coolie was a racial term it was the assault that was less favourable treatment and that the assault was not racially motivated.
  Outcome: The Employment Appeal Tribunal in a case along these lines ruled that it was impossible to separate the two and the company was guilty of racial discrimination.
- A man of mixed race had worked as a machine operator for just a month. During that time work colleagues racially harassed him; one colleague burnt his arm with a hot screwdriver, others called names like chimp and baboon. Metal bolts were thrown at his head; he was whipped with a piece of welt and a notice saying 'chipmunks are go' was stuck to his back. On leaving he claimed racial harassment. In a case incorporating such facts the court decided that the company was not liable for harassment. One of the requirements for harassment is that the acts must take place in the course of your employment while you undertake tasks for your employer.

The court decided that the acts were unrelated to work activities. The case was appealed to the Court of Appeal.

Outcome: Not surprisingly the Court of Appeal decided the employers were liable for the acts of racial harassment and the employee won his claim.

- A woman who worked for an advice line was subjected to sexual comments from her manager. The day before she had an interview with him for a promotion he had allegedly said that she should wear a short skirt and a see through blouse showing plenty of cleavage if she wanted to be successful. After the interview, she complained internally of sexual harassment. Her complaint was rejected after an investigation, and she then refused to return to her job unless her boss was moved to another department. When she was dismissed she lodged a sexual harassment complaint. Initially a tribunal found that as she had not objected to the comments, her boss could not have known that she found them offensive. The tribunal also took into account the fact that her boss was sexually vulgar to male employees. The case then went to appeal.

  Outcome: In a case incorporating such facts, such comments did amount to sexual harassment and had undermined the employee's dignity as a woman. The court in that case decided that it was simply not relevant that her boss was sexually vulgar towards male employees, since such comments might be vulgar to a man but would not be intimidating, as they would be to a woman. She won her claim.

- A homosexual office manager was nicknamed Sebastian by colleagues after a character in a comedy series and was subjected to ongoing homophobic abuse. He was called 'abnormal', 'queer' and 'queen' by fellow workers. He brought a claim against his employer.

  Outcome: In a similar case, the employee won a claim of unlawful sexual orientation discrimination and was awarded over £35,000.

Accused of harassment?

If you are accused of harassment – falsely or otherwise – your employer should take you through a disciplinary procedure. The company's harassment policy should be followed, or in its absence, the main disciplinary procedure should be used. So get hold of a copy of the relevant procedure immediately.

It is normal for employers to suspend employees from work while investigations take place. Before this happens you should be warned that the allegations are serious and that they may result in your dismissal, that detailed investigations will take place and statements taken, and you should be given enough information to fully understand the allegations against you. This information should be given to you in enough time for you to be able to read and absorb everything, and in accordance with your employer's procedures.

You will then be called to a disciplinary hearing at which you will have the opportunity to state your side of the story. You will also have the legal right to be accompanied by a fellow employee or trade union official. The hearing could be suspended to allow further investigations in light of what you tell them. At the end of the hearing, the panel – as specified in your company's procedure – will consider the evidence and come to a decision.

You may be fully vindicated, be given a warning, a final written warning or dismissed, depending on the evidence and who is believed. You will have the right to appeal the outcome.

If you are dismissed you could bring employment tribunal proceedings against your employer for unfair dismissal.

If you feel strongly that you have been set up, and/or unfairly treated, you could claim constructive dismissal (*see* Chapter 23) but you should take advice, as this is not an easy, or often advisable, course of action to take.

 ## Key Questions

Who does the law protect against harassment?
It is not just employees who are protected against harassment. Job applicants, contract workers and the self-employed are also protected.

What is harassment?
Examples typically include brushing up against someone, touching them including pinching, patting, sexually explicit comments, offensive jokes, and making rude gestures, which relate to a person's sex, race, religion, sexual orientation or disability.

What if I was harassed on only one occasion?
In most cases the worker is subjected to a series of acts of harassment, but one incident can be sufficient if it is serious.

Mini Case Study

An employee, who was an area supervisor, attended a meeting at which one of the company managers greeted her with 'Hiya big tits'. She was extremely distressed by this and claimed sexual harassment.

Outcome
This was harassment.

If a colleague harasses me, who is liable?
The harasser and, in most cases, your employer too. However, your employer can avoid liability if it can prove that it took all reasonably practicable steps to prevent the harasser from harassing. The harasser may still however be liable at employment tribunal even if the company escapes liability.

What if a client harasses me?
You may have a claim against the client and his or her company. Rather surprisingly, you may also have a claim against your own employer if you can show that your employer could have anticipated the acts of harassment were likely or failed to take steps to protect you once it was clear that the harassment was occurring.

Should my employer have an anti-harassment policy?
Not all employers have an anti-harassment policy and it is not a legal requirement. It is good practice and its very existence often forms part of an employer's defence against a claim of harassment.

Are there any exemptions?
There are no exemptions relating to harassment. The protection applies to all workers and there are no exceptional circumstances where harassment is permitted in law. And as a good employment practice the employer should attempt to prevent or reduce the harassment.

If I complain it may affect my standing at work. What do I do?
There is special protection against such fears. If you have a discrimination complaint and are worried that if you report it you may suffer in some way, this means that you are worried about being victimized. You could

bring a separate complaint at employment tribunal against your employer if this happens (*see* p. 141).

I've been having an office romance. Now he/she's harassing me. What is my position?

It depends on the nature of the harassment. The fact of your previous relationship should make no difference to your right to be protected against harassment at work. But you should take extra care to make notes of the events and what is said, as it is likely to be harder for you to explain and prove the nature of your complaint. Cases have shown that the reason for unfair treatment may not be related to a person's sex but to the breakdown in the intimate relationship.

When does harassment become a criminal offence?

If acts of harassment are reported to the police and they decided to press charges, it can be a criminal offence. Criminal liability is unrelated to whether the acts of harassment take place inside or outside the workplace, but there does need to be more than one incident for a criminal charge of harassment.

Bullying

One of the difficulties in dealing with the problem of workplace bullying, according to the Andrea Adams Trust, is that it is quite often hard to recognize, and its effects are attributed to something else. The Trust, which aims to reduce workplace bullying, says it can often be overlooked because euphemisms like 'harassment', 'intimidation', 'aggression', 'bad attitude', 'personality clash' and 'poor management style' are often used to describe it.

Establishing just how many people suffer from bullying in the workplace is difficult, because many prefer to suffer in silence. However, a recent study suggested at least one in ten people felt they had been bullied in the last six months. And in most cases it is a more senior member of staff or manager who bullies a more junior colleague, often leading to stress and absenteeism.

The main difference between harassment and bullying is that bullying is not based on the sex, race or disability of the person being bullied. It is general nasty, intimidating or violent workplace behaviour. There is no specific legal protection against such behaviour although there are things you can do if you are being subjected to bullying.

Bullying or discrimination?

Be sure that there is no sexual, racial, religious, sexual orientation or disability harassment element to the behaviour you are being subjected; if there is it will significantly strengthen your claim.

Informal resolution

Deal with the matter informally through your employer's internal grievance procedures. Remember you may be required to do this before you can bring a claim.

Constructive dismissal

If the bullying is bad enough you can leave and claim constructive dismissal (*see* Chapter 23). The disadvantage is that this is not an easy claim and you should seek advice before taking any action.

Personal injury claim

You may also be able to bring a personal injury claim if your employer fails to provide you with adequate protection from workplace bullying.

Criminal liability

Remember the Protection From Harassment Act does not require there to be any sex, race, religion, sexual orientation or disability element to the act of harassment. In particular, if the bullying is serious, and takes place on more than one occasion, an employee could report the matter to the police.

Your Rights

1 To be treated with dignity in the workplace and take action (for example, leave and claim constructive dismissal) if you are bullied.
2 Not to be harassed on the grounds of sex, race, religion, sexual orientation or disability.
3 To bring proceedings against the perpetrator and the organization if you are harassed.
4 To bring criminal proceedings against the harasser.

 Tactics and Tips

Codes and Guidance
These are very useful and easy to understand. Do get hold of a copy if you need further information. Also bear in mind that although they are not legally binding, employment tribunals are required to take them into account when determining issues relating to a disability claim. Their failure to do so will be classified as an error in law.

Time limits
The tribunal, in all discrimination matters including harassment, has a discretion to consider a complaint which is out of time if, in all the circumstances of the case, it considers that it is just and equitable to do so. The time limits are therefore not as strict as for an unfair dismissal claim.

Written records
You should keep a written record of all incidents of harassment. This will help make the position clearer if the matter ends up at employment tribunal.

Company procedure
You should be aware of the company harassment policy if there is one. Harassment should be reported and dealt with without delay, whether informally or formally.

Grievance procedure

Employees who are being harassed should raise a 'grievance'. The grievance procedure is an important tool in cases of harassment and also a means of bringing such serious allegations to the attention of an employer. You may be prevented from bringing a claim at employment tribunal if you don't first raise a grievance. The process is often set down in the contract or staff handbook, although a grievance can be raised even if there is no procedure in writing. In most cases this merely means writing a letter to the relevant manager raising the complaint.

 What next . . .

If you need advice on harassment at work, the first thing you should do is get ahead of the game and take advantage of the tactics and tips every worker and employer should know in Chapter 2. If you need to take things further see Part 5: Taking things further. Details of organizations that can assist you and further information are in Appendix B: Contact points.

16

Trade union membership

Total union membership in the UK is around 7 million

After almost two decades of decline, trade union membership has begun to gently rise again amid higher levels of industrial action and concern over working rights. Today about one in four of those who work belong to a union.

A trade union is defined in the law as an organization, whether temporary or permanent, which consists wholly or mainly of workers and whose principal purposes include the regulation of relations between workers and employers or employers' associations. It should have some sort of structure although a written constitution is not necessary. The regulation of industrial relations must be one of a union's principal objects but it is not actually necessary for it to have a negotiation function. Typically, however, trade unions are involved in collective bargaining, for example, on wages and hours on behalf of their members. Unions also often assist members by advising on rights and even undertaking legal representation and advocacy at employment tribunal. There is in place a mechanism by which recognition of a union can be imposed upon an employer, although many employers voluntarily recognize a union. When recognized (meaning the employer accepts the trade union as entitled to act on behalf of a particular group or groups of employees), unions are responsible for collective consultation with employers in the event of large-scale redundancies, or a sale or transfer of the business (*see* Chapter 22: Redundancy and Chapter 19).

Employees have the right to join a trade union. As members there are a number of rights to which employees are entitled. Members should not be denied employment because of their membership, and dismissal for trade union membership, membership activities or on union recognition grounds entitle members to claims of automatic unfair dismissal. Conversely employees cannot be forced to join, remain or cease to be a union member and protection extends not only to those dismissed in such circumstances, but also to those subjected to a detriment (unfairness), or selected for redundancy on these grounds. A breach of any of these rights entitles employees or ex-employees to bring a claim at employment tribunal for compensation.

Job applicants are also protected against being refused employment or discouraged from applying on the grounds of membership or non-membership of a union and a breach of this right again gives prospective employees the right to a claim for compensation at employment tribunal.

Employees have the right to time off work to take part in trade union activities (*see* Chapter 11), and in some instances employers must consult with union representatives of a recognized union on worker training. A trade union official of a recognized union also has the additional right to take time off work with pay to undertake trade union duties.

There are categories of worker excluded from these rights, including those seeking or engaged in self-employed work, such as independent contractors or freelancers and also those seeking employment as or engaged as members of the police, armed forces and parts of the security and intelligence services, as well as share fishermen.

It should be noted that there is also body of law relating to the constitution and regulation of trade unions. There are separate rules relating to the rights of trade union members in relation to their union as well as rights and duties of unions themselves. This overview doesn't address those issues but focuses on the rights of trade union members in relation to their employer.

Finally, a brief word on strikes. Those organizing strikes or industrial action would technically be exposed to legal action not only by employers but by customers and suppliers who potentially or actually suffer loss as a result of the action. But protection against legal action exists in the form of statutory immunities in certain instances. A number of conditions must however be satisfied before the immunities apply. If immunities do not apply, an employer can seek an injunction which operates to stop the strike from proceeding. If workers strike when an injunction is in place, the union faces heavy fines as well as other implications of being in contempt of court.

What if . . .

- An applicant for a job is told that it is a requirement to be a member of a particular union. She refuses to agree to become a member and is then told it isn't worth her applying.
  Outcome: This is an unlawful refusal to consider an application and the applicant can lodge a claim at employment tribunal to seek a declaration and compensation.
- An employee wished to join a trade union but his employer says that if he does so he will no longer be entitled to participate in the company bonus scheme.
  Outcome: This is unlawful and will entitle the employee to bring a claim at employment tribunal.

Key Questions

Do I have the right to belong to a union?
Yes, you do and you should not be prevented or discouraged by inducements or otherwise from taking up the union membership.

Must my employer recognize my union?
No, an employer does not need to recognize your union, but if it fails to do so voluntarily, then there are steps that unions can take to seek to compel statutory recognition for the purposes of collective bargaining on pay, hours and holidays, but the legal provisions and requirements are complex and detailed and certain conditions need to be satisfied. Applications can be made to the Central Arbitration Committee when problems arise or there is a breakdown in the process of statutory recognition.

What about staff associations – what is their status?
If a staff association represents the interests of workers and is responsible for the regulation of relations between workers and employers, it may qualify as a union. Some staff associations are formed just to decide on Christmas outings or other worker-related issues, and such organizations clearly do not fall into the category of a union. Staff associations or consultative committees are often formed for the specific purpose of consulting with employers and disseminating information to employees

in the event of larger-scale redundancies, or a sale or transfer of the business. There is a legal obligation to consult in such circumstances and such bodies can be formed specifically for these purposes.

Can I be sacked for taking industrial action?

Yes, but you may have the right to claim unfair dismissal. You could lose your right to claim unfair dismissal if you take part in industrial action that is not protected as the law does not allow an employment tribunal to consider a complaint of unfair dismissal in such unprotected industrial action.

Can I negotiate on my own behalf for pay or does the union do all bargaining?

It will depend on the arrangement within your organization for such matters as pay. There may be a collective agreement in place, which is incorporated into your contract of employment. In such a case the union will negotiate and reach agreement with regard to issues such as pay on your behalf. The changes agreed will apply to your contract with your employer even though you may not have had any involvement in the negotiations.

 ## Your Rights

There are many rights associated with trade union membership including the following:
- not to be denied employment on union membership or non-union membership grounds;
- not to be dismissed, subjected to a detriment or selected for redundancy on union membership or non-membership grounds;
- to belong to a trade union;
- not to belong to a trade union;
- not to be excluded or expelled from membership;
- to take part in membership activities;
- to take time off with pay if you are an official undertaking union duties;
- for a recognized union to be consulted in the event of large-scale redundancies or a transfer or sale of the business.

Contact Points

Trades Union Congress (TUC)
Address: Congress House, Great Russell Street, London WC1B 3LS
Telephone: 020 7636 4030
Website: www.tuc.org.uk

 What next . . .

If you need advice on trade union membership the first thing you should
do is get ahead of the game and take advantage of the tactics and tips
every worker and employer should know in Chapter 2. If you need to take
things further see Part 5: Taking things further. Details of organizations
that can assist you and further information are in Appendix B: Contact
points.

17

Health and safety

Employers have a duty to ensure your health, safety and welfare at work

We've all seen the ads: 'Had an injury at work?' asks an authoritative voice, 'Time to make a claim.' If your workplace is too noisy or too cramped, or if you've had an accident at work, your employer could be liable.

In general employers have a duty of care to ensure, *so far as reasonably practicable*, your health, safety and welfare at work. This means that the degree of risk you are exposed to needs to be balanced against the difficulty and cost of any measures needed to tackle the risk. As well as the many acts of Parliament and regulations on health and safety, there are also more general obligations on employers to ensure they are not negligent, which takes the form of ensuring they provide workers with a safe place, access and system of work, adequate equipment, competent fellow employees and protection from the unnecessary risk of injury, etc.

Unlike most other areas of law, the extensive regulation on health and safety aims to protect life and limb, but despite fairly wide-ranging obligations there are still a large number of workers whose health is adversely affected by work. Over one million people are injured at work each year and twice that number believe they suffer ill health caused by their work.

The Health and Safety Executive (HSE) and local authorities are responsible for the enforcement of much of the law on health and safety. Their inspectors can enforce improvement and prohibition notices if a company is in breach of the law. An employer in breach of health and safety obligations may be held criminally liable and personal liability may attach to any director or manager if the offence was committed with their consent or due to their negligence. The HSE publishes a 'name and shame' report which names companies and individuals convicted in the previous 12 months for flouting health and safety law. These names can also be accessed on its website.

The law lays down minimum standards to protect all workers, not just employees, and the protection extends to further protect members of the public affected by the activities of the employer as well as other sub-contracted workers working on the premises. The law requires every employer to undertake an assessment of risk in relation to the workplace to identify measures necessary to comply with health, safety and fire precautions.

Minimum standards must also be observed for all new buildings and modifications in relation to matters such as ventilation, lighting and sanitary facilities.

There are numerous regulations that cover a multitude of concerns such as particularly hazardous work, noise and electricity at work, the use of computers, the regulation of construction sites, manual handling of loads, fire precautions and first aid at work – to name just a few. And employers should have in place special insurance in the event of work-related injuries and other health and safety related claims. The full extent of the law on health and safety cannot be covered here, but aspects of health and safety law relevant to work include the following.

Health-and-safety-related dismissals

Employees who are dismissed on health and safety grounds would have an automatic unfair dismissal complaint against their employer. There is no upper limit on the amount of compensation that can be awarded in such a dismissal (*see* Chapter 22: Being dismissed). Employees are also protected against being subjected to a detriment (unfairness) on health and safety grounds and can resign and claim constructive dismissal if employers breach their duty of care. Further rights exist where legal obligations (which can include these on health and safety) are flouted and a worker is dismissed on disclosing such breaches of the law (*see* Chapter 21).

Health and safety suspension

Employees are entitled to paid suspension from work for up to 26 weeks if they are unable to work in order for their employer to comply with any law or regulation on health and safety. You may lose the right to payment in certain circumstances, for example, if you unreasonably refuse to do suitable alternative work.

Violence at work

If there is a risk that you may suffer violence at work your employer must provide adequate precautions to protect your safety. The same applies to an employee being exposed to bullying and harassment at work, which can be a criminal offence (*see* Chapter 15).

The Health and Safety Executive's definition of work-related violence is 'any incident in which a person is abused, threatened or assaulted in circumstances related to their work'. So this means that verbal abuse and harassment, the most common form of violent behaviour is caught within the definition. Workers most at risk are those who provide a service to the public. Some health and safety policy statements may set out how to deal with workplace violence and this may include being given time off work to recover either from the physical impact and/or the trauma.

Dangerous substances

Certain substances are hazardous to health and there are regulations controlling the maximum exposure limits permitted. Such substances include toxic, harmful corrosive substances, irritants, biological agents and dust of any kind. A risk assessment would need to be carried out and, in some instances, the exposure may need to be monitored under suitable medical surveillance.

Information instruction and training should be provided to you if you are exposed to hazardous substances so that you are aware of the risk of exposure and the precautions that must be taken. The HSE produces a number of codes of practice in this area (*see* Appendix B: Contact points).

Corporate killing

A conviction for corporate manslaughter presently only applies if there is a senior individual who is identified as being responsible for the fatal incident and it can be shown that he or she had been grossly negligent. The first conviction for corporate manslaughter occurred in 1994 when a managing director was held responsible for the deaths of four children in the care of his company on a canoeing trip. The government proposed in 2000 the introduction of a new offence of corporate killing, and reckless and careless killing.

Stress at work

This can result in psychological injury and a landmark case brought home the fact that employers are as accountable for our mental health as they are for our physical health at work (*see* Chapter 18).

Repetitive strain injury

The number of people developing repetitive strain injury (RSI) because of their work is rising. RSI is also known as work-related upper limb disorder. The problem is associated not only with manual workers, but is also rising among office workers doing extensive work on computers. There are a variety of conditions that fall into this category such as tennis elbow, tendonitis and trigger finger, to name a few. The TUC says that more than 150,000 workers are suffering from RSI with numerous successful claims arising as a result. RSI may also be a disability (*see* Chapter 14: Disability discrimination).

Smoking at work

It is established that passive smoking, meaning the unavoidable inhalation of smoke from sharing a room with smokers, can be harmful to the health of those that don't smoke. And that has given new impetus to the need for employers to protect their workers against harm to health caused by passive smoking. Gone are the days when smoky offices were the norm. Now it is the smokers who are relegated to designated smoking areas and kept apart from non-smokers. And being forced to work in a smoke-filled room has even enabled an employee to claim constructive dismissal (*see* Chapter 23).

One difficulty employers may face is the phasing-out of smoking facilities in the workplace. An employer should use a reasonable process to implement the change, which would include a phased implementation and consultation with workers. It is unlikely that an employee can claim constructive dismissal because of the removal of his right to smoke at work if the employer carries out a proper procedure.

Hours of work

The regulation of time you spend at work, your rest breaks and the holidays you take are measures designed to protect your health and safety at work. There are extensive rights in this respect (*see* Chapter 8).

Accident reporting

From 1 April 2001 a central reporting system for the whole of the UK came into effect. Accidents can be reported by telephone, e-mail, fax and post.

What employers must do

Among other measures the Health and Safety Executive says employers must:
- provide a safe workplace without risks, so far as reasonably possible;
- assess the risks to health and safety;
- make arrangements for implementing the measures identified as necessary;
- if there are more than five employees record the findings of the risk assessment and the arrangements;
- draw up a health and safety policy if there are more than five employees. It should include all measures in force, and be made available to the workforce;
- consult on any changes that may substantially affect your health and safety;
- consult on arrangements to get competent people to help the company satisfy health and safety laws;
- consult on the information given to staff on the risks involved with their work and measures to reduce or get rid of it, and what to do if staff have to deal with a risk or danger;
- consult on the planning of health and safety, and the health and safety consequences of introducing new technology;
- ensure machinery is safe and that safe working practices are followed;
- give workers any necessary information, training or supervision;
- appoint someone competent to assist with health and safety matters;
- co-operate on health and safety with other employers sharing the workplace;

- set up emergency procedures;
- provide adequate first-aid facilities;
- make sure the workplace satisfies health, safety and welfare requirements in areas such as ventilation, temperature, lighting and sanitary facilities;
- make sure equipment is suitable for its intended use, as far as health and safety is concerned, and that it is properly maintained and used;
- prevent, or adequately control, exposure to substances which may damage health;
- take precautions against flammable or explosive hazards, electrical equipment, noise and radiation;
- avoid hazardous manual handling operations, or where they cannot be avoided, reduce the risk of injury;
- provide health monitoring as appropriate;
- provide free protective clothing or equipment where necessary;
- ensure appropriate safety signs are provided and maintained;
- report certain injuries, diseases and dangerous occurrences to the appropriate authority.

 ## Contact Points

Health and Safety Executive (HSE)
Information line: 08701 545500 – will also give contact details of regional offices.
Website: www.hse.gov.uk

 ## What next . . .

If you need advice on health and safety at work, the first thing you should do is get ahead of the game and take advantage of the tactics and tips every worker and employer should know in Chapter 2. Also make enquiries with the Health and Safety Executive who have extensive publications and information that is easily available. If you need to take things further *see* Part 5: Taking things further. Details of organizations that can assist you and further information are in Appendix B: Contact points.

18

Stress at work

13 million working days per year are lost through stress-related illness
The Health and Safety Executive

Rarely is stress ever out of the headlines. A new survey, a record compensation or settlement award, a lifestyle tip to help try and beat it.

There can be no question though that work-related stress is a serious and growing problem that is here to stay. Why? Well, experts seem to have differing views but most agree it is partly to do with the way we work. Growing workloads, long hours (*see* Chapter 8), short breaks and a 24-hour working culture driven by instant communications mean we can all be available round the clock. All this is coupled with a lack of job security – no surprise then that the phrase *stressed out* emerged in the hectic 1980s.

Stress is our natural reaction to pressure but, in extreme or sustained circumstances, it can lead to mental or physical illness, manifested as an inability to concentrate, irritability, dizziness, back pain, tiredness, depression, emotional instability, high blood pressure and worse. Stress affects everybody at times but some people cope with it better than others; in many cases it can also lead to heavier dependency on cigarettes, alcohol or drugs. It can also have a corrosive effect on family life.

Employers are becoming increasingly aware that it is in their interests to alleviate stress, as it often leads to low morale, poor staff performance, an increase in sickness absence and staff turnover, all of which end up costing them dear. If employers do nothing to tackle the problem they lay themselves open to claims in the courts.

So, along with the headlines what do the rash of surveys tell us about stress in the workplace?
• the Health and Safety Executive says around one in five workers experiences serious stress at work;
• teachers, nurses, health professionals, social workers, as well as white-

collar workers, managers and professionals have the highest levels of stress;
- there was little difference in reported stress levels between men and women;
- a CBI/PPP survey found stress was perceived as the second most important cause of absence after minor illness. The survey found it was not a major factor for manual employees;
- every year 25,000 people stop work completely because of work-related illness.

There is no law directly dealing with stress at work, but there is law requiring employers to look after your well-being, health and safety at work. The law protects you if you become ill as a result of stress caused by your job. But you have to show your illness was 'reasonably foreseeable' in that you made your employer aware of the effect of the stress or it was obvious and your employer ought to have known anyway.

A number of different categories of law can be used in the battle against stress, including health and safety law, negligence claims and common law. The common law consists of age-old principles developed over time, and includes your employer's obligation to provide a safe place and system of work, and to protect you from any unnecessary risk or injury.

The fact that an employer's obligations in negligence extend to caring for your mental as well as physical health became clear from the landmark case of *Walker* v *Northumberland County Council*. In this case a social worker who suffered two nervous breakdowns because of his work sued his employer. He argued his employer should have known about the stress, and that it had failed to do anything about his complaints. He was awarded nearly £200,000. But there are specific requirements needed for a complaint such as this to succeed and not all will satisfy them.

A claim as a result of stress-related injury or illness is not an easy claim to bring. You need to have actually suffered an illness arising from the stress. So, ironically the more you are able to cope, the less likely it is that you will have a claim. The stress leading to the illness needs to be directly related to your job – and not as a result of personal circumstances, and it also needs to pass the difficult 'foreseeability' test. The courts require that it was reasonably foreseeable that illness would be the resulting impact of the stress. There must be a foreseeable and reasonable connection between the job stress and the illness. For example, if someone has already suffered a nervous breakdown because of overwork in the past, the employer must know that the same thing could happen if the employee is again overworked. If there was no way of foreseeing that illness could have arisen from the stress, it is unlikely you will have a claim. Just feeling stressed does not give you a claim. In a recent case, *Sutherland* v *Hatton*, important guidelines were given to employers, the courts and those claiming stress which should prevent claims which have no reasonable prospect of success.

Remember your company's grievance procedure – it is a valuable tool to get yourself heard if you feel your concerns are being ignored.

The Health and Safety Executive regard stress in the workplace as a priority area. They produced guidance for employers on how to assess and deal with stress in the workplace such as their publication *Management Standards for Tackling Work-related Stress*. For more details *see* Appendix B: Contact points.

Dutch comparison

If stress in the workplace is a growing issue here, much may be learnt from the Dutch experience, where work-related stress is close to becoming pandemic. The Netherlands has the highest number of workers taking long-term sickness leave in the world, with one study showing 60 per cent of Dutch employees suffer from work-related stress. Almost 100,000 workers are diagnosed as being *overspannen* each year, supported by a welfare state that provides a year off on full pay for those diagnosed with such work-related stress.

 What if . . .

- A social worker has a heavy workload dealing with numerous child abuse problems. His workload continues to increase but no additional staff are taken on to help out. He complains about the situation, but nothing is done about it. He then suffers a nervous breakdown as a result of being overworked. On his return to work he is told that he will be assisted in his work, although any assistance will be short-term. As a result of overwork he starts to suffer stress symptoms again. He goes on sick leave for stress-related anxiety and then suffers a second nervous breakdown. He is dismissed due to his illness. He brings a claim against his employer because they failed to prevent him being exposed to a workload that was harmful to his health. He also claims that his employer should have known that this would risk his health. His employer argues that they could not have foreseen that the employee's workload exposed him to a risk of mental injury and in any event there were financial constraints in the engagement of more staff.

Outcome: The employers had breached their duty of care of the employee's mental health – but only in relation to the second mental breakdown, not the first. This is because it is reasonably foreseeable that overwork may cause the employee a mental injury as he had previously suffered a nervous breakdown on this basis. In a similar case an employee eventually accepted an out of court settlement of £175,000 shortly after his former employers lodged an appeal to the decision.

- A relief warden for 16 gipsy sites suffers stress as a result of his job. He is frequently threatened, verbally abused by the gipsies and once shot at! He leaves his job on the grounds of ill health, which is caused by this stress, and then suffers a nervous breakdown. He brings a claim against his employers.

  Outcome: In a similar case employers settled a claim out of court paying the employee £203,000.

- A pub manager claims to have suffered permanent psychiatric injury, much like post-traumatic stress disorder, because of his job. As a result he says he is now unable to work. He claims that his wife and staff were subjected to offensive conduct as well as violence and threats, theft and burglary. His employment is terminated as a result of his sickness and he brings a claim against his employer.

  Outcome: It is reasonable expectation that he can run the pub despite its difficulties, and he was aware of the internal management and training and assistance programmes as well as the grievance procedure. In a similar case the employee failed. He had not properly notified his employer of his difficulties or illness and never put his concerns in writing. The brewery also had comprehensive arrangements designed to protect managers in his position who suffer in such a way. His claim failed.

 Key Questions

What is stress?

Stress does not have an official definition, but is used to describe extreme and, in some circumstances, harmful pressure. The HSE have defined it as 'the adverse reaction people have to excessive pressures or other types of demand placed on them'. Many people are subjected to pressure – some thrive on it but others are stressed by it.

Isn't my employer obliged to look after my well-being?
Yes, your employer is obliged to look after your health and safety at work as well as make sure your work practices are not harmful to you.

I have to take time off because of stress – what are my rights?
If work-related stress is causing you to feel unwell, then this is an illness like any other and you would be entitled to sick leave as indicated by your doctor and in line with your terms and conditions. If the stress ultimately causes you to be ill or injures your mental health, then you may have a claim against your employer.

Stress made me difficult to deal with, or less productive, at work and I was dismissed. What are my rights?
If the stress made you unpleasant and less productive, it is probably just an indication that you could not cope with the pressure of your job. You would not have a claim unless the work-related stress you were suffering caused some harm to your health.

What if I am stressed but my employer does nothing to help?
You could be on the road to a claim if it impacts on your health. But before things get that bad, you should lodge a grievance, consult personnel or the welfare department if your organization has one. Put your concerns down in a letter to your employer as this could help if the matter escalates to a claim. Before taking any action, you should make every effort to make sure your employer is aware of your concerns. Employers who offer a confidential advice service with referral to appropriate counselling are unlikely to be found in breach of their duty to care for their employees.

What should my employer do?
A responsible employer would address the cause of your stress at work. However, if you are just stressed and it is not affecting your health, they may think that you are just not able to cope with the pressure of the job, in which case they may consider dismissing you ultimately if they perceive that you cannot do the job. It is only if the stress is impacting on your health that you have a legal issue of concern to your employer.

I've suffered ill-health since I left work because of stress at work – do I still have a claim?
Yes, you may still have a claim. The period of time in which to bring a claim is three years from the date of the injury, although this can be extended if the condition is latent (such as asbestosis).

How do I prove stress-related illness or injury?

You will need expert medical opinions to prove that you are ill and that the illness was caused by your job. If you are to bring a claim or indicate to your employer that you may do so, such evidence is essential.

I am being bullied and harassed at work and it is really stressing me out – do I have a stress claim?

If you are being bullied or harassed you may have a separate claim against your employer that is more appropriate than a stress claim (*see* Chapter 15). If you are successful in a claim against your employer based on sex, race or disability discrimination then you may in addition to compensation for financial losses receive an award for injury to feelings. A discrimination award can take account of stress-related injury to feelings.

 ## Your Rights

For your employer to take care of both your physical and mental health and safety at work, including providing you with a safe system of work.

 ## Tactics and Tips

Claiming is not easy – take advice

A negligence claim is not straightforward and does not take place at employment tribunal but in the High Court and county courts. You should, therefore, take advice before taking any action to establish the likelihood of your claim being successful.

Your health should come first

If your health is being affected by work, you should take action immediately – both directly with your employer and by seeking external advice from your medical practitioner, or one of the contacts listed in Appendix B: Contact points. Your health should come first and while you may eventually be able to obtain some money through the law, money must take second place as compared to resolving the situation and maintaining your health.

Time limits

You do not need to lodge a negligence claim within three months of your illness; the time period is three years from the date your cause of action arose, which means the date on which you became ill as a result of the stress. There are some circumstances where this time limit can be varied. Be careful if you are also wishing to bring an unfair/constructive dismissal claim against your employer; you will only have three months from the date you are dismissed or forced to leave.

Grievance procedure

If you are not satisfied with the way in which matters causing you stress are being handled you could raise a 'grievance' against your employer. A grievance procedure is a way of making a formal complaint within your company. The process is often set down in the law and often also in your contract or staff handbook, although you can still raise a grievance even if there is no procedure in writing. In most cases this merely means a letter to your boss raising the complaint.

 What next . . .

If you need advice on stress at work, the first thing you should do is get ahead of the game and take advantage of the tactics and tips every worker and employer should know in Chapter 2. If you need to take things further *see* Part 5: Taking things further. Details of organizations that can assist you and further information are in Appendix B: Contact points.

19

Business transfers: when your employer changes hands

If your company is sold or transferred your position is protected

If the firm or the service you work for is sold, contracted out or privatized or changes hands by any other process, the law protects both your job and the terms and conditions you originally signed up to.

In the past, before this protection existed, a business changing hands meant employees lost their job and had no automatic right to continue to work. The new owners could take you on – but it was their choice whether they did so, and they had every right to offer you less favourable terms if they did.

There are no official figures kept for how many businesses change hands, but the constant spate of mergers and restructuring means that hundreds of thousands of employees face this sort of situation each year.

The main rules that safeguard your rights in the event of a transfer are in the Transfer of Undertakings (Protection of Employment) Regulations 1981, known commonly as TUPE. These Regulations were put into place as a result of a European directive referred to as the Acquired Rights Directive.

So what does TUPE do? If the business transfer falls within the protection of TUPE (*see* Key Questions below for what qualifies as a protected transfer), you automatically become an employee of the new owner and your employment will continue as normal, without a break and on the same terms and conditions you had before. In certain instances even collective agreements made with trade unions pass to the new employer, and the new employer will need to recognize those same trade unions.

Before TUPE, such a transfer meant that employees could lose their jobs or the terms they were on.

The protection you benefit from is quite extensive. If you are dismissed for a reason connected to the transfer you have the right to claim automatic unfair dismissal (unless a special defence referred to as an 'economic, technical or organizational reason entailing changes in the workforce' applies). Employees, staff associations or unions must also be given information before the transfer takes place.

If you do not want to work for your new employer, the law gives you the right to object to the transfer and just not be taken on. You have to be sure of your decision as an objection is not classed as a dismissal, and, depending on your reasons for objecting, in many circumstances you will not have any rights against your employer if you do object.

You should get advice if you have any doubts, especially given the complexity of this law and the fact it may be difficult to establish if you qualify for protection.

 ## What if . . .

- An insurance firm is taken over (in a protected transfer) and the new owner asks the employees to take a pay rise in place of their guaranteed contractual bonuses. They agree, but then change their minds and bring a claim for the reinstatement of their bonuses at employment tribunal.
  Outcome: They are likely to be entitled to have their bonus reinstated if it was taken away as a result of the transfer. They will also be able to keep their higher salaries even though they agreed to the changes.
- An employee was dismissed two years after a protected transfer for refusing to give up his generous contractual redundancy pay entitlement. He brought a claim against his employer saying the change in his terms and conditions was due to the transfer and was therefore unlawful – making his dismissal unfair.
  Outcome: In a similar case the court found that the dismissal came about because of the transfer even though the transfer took place two years ago. The dismissal was therefore unfair.
- The catering services in your company are to be contracted out to another business instead of being provided internally by your employer.
  Outcome: In this case the employees in the catering services would transfer to a new employer. They will be entitled to enjoy the same terms and conditions as before. Any attempts to change their terms because of the transfer will be unlawful, unless a legitimate redundancy situation exists.

Key Questions

Am I protected when my employer changes hands?
If in any doubt you should seek legal advice, as the law here is very complex.

The law says there is a transfer of an undertaking where there is a transfer of an economic entity which retains its identity, meaning an organized group of resources which has the objective of pursuing an economic activity whether that activity is central or ancillary. So TUPE protects you if there is a change in the employer or person responsible for carrying on a business and there is an economic entity, which retains its identity after the change of hands.

The transfer can be between two companies in the same group although the most common cases are where there is a sale of a business or part of a business or an outsourcing or contracting out of a department or function.

The circumstances in which TUPE applies can be far from clear at times and if in doubt, advice should be sought.

Is there a qualifying length of service for rights under a protected transfer?
You need one year's continuous service in order to bring a claim against your employer for unfair dismissal connected to a protected transfer. An employee could bring a breach of contract claim without completing one year's continuous service if, for example, there is a reduction in salary as there is no qualifying period for such a claim.

Are any transfers excluded?
Specifically excluded from protection are certain transactions, including a transfer of shares. This is when shares in your company are bought by new owners.

Who is not protected?
At present only employees are protected so if you do not fall into this category, you are not protected (*see* Chapter 3 to check that you qualify).

What information must unions or employee representatives receive?
Appropriate representatives (either your recognized trade union or elected employee representatives) should be informed of the following far enough ahead of the transfer to allow consultations to take place:

- the fact of the transfer;
- when it is to take place;
- the reason for the transfer;
- the legal, economic and social implications for affected employees;
- the measures your *present* employer envisages taking in relation to the affected employees – if there are none this should be stated;
- the measures your *new* employer envisages taking in relation to the employees it acquires automatically – again, if none this should be stated.

What should union/employee representatives do with this information?
It is their responsibility to disseminate this information to all employees in the workforce affected by the TUPE transfer.

What claims can I make if my employer doesn't inform and consult?
You or your union or employee representative have the right to bring a claim at employment tribunal. The claim would be for what is called a 'protective award'. This is up to 13 weeks' actual pay.

What about contracting out and privatization?
These sorts of transactions may qualify for protection because an economic activity may be transferred and it may retain its identity after the transfer. So the requirements of TUPE may be satisfied.

How long are my terms and conditions specially protected by TUPE?
In theory there is no time limit, but as time passes it becomes harder to prove the changes are linked to the transfer (*see* What if . . . above).

What if I am dismissed prior to the transfer?
If you are dismissed before the transfer, you may still have the right to claim what is known as automatic unfair dismissal. The key factor is whether you were dismissed in connection with the transfer.

Can I refuse to be transferred?
You cannot be transferred to the new organization if it is against your wishes and you refuse. You need to inform your employer that you object to being employed by the new organization. If you object, the transfer

terminates your contract of employment, but you are not treated as having been dismissed, you are treated as having resigned. If you are objecting because there is a substantial and detrimental change to your working conditions then you may have a claim against your employer and be able to seek compensation. Otherwise you will not, and are effectively just deciding to leave your job.

Are there any rights or liabilities that do not transfer?

Any criminal liability (for example, in relation to a health and safety matter) remains with the old employer and does not transfer under TUPE to the new employer. Similarly, rights and liabilities relating to occupational pension schemes do not transfer. In reality, the organization to which the employees transfer may have pension arrangements in place, but there is no legal obligation to provide these to the transferred employees. However, members of an occupational pension scheme before a TUPE transfer will soon be entitled to have a scheme provided by their new employer, although there will be no obligation to match the type and value of the scheme provided by their former employer.

In reality, mergers and takeovers lead to changes and redundancies. What are my rights?

If you are dismissed in connection with the transfer before or after the transfer, you may be able to bring a claim for unfair dismissal and/or a redundancy payment.

The dismissal will be automatically unfair unless it satisfies the defence of being for an 'economic, technical or organizational reason entailing changes in the workforce'. If your employer can prove the dismissal was for one of these reasons, the dismissal will be fair, but there must be a real business case for the need to reduce, or change, the structure of the workforce. In this case you will only be entitled to work your notice, or be paid in lieu and a redundancy payment.

If your terms and conditions are substantially changed, you may resign and claim constructive dismissal (*see* Chapter 23).

In certain, very rare, cases you can resign and claim constructive dismissal even if your terms and conditions remain unchanged. The change in the identity of your employer may in itself constitute a significant and detrimental change, for example, if your high-class organization, Top Quality Supplies, is acquired by the fly-by-night Farmer Nasty Joe's Potatoes.

Your Rights

1 To continue to be employed on the same terms and conditions if your employer changes hands.

2 Your new employer in specialized circumstances must recognize the same trade unions as your old employer, and any collective agreements must still apply.

3 Trade union or employee representatives must be provided with information and in certain instances consulted ahead of a transfer.

4 To bring a claim at employment tribunal if there is failure to inform or consult over the transfer.

5 To object to the transfer in which case your employment ceases.

6 To claim automatic unfair dismissal at employment tribunal if you are dismissed because of the transfer, unless your employer can justify the dismissal on what the Act describes as 'economic, technical or organizational reason entailing changes in the workforce'. In reality this means an employer must have an overriding case for needing to reduce the workforce based on sound business reasons. In this case you would be entitled to redundancy pay and to either serve your notice or be paid in lieu according to your terms and conditions.

Tactics and Tips

Changes to your contract

Remember – unique to this area of law – detrimental changes, even if agreed, have no legal effect if they arise as a result of a protected transfer. If you agree to changes to your contract as a result of a protected transfer you can still go back on the agreement and get your original more beneficial terms back.

Objection or opt-out

Also unique to this area of law is your right to object to being transferred. Remember that this is an option available to you, because you do not want to work for the new organization.

Substantial and detrimental change to working conditions

You can bring a claim based on the above but be sure to take advice, as such a claim is both uncommon and not straightforward.

Written records

You should keep a written record of all the discussions you have with your employer or employee/trade union representatives concerning a transfer. This will help make both an employee's and employer's position more robust if a case is brought to employment tribunal as a result of the transfer.

Grievance procedure

If you are not satisfied with the way in which matters are being handled you could raise a 'grievance' against your employer. A grievance procedure is a way of making a formal complaint within your company, and the process is often set down in the law and should also be in your contract or staff handbook, although you can still raise a grievance even if there is no procedure in writing. In most cases this merely means writing a letter to your boss raising the complaint.

 What next . . .

If you need advice on TUPE, the first thing you should do is get ahead of the game and take advantage of the tactics and tips every worker and employer should know in Chapter 2. If you need to take things further *see* Part 5: Taking things further. Details of organizations that can assist you and further information are in Appendix B: Contact points.

20

Privacy: e-mail and the Internet

Your employer can legally monitor your e-mails, Internet use and phone calls

We live in an Orwellian world where Big Brother always seems to be watching. The question of how individual privacy should be protected after the explosion in e-mail and Internet usage is a vexed one, complicated by globalization and the ease with which information can now be stored and moved around. As technology changes at breakneck speed the law struggles to catch up.

In this country claims are not yet as extreme or extensive as in the USA, but dismissals for misuse of the Internet and communication systems at work regularly make headline news: whether it's the group of colleagues sacked for downloading and forwarding pornographic e-mails to each other in breach of their employer's policy or the employee caught leaking confidential information to a competitor.

So do you know your rights – do employers have *carte blanche* to snoop on their workforce?

Not only is the law struggling to catch up, it is presently a rather confused area. The law says it is unlawful for communications to be intercepted unless the sender and recipient consent to the interception or there are reasonable grounds to believe that they did. However, in support of employers, there's the controversial Lawful Business Practice Regulations, introduced to allow employers to read certain communications without the express consent of employees. This law has been roundly criticized by civil liberties groups. In the employee's corner sits the code of practice under the Data Protection Act as well as the Human Rights Act, and nobody quite knows how the conflict will be resolved. The Human Rights Act confers the right to respect for private and family life, which could curtail employers' monitoring of their staff, and the data protection code of practice also leans in favour of the safeguarding of employee rights. Until cases test and clarify the law in this area employers and employees have little choice but to pick their way through the maze.

But where there is business justification the position is different. Calls, e-mails and faxes that you send and receive at work can be intercepted for certain reasons *without* the direct consent of employees – *see* below for detail of when 'snooping' is permitted. So, on balance, in most circumstances it is likely that your employer will be able to justify checking out employee communications.

It is worth noting that e-mails are also a valuable source of evidence of 'on-goings' at work and frequently form part of the bundle of evidence used at employment tribunal. Both parties have the right to request disclosure of such evidence as part of the proceedings.

Internet abuse

Use of the Internet in the workplace has been the cause of much controversy. Many employers have dismissed staff for abuse of the Internet at work. Most commonly, dismissals have arisen as a result of employees downloading pornographic or indecent material from the Internet or forwarding lewd material to colleagues and friends.

Employers can dismiss staff if they have in place an Internet policy warning employees not to use it for unauthorized purposes. Often the policy will specifically state that downloading pornography will be classified as gross misconduct, which can result in summary dismissal (*see* Chapter 22: Being dismissed). Employers tend to be robust in disciplining abusers of the Internet – so there is no point in employees taking any risks.

 What if . . .

• An employee discovers that her company was tapping her private calls made while at work without her knowledge or consent, direct or indirect. She was unaware that this was happening and brought a claim to the European Court of Human Rights when she found out.
  Outcome: In a similar case some years ago the employee had a reasonable expectation of privacy and this had been breached. She won her claim.
• An employee is dismissed on the grounds of gross misconduct when it

is discovered that he used the Internet at work to access sexually explicit pictures and moving images. He admits that he did but said that he accessed the site by mistake and then got stuck in it and only revisited it because of his concern that children could easily access it. His employer dismissed him after an investigation.

Outcome: The dismissal in a similar case was fair as his employer had an established code of practice on use of the Internet and had followed a fair procedure in dismissing him.

 Key Questions

In what circumstances can my employer monitor my e-mails and calls?
When business communications such as telephone calls, e-mails and faxes are sent from business premises, your employer can monitor them without your express consent. Your employer should, however, make all reasonable efforts to inform users that their communications may be read. In practical terms this means your employer either has a policy which highlights that your communications may be read for certain reasons or has posted a notice on the staff notice board. The circumstances in which your employer can do this are:

- to establish facts;
- to check for compliance with regulatory practices;
- to ascertain or demonstrate the standards that the company is achieving or ought to be achieving;
- if it is in the interests of national security;
- to prevent or detect crime;
- to detect or investigate unauthorized use of the system;
- for the effective operation of the computer/telephone system or if it is an inherent part of the way the system operates. This may include monitoring for viruses;
- to establish if the communication is relevant to your employer's business. This may apply where someone is off sick or on holiday and their voicemail is checked;
- if the communication is a free service to the public offering counselling or support services.

What can I do if my rights are breached?
If your employer accesses your communications and their reasons for doing so do not fall into one of the lawful exceptions, then you could seek an injunction for unlawful monitoring and even sue for damages if the monitoring has caused you loss. This is extremely unlikely in reality.

What if I discover that my employer has been monitoring my private communications at work without any notification at all that this may be happening?
You may have a human rights claim against them as this may be a human rights breach.

Should my company have a privacy and monitoring policy?
Responsible employers should have an Internet, e-mail and communication policy in place and accessible to all employees.

Can I see the records that they keep on me?
Under the Data Protection Act you have extensive rights to access both electronic and paper data kept on you.

Surveillance in the workplace

Many forms of surveillance in the workplace are becoming standard. CCTV and video surveillance, which has been around for a while is used not only to observe the movements of workers, guarding against theft and vandalism but also as evidence of employee behaviour at employment tribunal. If any evidence from such devices is used, you must be aware that the surveillance is taking place. Evidence from covert surveillance is unlikely to be much help to an employer in light of the right to respect for private and family life under the Human Rights Act.

Inspection and scrutiny also takes the form of drugs and alcohol testing, telephone monitoring and even genetic testing. All of these may have a sound basis in law. (For more on genetic testing *see* pp. 169–70.)

Your Rights

1 To be made aware if your employer is going to read your communications at work, such as through a company policy.
2 To bring a claim if your rights to privacy have been breached and you were not made aware through company policy or otherwise of your employer's actions.

 Tactics and Tips

Policy or notification
Remember that your employer needs to make every effort to inform you if they are monitoring your communications at work. It has been suggested that where this is happening, private phones should be available for employee use where they can be sure they are not listened into. Remember the notification from your employer may be in your contract or in the staff handbook.

Conflicting laws
There are three major areas of the law which appear to conflict on the issue of privacy at work. As a result cases arising from claims in this are likely to lead to clarification of the law. If you feel you have been wronged, this may be a bargaining card in your favour. No employer wants to make the headlines in a landmark case which clarifies the position in law.

 Contact Points

Information Commissioner – deals with data protection and freedom of information
Address: Wycliffe House, Water Lane, Wilmslow, Cheshire SK9 5AF
Telephone: 01625 545700 **Information line:** 01625 545745
Website: www.dataprotection.gov.uk

What next . . .

If you need advice on privacy at work, the first thing you should do is get ahead of the game and take advantage of the tactics and tips every employer and worker should know in Chapter 2. If you need to take things further *see* Part 5: Taking things further. Details of organizations that can assist you and further information are in Appendix B: Contact points.

21

Whistleblowing

One employee was awarded £293,000 after getting the sack for reporting the illegal acts of his boss

Your boss is secretly siphoning off company money, illegally flushing industrial waste into a river, or worse. You want to report the matter, but fear for your job – so what do you do?

Any number of high-profile cases of this kind have been reported in the media, many of them involving the public services. Among them, the doctor who blew the whistle on the NHS Bristol babies heart surgery scandal, or the true story dramatized by the Hollywood blockbuster *The Insider*. It tells of a tobacco company scientist becoming aware of addictive chemicals being placed in cigarettes who reveals all to the media, and loses all as a result.

For years there was little protection from such treatment, but the Public Interest Disclosure Act now protects most workers in these sorts of situations. One of the first successful cases brought under this legislation in 2000 was that of an accountant sacked from his £70,000-a-year job for exposing his boss's expense fiddles – he won £293,000.

The law operates to protect workers from being dismissed or suffering reprisals (known as detriments) if they report certain wrongdoings that they become aware of. If they lose their jobs they can bring a claim for unfair dismissal (and in these cases the normal qualifying period and upper limit of £56,800 (2005) do not apply – *see* Chapter 22: Being dismissed).

However, the Public Interest Disclosure Act is not straightforward and you need to check carefully whether the requirements qualifying you for protection are satisfied, and follow set procedures that determine whether you should report a case internally, within your organization, or externally, to prescribed individuals or organizations.

There are three things you need to establish:

1 Have you made what is referred to as a 'qualifying disclosure', i.e. one that is protected?

2 Have you followed the correct procedure?

3 Have you been dismissed or suffered a detriment as a result of disclosing the information?

 What if . . .

- An employee was responsible for the accounts of a company. Senior employees of the company regularly travelled the world and had large expenses to match, and the employee had to check receipts for these expenses. When the managing director of the company did not provide receipts for six months the accountant decided to notify someone more senior of the managing director's default by fax. However, he was told to destroy the fax and that no action would be taken. When he reported the matter to others he was told he was a bad accountant, was told to resign and threatened with criminal prosecution. He was later called to a disciplinary hearing and dismissed. He claimed automatic unfair dismissal under these provisions. (Automatic unfair dismissal is explained below; also *see* Chapter 22: Being dismissed.)

  Outcome: The tribunal found that he had been unfairly dismissed for making a protected disclosure to his employers. He was awarded £293,441 compensation, as he was 58 years old and it was felt that he would not work in a similar job again. His compensation was, therefore, calculated to see him through to retirement age.

- A care home worker telephoned Social Services to express concern about the treatment of a resident. She was dismissed a short time afterwards and claimed automatic unfair dismissal under these provisions.

  Outcome: The tribunal felt that she did not follow the correct procedure. The matter was not serious enough to be reported outside the company in the first instance, and she did not have a good enough reason for not reporting the matter internally. Her claim failed.

- A council worker discovered a colleague, with whom he shared an office, had pornographic images on his PC. He reported his findings to a director and the employee with the offending images on his screen was suspended. The employee who reported the matter was moved out of his office into an open plan area and his job responsibilities were changed. He brought a claim at employment tribunal saying that the changes amounted to a detriment after he had made a protected disclosure.

Outcome: The disclosure was a protected one but the council worker had not been subjected to a detriment. The Council had acted reasonably, and there were good reasons for the changes imposed on him.

 Key Questions

Who qualifies for protection under the Public Interest Disclosure Act?
This Act covers workers, not just employees. This means that contractors, consultants and the self-employed (unless they are genuinely in business on their own account) are also protected. Police officers and those that work outside the UK are excluded.

What is a protected or qualifying disclosure?
To make a qualifying disclosure you need to show that you believe the information you are revealing shows one of the following:
• a crime has been committed;
• a failure to comply with legal obligations;
• a miscarriage of justice;
• a health and safety risk;
• damage to the environment;
• a cover-up. Information on any of the above has been deliberately concealed.

What if I wanted to make a qualifying disclosure on a future event?
The law protects you. For example, if you believed that someone's health and safety was likely to be in danger, that would be a protected disclosure.

How can I be sure I am protected under the Public Interest Disclosure Act?
There are six types of disclosure that are protected:

1 When you disclose the matter to your *employer* in good faith. For example, disclosing the matter to your line manager or someone more senior than you. Or the disclosure can be made to another person if you think that other person is the appropriate and *legally responsible person* to whom the matter should be disclosed. An example is a nurse employed by an agency reporting a matter to the hospital at which she is placed.

2 When you disclose the matter to a *legal adviser*, in the course of obtaining legal advice.

3 When you disclose the matter in good faith to a *Minister of the Crown* where your employer is either an individual appointed by a Minister of the Crown or a body where any one of its members have been appointed by a Minister of the Crown. This applies to government employees/civil servants, employees of utilities regulators such as OFTEL as well as employees of NHS trusts and tribunals.

4 When you disclose the matter to a *prescribed regulator/body* referred to as a 'prescribed person' – individuals and organizations selected by order of the Secretary of State for Trade and Industry. The Health and Safety Executive is one such example. For a full list *see* Contact Points below.

5 When you make a disclosure externally – *outside your company*, if you believe that you will be subjected to a detriment if you disclose the matter internally, *or* there is no prescribed person and you think your employer will destroy the evidence if you disclose the matter, *or* you have already disclosed the matter to a prescribed person or your employer.

You also need to show you made the disclosure in good faith, you believe the information is true, you are not out to make money or gain from the disclosure, and it is reasonable for you to disclose the matter.

An external disclosure could be to the media, a non-prescribed regulator a union official, or even a relative of the person concerned. It would be for the tribunal to assess whether it was reasonable for you to report the matter to the person you chose.

6 When you make an *exceptionally serious disclosure*. In cases where the matter, which you believe to be true, is exceptionally serious and the disclosure is made in good faith, and not for personal gain, it may be reasonable for you to bypass one of the above methods and go directly to an outsider. For example, if you were concerned that a child was being sexually abused at a nursery, you would be protected if you went directly to the police. One word of warning – it may be viewed as unreasonable for you to go directly to the press if there is a less damaging route by which you could seek to resolve the matter.

What do I do if my contract contains gagging clauses?
Any clause in a contract that attempts to prevent the operation of this Act will be void.

What if there is a clause on confidentiality in my contract?

Employees are not permitted to disclose information that is a trade secret or so highly confidential that it needs the same protection as a trade secret. The law is often supplemented by a clause in the contract of employment further increasing an employee's obligation of confidentiality. These clauses will not prevent you from making a protected disclosure but will apply in all other respects. Remember that the disclosure needs to satisfy the requirements above to be protected. If you get it wrong you could be disciplined, dismissed or taken to court for breach of contract.

What if, by making the disclosure, I am breaking the law?

If that is the case then you will not be protected by the Act. For example, if making the disclosure means that you will break the Official Secrets Act then you will not be protected.

What is a detriment?

The protection you may qualify for is protection against dismissal or a detriment. A detriment can be anything negative that happens after you make the disclosure including loss of a benefit or opportunity. You may need to persuade a tribunal that the reason for your dismissal, the loss of benefits or bad treatment is because you made the qualifying disclosure. If you can show this then you may qualify for protection. Remember, as the claim is *automatic* unfair dismissal, you only need to show the reason for your dismissal, there is no upper limit on the size of the award and you do not need to have been employed for any length of time.

 Your Rights

1 To bring automatic unfair dismissal proceedings if you are dismissed for a protected or qualifying disclosure.

2 To make a claim if you have suffered any detriment, and to have the position rectified.

3 There is no limit to the compensation you can be awarded, so you could be awarded compensation above the usual upper limit of £56,800 (2005).

4 To bring a claim without the need to have worked for any length of time.

Tactics and Tips

Take advice
A number of cases have failed for a variety of reasons including that the disclosure made was not a protected disclosure, or the wrong procedure was followed in that the worker went immediately to someone outside the organization without justification. So it is advisable to take advice before taking any action or lodging a claim.

Be as sure as you can
Remember that in the real world there may be an impact on your future career despite the existence of the law.

The stakes are high
Your employer will be obliged to take your claim seriously as there is no upper limit on the size of the award, and no qualifying period of employment needed before you can commence proceedings. But it may also mean that your employer is more open to agreeing a deal by offering you a settlement.

Company policy
Your company may have a policy on whistleblowing. If so – be sure you have read it before taking any action.

Written records
You should keep written records of all the discussions you have with your employer or a prescribed regulator or body concerning any such disclosure. This will help make your position more robust if the matter ends up at employment tribunal.

Grievance procedure
Remember that if you are not satisfied with the way your disclosure is being handled you could raise a 'grievance' against your employer. A grievance procedure is a way of making a formal complaint within your organization, and the process set out in the law and should also be set down in your contract or staff handbook, although you can still raise a grievance even if there is no procedure in writing. It may strengthen your position at employment tribunal if you are dismissed as a result of the disclosure.

Making a claim

Beware. You have only three months from the date of a dismissal for such a disclosure in which to lodge a claim at employment tribunal for automatic unfair dismissal. Remember that there is no qualifying period needed for you to bring such a claim and that there is no limit to the compensation that you could be awarded if you succeed.

Special relief

If you are dismissed as a result of making a protected disclosure, then you are entitled to apply for special interim relief – which is either to have your pay and conditions continue or be reinstated up until the date of the hearing. Be warned, however – you have to make a claim for this interim relief within seven days of your dismissal date.

 ## Contact Points

Public Concern at Work – an independent charity specializing in public interest whistleblowing
Address: Suite 306, 16 Baldwins Gardens, London EC1N 7RJ
Telephone: 020 7404 6609
Website: www.pcaw.co.uk

Prescribed Person – a full list of prescribed persons is contained in the Public Interest Disclosure (Prescribed Persons) Order. Details can be obtained from the DTI pamphlet, *Guide to the Public Interest Disclosure Act*, (URN 99/511)
Orderline: 0870 1502 500
DTI **website:** www.dti.gov.uk

 ## What next . . .

If you need advice on blowing the whistle, you should take advice and also take advantage of the tactics and tips every worker and employer should know in Chapter 2. If you need to take things further *see* Part 5: Taking things further. Details of organizations that can assist you and further information are in Appendix B: Contact points.

22

Losing or giving up your job

There are only five legal ways in which you can be dismissed

This section of *The Penguin Guide to Employment Rights* covers almost all forms of losing or giving up your job, from redundancy through to 'heat-of-the-moment termination', which, although it sounds like the title of a 'B'-class action movie, is one of the rare legal phrases to actually convey a little of the sound and fury often involved.

It begins by taking an overview of what constitutes fair dismissal, before looking at the five main ways you can lawfully be dismissed. Not surprisingly dismissal in all its forms is one of the most controversial and hotly disputed parts of employment law. It is also one of the most commonly experienced – almost everybody seems to know somebody who believes they have lost their job unfairly.

Subsequent sections focus on other ways people leave employment such as the much-misunderstood constructive dismissal, when you resign because you feel you have been forced to do so because of the way your employer has acted. Also covered are notice periods, restrictions and confidentiality agreements.

Being dismissed

There are no exact figures for the numbers of employees dismissed each year, but hundreds of thousands of calls are recorded by the ACAS helpline each year for work-related problems, and ACAS are involved in thousands of employment tribunal and potential employment tribunal cases annually.

Although the terminology may seem strange, if an employer is going to dispense with an employee's services the employee is entitled to be 'fairly dismissed'.

That means employers must act reasonably, which includes following a statutory disciplinary procedure, and the dismissal must be for one of the five following reasons:

1 *redundancy* – because the role is redundant;
2 *under-performance or sickness* – if an employee is under-performing, sick or absent, or their qualifications are at issue;
3 *misconduct* – the way an employee behaves;
4 *legal barrier to work* – such as if an employee employed as a driver loses his driver's licence and cannot continue to work;
5 *other reasons* – a catch-all category of other reasons which can justify the dismissal.

The requirement to follow, as a minimum, disciplinary procedures prescribed by the law means that a dismissal would be automatically unfair if these procedures are not followed. Most employers would have incorporated these statutory disciplinary procedures into their own company procedures. The procedures oblige employers, for example, to write to employees inviting them to a disciplinary hearing as well as offer the right to appeal any decision reached as a result of a disciplinary hearing.

What constitutes reasonableness depends on the exact circumstances of the case. For example, if an employee were dismissed for poor performance, one factor to be taken into account would be whether they were given enough time to improve.

But there are some more general factors that define reasonableness too, such as the size of your company. If your company is a multinational it would have to prove that it has been more meticulous and thorough in its dealings than a smaller company might have been expected to be.

Your employer must also follow a fair procedure in dismissing an employee – what a fair procedure actually is in practical terms also depends on the exact reason for the dismissal. However, it would be unfair if an employer fails to follow a fair procedure in dismissing an employee, even if the dismissal is for one of the five permitted reasons.

 Key Questions

Can I bring a claim for unfair dismissal?
Employees can bring a claim for unfair dismissal if they have at least one year's continuous service with their employer. There are certain situations

in which one whole year's service is not required, such as if dismissal is on health and safety grounds. Such a dismissal is called an automatically unfair dismissal (*see* below).

What if I am dismissed for what is clearly an unfair reason?

Some dismissals are 'automatically unfair' when they are for unlawful reasons, and these can include being dismissed for being pregnant, or as a result of sex, or disability discrimination, for example. Sometimes employers may get the reason for a dismissal wrong, but this does not necessarily mean it is unfair if it is a genuine mistake. Alternatively, employers may get the reason wrong deliberately, either out of kindness or to cover up a reason that is not permitted. If it is the latter it is unfair.

Do I have the right to know the reason why I'm being dismissed?

If you have one year of continuous employment you are entitled to a written statement of the reason for your dismissal. You must request the statement and your employer must reply to you within 14 days. If you do not get a reply, you are entitled to claim two weeks' pay at employment tribunal. If you have less than one year's service you have no such right although it is good practice for your employer to tell you the reason.

Am I entitled to warnings before being dismissed?

You should be warned, or made aware, of the issues surrounding your dismissal, as employers are required to follow a statutory procedure in order to dismiss you fairly. If it is a matter of misconduct involving theft or disobedience, for example, your employer should follow the company's disciplinary procedure. If it is a matter of under-performance, you should be given a warning that failure to improve may lead to your dismissal. Exactly how much warning you should get really does depend on the case and is not prescribed in law.

My final payment – what am I entitled to?

If you are dismissed for gross (i.e. very serious) misconduct then you are only entitled to your pay and benefits to the day of your dismissal – you are not entitled to any payment for your notice period. In all other cases you are entitled either to work your notice or receive compensation (both in pay and benefits) in lieu of your notice period. If you are being made redundant then you are also entitled to a redundancy payment if you have been employed for two years or more.

I've been unfairly dismissed – what do I do next?

The first thing is to remember that you only have three months from the date of your dismissal to lodge a claim at employment tribunal, although there are circumstances where this time limit can be extended. You may lose your right to bring a claim if you miss this deadline.

What sort of compensation might I be entitled to?

If you win an unfair dismissal claim at employment tribunal you will be entitled to a basic award and a compensatory award. The basic award is calculated in the same way as a statutory redundancy payment – with reference to age and years of service – to a current maximum of £8,400 (2005).

You can be awarded up to a maximum of £56,800 additional compensation (called the compensatory award) and this payment is designed to compensate you for the losses that you incur as a result of your unfair dismissal. This means that if you get a job on the same pay immediately, your right to this award may be reduced to nil.

Could I be reinstated in my job?

An employment tribunal has the power to order your reinstatement (going back to your old job), re-engagement (being assigned a different job) or compensation. The vast majority of employees choose compensation rather than returning to their employer. You can also get reinstated if you successfully appeal against your dismissal as part of your employer's internal dismissal procedure.

 Your Rights

If you face losing your job your basic rights may include:
1 To be dismissed for one of five legally permitted reasons.
2 The right to know the reason for your dismissal.
3 Fairness in the dismissal procedure.
4 To make an internal appeal.
5 To make a claim to employment tribunal.

What next . . .

If you need advice on dismissal as set out here or in the subsequent chapters, the first thing you should do is get ahead of the game and take advantage of the tactics and tips every worker should know in Chapter 2. Details of other organizations that can assist you and where you can obtain further information are in Appendix B: Contact points.

Redundancy

In recent years around 750,000 workers have been made redundant each year. This compares with a peak of around 1.5 million redundancies in the peak recession years of the 1980s and 1990s. Over 40 per cent of those made redundant are back in work within three months.

Redundancy is perhaps one of the most feared words in the English language. 'I'm sorry, we're going to have to let you go,' is the stereotypical version of how the news is broken.

People use scores of terms to describe it, only some helping cloak its bitter reality: downsized, laid-off, out-placed, restructured, shed, wasted, P45ed. The Americans call it being 'pink-slipped'. Today, redundancy remains one of the most talked and written about areas of working life, and it is one of the most frequently used reasons for dismissing employees.

The exact number and type of redundancies depend on changes in the structure of the economy, and the economic cycle itself. The continuing decline in manufacturing industry is often cited as one of the biggest causes of job losses and this remains so. But the strength of the pound, the impact of new technology and a huge spate of mergers and takeovers in the wake of globalization have all also taken their toll.

A common misunderstanding can arise over the definition of redundancy and when it applies. Although redundancy has become associated with all forms of dismissal it actually has a precise legal definition and is just one of five ways an employee can be legally dismissed.

Establishing whether a certain situation fits the definition of a redundancy can be difficult.

Generally a redundancy occurs if:
• your employer has stopped or intends to stop doing business; or

- your employer has stopped or intends to stop doing business in the same location; or
- there has been a reduction in the need for employees to undertake the particular kind of work they do.

Understanding what is meant by reduced work can be tricky. If new technology for inputting data means that one person can carry out twice the work, this gives rise to a redundancy. There would be a reduced need for employees to carry out the data input work.

Employers often disguise a dismissal as redundancy, when in fact it is due to poor performance or a personality clash. This is partly because redundancy is often perceived as a kinder reason for dismissing an employee than the genuine reason.

Alternatively, employers may see a redundancy as less time-consuming and involving less effort than, for example, a dismissal for under-performance. Redundancy dismissals can also take place for unlawful or discriminatory reasons such as the pregnancy of a worker.

 What if . . .

- A college spent £30,000 installing a new heating system with electronic controls. The college then decided to appoint a heating engineer who could also do some general plumbing and made a resident plumber based at the college redundant.
  Outcome: In a similar case, the need for a heating engineer who could do plumbing instead of just a plumber gave rise to a legitimate redundancy. This was despite the fact that there had been no reduction in the amount of work to be done and no reduction in the number of employees required to do it. The court decided there was a reduced need for employees to do work of that particular kind, i.e. plumbing.
- A manager goes into hospital and the managing director takes over his work as well as doing his own work, and finds he can do both jobs. The manager is then made redundant.
  Outcome: The courts in a similar case decided that it was a genuine redundancy because there was a reduced need for managers.
- A lecturer is made redundant when the university runs out of funding. There was still a need for employees to carry out this work, but no money to pay them.
  Outcome: This is likely to be a legitimate redundancy because while

there was still a demand for the course, there was a need to reduce the number of lecturers.

• A barmaid in her fifties is dismissed because her employer wants a younger and more glamorous variety of barmaid.

  Outcome: The barmaid's attempt to claim a redundancy payment in a similar case failed because there was no reduction in the work of a particular kind that she did. She would however be able to claim unfair dismissal.

Job hunting on being made redundant

If you are being made redundant, and have been given notice of redundancy, you are entitled to take time off to look for work as well as to arrange training for future employment. You don't need to have an interview planned; it can be just to look for work. To qualify for this right you need to have had two years' continuous employment up to the date you will be made redundant or would leave if you were given your statutory minimum notice entitlement (*see* pp. 260–61: Notice periods).

Your employer should pay you and you are entitled to take reasonable time off. If your employer refuses to allow you this time off or refuses to pay you, you should raise a grievance. If the matter is not resolved you have the right to bring a claim at employment tribunal, but you should do it within three months. If successful, you will be awarded money for the time you should have been allowed to take, or the pay you should have received (*see* Part 5: Taking things further).

 Key Questions

What is fair redundancy dismissal and procedure?

Being treated fairly means there has to be a fair reason to make you redundant in the first place, and a fair procedure must then be followed. That means that at least, the statutory disciplinary procedure should be followed and you should be given as much warning as possible of impending redundancies. Your employer should consult about how to minimize hardship to employees and achieve the company's objectives fairly.

The criteria for selection of employees to be made redundant should also be agreed, and be based on objective measures like attendance records and length of service. Your employer should try and find you alternative employment within your organization. If you are not found another job by the end of the consultation period you should be served notice or paid in lieu.

How should I be told that I've been made redundant?

There is no set way in which you should be told you have been made redundant. However, if a true consultation exercise is being undertaken then the first time you are spoken to should be to inform you of the possibility of your redundancy rather than the final decision. You should be made aware of all the relevant issues such as the reason for the redundancies, how many people are affected, and what options are being considered.

How long should I be consulted prior to my possible redundancy?

You should be consulted for a reasonable period of time. There is no specified minimum period of time and what is reasonable varies. It is best if it is a few weeks at least. In cases where more than 20 people are made redundant your employer must consult over at least one month. Not consulting is seen as unreasonable and could mean your dismissal is unfair. In reality people are often dismissed without consultation because employers know they can get away with it. Companies sometimes just give staff a general warning then tell individuals to leave, paying them in lieu of notice.

Can I get compensation for the way I was told about being made redundant?

No, you cannot claim compensation for hurt feelings.

How much notice should I get prior to my redundancy?

You are entitled to the greater of either statutory minimum notice, or the amount of notice set out in your contract. Statutory minimum notice is one week for each year of continuous service to a maximum of 12 weeks. So, for example, if you have worked with your employer for 10 years but your contract says you are entitled to one month's notice, you will in fact be entitled to ten weeks' notice. If you are not served adequate notice you can take your employer to employment tribunal and claim wrongful dismissal. Be careful to ensure that you have actually been served notice verbally or in writing. It should be clear and definite, not a general statement of the possibility of losing your job, as that would not constitute a notice of redundancy.

Do I qualify for a redundancy payment?

You qualify for a redundancy payment if you have been made redundant after at least two years' continuous work with your employer. You also have to be an employee and not within the excluded category set out below. The law entitles you to a minimum redundancy payment based on your age and years of service. This is called the statutory redundancy payment.

Although rare, you may also have a separate right to a redundancy payment under your contract of employment, which is calculated in a different way from your statutory payment. While the law sets a limit on the statutory amount you can be paid, the contractual payment is set out in your contract, company handbook or set by custom and practice within your firm or industry. It may well enhance your redundancy entitlements and can be fairly generous.

Who is excluded from claiming a redundancy payment?

There are a number of categories of workers who are excluded from payments including employees who reach retirement age or are under the age of 18 years, masters or crew of fishing vessels paid by a share of the profits alone, civil servants and public employees, employees working outside the country unless they can be regarded as ordinarily working here, employees offered suitable alternative employment, employees who unreasonably leave during the trial period of suitable alternative employment, employees dismissed for misconduct, employees subject to an exemption order, employees who receive a pension instead of redundancy under particular regulations, and employees who have signed a waiver within a fixed term contract of over two years.

What if my employer decides to move to a different location?

It can be argued that a clause in your contract saying you can be required to work elsewhere takes away your right to a redundancy payment if you refuse to transfer. Although much depends on each individual case, the courts have found that these so-called mobility clauses should not take this right away.

How is my statutory redundancy payment calculated?

Your redundancy payment is based on your age and number of years of service. You receive a multiplier of the maximum weekly pay, which is currently £280 but is increased from time to time. Read off your age and years of service from the redundancy calculator in Appendix A and multiply the number set out by £280, or the actual amount of your weekly pay if it is less than £280. For example, a 45-year-old employee who has worked for 16 years is entitled to £5,040 (2005) statutory redundancy pay.

Does my employer have to offer me another job?

No, your employer does not have to offer you another job. The obligation upon your employer is to show that appropriate efforts were made to investigate the availability of a suitable alternative job. The suitability of an alternative job depends on how similar it is to the redundant job. Factors such as pay, status, hours of work and location are relevant. If a suitable alternative job is found, you are entitled to a trial period. If you unreasonably refuse suitable alternative employment, you will lose your right to a redundancy payment. Whether your refusal is reasonable depends on your exact circumstances, but factors such as domestic problems, housing and schooling considerations and medical reasons are relevant. In one case an employee was found to have reasonably refused alternative employment in a different location because it would have required moving his family, including his children who were both about to sit exams.

What about voluntary redundancy?

People often wonder whether a voluntary redundancy is a redundancy in the same way as an imposed redundancy. It seems as if it is simply a mutually agreed termination as opposed to a redundancy. This is not the case. Accepting an offer of voluntary redundancy is broadly accepted as a genuine redundancy dismissal. It is legally recognized as a redundancy even though the employee has willingly participated in the scheme.

Can I be made redundant during maternity leave?

Yes, you can be made redundant if you are pregnant. But the law recognizes that pregnant women are particularly exposed to being made redundant because of prejudice within the workplace as well as commonly held beliefs that women will want to stay home to look after the baby or lose interest in their job. If a woman is made redundant during maternity leave an employer is required to offer her an alternative job ahead of other employees.

What if I think my employers have used redundancy as an excuse?

If the reason for your redundancy is not genuine you can claim unfair dismissal at employment tribunal and could get compensation of up to £56,800. However, such a claim may be difficult to prove.

Are the rules different if lots of people are being made redundant?

Yes. If more than 20 employees are being made redundant at one location in a 90-day period then there are additional obligations in relation to information, consultation and also notification. The consultation must be over a period of at least one month and specific information must be provided to workforce representatives. The consultation period goes up to 90 days if there are more than 100 people being made redundant. Your employer must also notify the DTI. Failure to do so may lead to your employer getting a criminal conviction.

Can I leave before my notice period is completed?

Beware that while you are able to give your employer notice to leave early and not lose your right to a redundancy payment, you must be sure that the period in which you decide to leave is within your statutory or contractual notice period. If your employer has served a longer notice than necessary and you choose to leave within that period, you will lose your right to a redundancy payment. You can also lose your right to a redundancy payment if your employer serves a counternotice on you but you still leave.

Am I compensated for my loss of benefits due to being made redundant?

You are entitled to compensation for all benefits during the notice period including pensions. Sometimes you can negotiate with your employer for certain benefits such as your health insurance and company car to continue for a period after the end of your employment.

What about my reference?

Your employer is not obliged to provide a reference to any prospective employers (except in a few sectors such as certain jobs in financial services). But if a reference is provided it must be a true accurate and fair reference. If your employer does not provide you with this and you suffer a loss as a result you could take legal action (*see* Chapter 6).

Your Rights

If you are facing redundancy your basic rights may include:

1 Fairness in the redundancy procedure.
2 A redundancy payment.
3 The right to make a claim to employment tribunal for a redundancy payment and/or for unfair dismissal.
4 A trial period to assess the suitability of an alternative job.
5 Time off to look for work or for training.
6 Certain additional rights where large-scale redundancies are taking place.

Bear in mind for most of these rights you need either one or two years of continuous employment with your employer.

What next . . .

If you need advice on redundancy, the first thing you should do is get ahead of the game and take advantage of the tactics and tips every worker and employer should know in Chapter 2. If you need to take things further *see* Part 5: Taking things further. Details of organizations that can assist you and further information are in Appendix B: Contact points.

Under-performance and sickness

I like work; it fascinates me. I can sit and look at it for hours. I love to keep it by me; the idea of getting rid of it really breaks my heart
Jerome K. Jerome, *Three Men in a Boat*

Does your boss say that you are under-performing, that your work is not up to standard, or that you're just not up to it? Are you frequently sick or is your attendance erratic and timekeeping poor? Or have you failed to achieve the qualifications needed for your job? If you fall into any or all of the above categories, and if it can be shown this has had a negative impact on your company, you could be dismissed.

Your employer could say that you simply do not have the aptitude to do the work, or even that you're sick and absent so much that it is affecting the smooth running of the business.

In law this is referred to as lack of *capability* or *qualifications*.

Capability is defined by skill, aptitude, health or any other physical or mental quality. In all cases, lack of ability must relate to the work that you are currently contractually required to do.

Qualifications are defined as any degree, diploma or other academic, technical or professional qualification relevant to the position that you hold. This sort of dismissal normally occurs when an employee is given a job on the understanding that he will obtain a particular qualification and then fails to achieve that qualification.

Chapter 12 takes a look at sickness in more detail and highlights how different sorts of sickness should be managed in the workplace, as well as touching on entitlements to statutory sick pay.

 What if . . .

- A pilot risks the lives of his passengers when he lands the aircraft so hard that there is serious damage to the plane. The airline feels he has been negligent and that pilot error is to blame. He is dismissed.

  Outcome: In a similar case, the court found the pilot had been fairly dismissed. It said that the job of pilot was one in which the degree of professional skill required was so high, and the consequences of the smallest departure from that standard so serious, that the dismissal was justified.

 Key Questions

What constitutes under-performance?
Under-performance can include employees who are slow or inflexible, who fail to meet standards or hit prescribed targets (even if the standards set are new or new targets are brought in by management), whose sickness absence level is so great that it is not possible for them to perform their job satisfactorily, who fail to establish good working relationships, and those who are difficult or abrasive and whose work is affected by this attitude.

How much of a chance to improve should I be given?
You should be given a reasonable period of time in which to improve, but what is meant by reasonable depends entirely on the circumstances of your case – the courts have ruled that it could be anything between a few weeks to several months. The factors taken into account in determining a reasonable period are the length of your service, your overall performance during that time, exactly how bad your performance has been, and how much warning you were given of your employer's dissatisfaction.

Who decides if I've improved – and how?
Your line manager or any other appropriate person chosen by your employer decides if you have improved. Their assessment should be as objective as possible. Objective criteria are those that can be measured – for example, speed and accuracy in the case of a secretary.

I've been off sick intermittently – can I be dismissed?
Yes, you can be dismissed. Your employer may be able to show that your absences adversely affect the smooth running of the business making you incapable of satisfying its needs. If you are being dismissed because of an unacceptable number of absences due to minor ailments your employer should follow a sickness absence procedure. This usually begins with a review of your attendance record and the reasons for your absence. You will be given a chance to provide an explanation and if you do not improve you may be given a formal warning. Your absence level is likely to be monitored during a trial period, and if things do not get better you could be dismissed.

What if I'm seriously ill?
If you are seriously ill you may be dismissed for your sickness absence but your employer should use a different approach and procedure. But you also have certain rights, and the Disability Discrimination Act may apply to employees with serious conditions. These issues are covered in Chapter 14: Disability discrimination.

How long can I be off sick before I'm dismissed?
There is no set period for how long you can be sick and off work before being dismissed. It all depends on the nature and size of the business you work for. Large employers often have guidelines to ensure consistency within their organizations, but there are no set rules. If you are sick contact your human resources department or your boss. Also remember you may qualify for protection under the Disability Discrimination Act.

Can I be dismissed for pulling 'sickies'?

Yes, although this is really a misconduct matter as opposed to one of under-performance and sickness. Your employer would still need to follow a fair procedure in dismissing you and would need to prove you were not actually sick.

Can my employer dismiss me for being 'difficult'?

You can be dismissed if your employer can prove your attitude is affecting your performance, or relationships with staff or customers. In particular, if clients are refusing to work with you because of your attitude then you could be dismissed by your employers even if you are really good at the work that you do. If the problem is a personality clash or your conduct seriously affects staff morale, then you could be dismissed for under-performance, misconduct or under a catch-all category known as other reasons.

Can I be dismissed for one action alone?

Yes, it is possible for one action to be relied upon to establish your incapability if the act is extreme and serious. The ruling in the case of the pilot mentioned above is again relevant. It said, 'there are activities in which the degree of professional skill which must be required is so high, and the potential consequences of the smallest departure from that high standard are so serious, that one failure to perform in accordance with those standards is enough to justify dismissal. The passenger-carrying airline pilot, the scientist operating the nuclear reactor, the chemist in charge of research into the possible effects of, for example, thalidomide, the driver of the Manchester to London express, the driver of an articulated lorry full of sulphuric acid, are all in the situation in which one failure to maintain the proper standard of professional skill can bring about a major disaster.'

What if my employer says that I am capable – but just being lazy?

Sometimes the real reason for a dismissal is misconduct not under-performance or capability. This is the case when an employee is deliberately being idle or refusing to pull their weight. In practice it can be hard for an employer to prove an employee is deliberately under-performing.

What if my appraisal suggests that I've performed well?

It is not uncommon for employees to be dismissed for poor performance even though their appraisals suggest there is no problem with their work. This is because employers often take the easier route of ignoring problems rather than addressing them. If this is the case it could help you, since it will make it harder for your employer to prove your dismissal is fair.

What if my employer is just using poor performance as an excuse?
If your employer is just using poor performance as an excuse to get rid of you then your dismissal is likely to be unfair and you could lodge a claim at employment tribunal. Be warned, however, that it may be difficult to prove if your employer has had the foresight to create a paper trail. A paper trail is paperwork like memos and notes that highlight your poor performance.

What if I lied about my qualifications?
This would be misconduct. If you are found out you could be dismissed.

Should I be offered alternative employment?
No, there is no actual right to be offered alternative employment. This is the case even if you cannot make the grade in a job you have just been promoted into – there is no automatic right to be given your old job back. However, in the case of a very large employer an employment tribunal may consider it unreasonable for an employee to be dismissed for the reason of under-performance or sickness without giving any consideration to the possibility of an alternative job that may be available in the organization.

What about my pay and benefits if I am dismissed?
If you are dismissed for incapability you are entitled to work your notice or be paid salary and benefits in lieu of notice.

What about my reference?
Your employer does not have to provide a reference but if one is provided then it must be true, accurate and fair. Failure to take reasonable care to be true, accurate and fair in writing a reference could lead you to lose a prospective job. If you suffer a loss in this way, you could sue your employer for negligence. There is no legal requirement for an employer to provide a detailed reference – in practice employers often just write a basic factual reference (*see* Chapter 6).

Your Rights

If you are facing dismissal for under-performance or frequent sickness:

1 Your employer should follow procedures, should have given you warnings and spelt out the consequences.
2 In the case of sickness this should include a comparison of your level of absence with others in your department.
3 In the case of under-performance your employer should undertake an objective assessment of your performance and highlight the problems.
4 You should be given a chance to improve and any appropriate training.
5 You should be warned of the consequences of failing to improve.
6 You can be accompanied to any disciplinary hearing.
7 You should be offered the right to appeal if you are dismissed.

Bear in mind, however, that you can only claim unfair dismissal if you have been employed for one year or more.

 Tactics and Tips

Written records
Both employer and employee should keep a written record of all the discussions concerning under-performance or sickness. This will help make the position clearer and more robust if the matter ends up at employment tribunal.

Appraisals
Employees should keep copies of all appraisals in a safe place. It is not uncommon for employers to dismiss people for under-performance even when their appraisals are glowing. This could help an employee's case as he or she should have been warned about any concerns.

Grievance procedure
If you are not satisfied with the way in which matters are being handled you could raise a 'grievance' against your employer. A grievance procedure is a way of making a formal complaint within your company, and the process is often set down in your contract or staff handbook, although

you can still raise a grievance even if there is no procedure in writing since the right to raise one is a legal entitlement. In most cases this merely means a letter to your boss raising the complaint.

Serious under-performance
Remember that there is no such thing as an 'instant dismissal' and that even if you are being dismissed as a result of under-performance so serious that it has drastic consequences, your employer should still investigate the matter, give you the opportunity to state your case, and hold a disciplinary hearing.

References
The whole business of getting a helpful reference is obviously a particular worry for those facing dismissal for poor performance or frequent absence due to minor ailments. If you are in this position it is a good idea to ask your current employer to agree the wording of your reference before you leave. Often an employer will agree to provide just a basic factual reference stating start and end dates and the duties you undertook. Remember they are under an obligation to be honest and may be contacted for further information (*see* Chapter 6).

 What next . . .

If you need advice on under-performance or sickness, the first thing you should do is get ahead of the game and take advantage of the tactics and tips every employer and worker should know in Chapter 2. If you need to take things further *see* Part 5: Taking things further. Details of organizations that can assist you and further information are in Appendix B: Contact points.

Misconduct

Misconduct may sound like something that goes on behind the school bike sheds but in the world of work it is a term that describes behaviour so unacceptable that it could cost you your job.

In general, misconduct is deemed to be serious or not serious. If the offence is not too serious, such as regularly being late for work, then it is likely that you will just be given a verbal or written warning. However, if this sort of behaviour persists you may eventually be dismissed.

The most serious cases of misconduct like theft, falsifying expense claims and violence at work are classified as *gross misconduct*. Gross misconduct is likely to result in your dismissal and cost you your entitlement to notice or pay in lieu of notice too.

Your contract or staff handbook should spell out your company's position; it should give an indication of what constitutes gross misconduct, explain the possible consequences of breaking the rules, and provide details of the procedure that applies in such cases.

The following offences are usually classed as gross misconduct:
- theft;
- fighting and violence;
- fraud;
- falsification of records;
- bullying or harassment;
- alcohol and drugs abuse;
- disobedience and insubordination;
- deliberate damage to property;
- e-mail and Internet abuse;
- disloyalty and breaches of confidence;
- bringing your employer into serious disrepute.

Contrary to popular belief, a dismissal for gross misconduct is not (or should not be) instant: a formal investigation should still always take place first. Indeed, it is central to the fairness of such a dismissal that an employer follows its disciplinary procedure, and the employee is given the right to be accompanied by a fellow employee or trade union representative at any disciplinary hearing.

If your employer has not adopted a specific disciplinary procedure then, as a matter of good practice, the ACAS code of practice on disciplinary and grievance procedures should be followed, both in the case of misconduct and gross misconduct. Disciplinary procedures should generally start with an investigation of the facts and an informal chat with the employee should be considered. In the case of gross misconduct it may be appropriate to suspend an employee on full pay. Before any decision is reached procedures should be followed which means an employee should be written to concerning the misconduct and should be fully aware of the case against him. A hearing should be arranged for the employee to put his case, and remember, the employee also has a legal right to be accompanied to such a hearing. Ultimate sanctions include a verbal, written or final written warning, and dismissal. The employee should always be given the right to appeal.

An employer must show that it formed a genuine belief that misconduct, whether gross or otherwise, has taken place before dismissing an employee. It is not necessary to have conclusive proof, just that on balance, the employer genuinely believes the employee is guilty. The employer having to form this 'reasonable belief' is different from the test in criminal cases where a jury needs to have reached a view of guilt 'beyond reasonable doubt'. However, a dismissal can also be procedurally unfair even if misconduct is ultimately proved.

In summary, a dismissal for misconduct is fair if, following a fair procedure and reasonable investigations, the employer formed the view that the employee was guilty of misconduct. This holds true even if after the dismissal it is established that the employee wasn't guilty after all. This is because only facts known at the time of the dismissal are relevant to fairness.

 What if . . .

- After six years of service as a driver and fitter, an employee is dismissed after a row with his manager that ended in him telling his manager to 'fuck off'.

  Outcome: The length of satisfactory service is likely to lead the court to decide that the act was not one of gross misconduct but one that merited a final warning.

- A drama teacher was dismissed after reporting to his employer he had been convicted for the possession and cultivation of cannabis under the Misuse of Drugs Act. His employer felt he was unsuitable for employment as a teacher.

  Outcome: An employment tribunal is likely to find his dismissal is unfair and in a similar case the employment tribunal said a teacher should be reinstated in his job. The court summarized the position relating to a conviction for an offence outside work as follows: dismissal may be justified if the situation seriously affects employment relationships, makes an employee a danger to others, particularly children, or has a negative effect on an employer's reputation.

- A company receives a complaint that one of their lorry drivers exposed himself to a young girl. The employee explains that he had had an urgent need to relieve himself and had not deliberately exposed himself.

His employer accepted the explanation and took no further action. Some time later, the company receives another complaint saying the same driver had made gestures of a sexual nature to a woman driver and had prevented her from overtaking his vehicle. He denies making obscene gestures saying he was trying to signal to the other driver to overtake. Again no further action is taken. The organization was next informed that reports had been made to the police that the driver had exposed himself to women on two separate occasions in the same lay-by, and the driver admitted that he had been relieving himself in the lay-by on the dates in question. When questioned further, the driver gives no reply and is then suspended without pay and sent home. When the police charged the man, his employer dismissed him.

Outcome: In a case along the lines of the above the company was found to have acted unfairly in dismissing the driver even though the offences he'd been charged with occurred in circumstances relating to his employment. This is because he was not given a further opportunity to explain his conduct. The dismissal was unfair on procedural grounds – not because the employee had not committed gross misconduct.

- An employee is dismissed from his job as a computer engineer for head-butting another employee and takes his employer to employment tribunal. The employee concerned does not see statements taken as part of the investigation.

  Outcome: The employer in a similar case had carried out a reasonable investigation, adopted a fair procedure and the dismissal was fair. The employee was aware of what he was being accused so the witness statements added little to the allegations.

Alcohol

Drinking causes as much of a problem in the workplace as it does in other areas of life – affecting performance and behaviour, and leading to erratic time-keeping, sickness and absenteeism; it often compromises safety too. According to the charity Alcohol Concern, over two-thirds of employees say alcohol misuse is a problem in their organizations. Surveys have found that those who drink a lot take far more sick leave, and that over 20 per cent of workplace accidents involved intoxicated workers.

Legal position

Employees whose work is affected by alcohol leave themselves open to dismissal for misconduct. An employee is at greater risk of being dismissed if being under the influence compromises health and safety. For example, one lunchtime the manager of a jewellery shop went to the local pub to watch a football match on TV. He later admitted to having a few too many pints. When he returned to work in the afternoon he forgot to lock the shop and it was subsequently burgled. If properly carried out, a dismissal for gross misconduct in such circumstances is likely to be fair.

For those with a 'drinking problem' the situation may be different as there is a growing tendency for employers to treat alcoholism as an illness and offer medical treatment and counselling to deal with such problems.

Contracts of employment often include the right to test employees for alcohol – if they do not it would be a breach of contract, and even possibly assault, if an employee is tested against his will.

Drugs

The main difference between alcohol and drugs is that while the consumption of the former is legal, taking the latter is against the law. They can both lead to serious problems in the workplace and affect the safety of the employee concerned, colleagues and members of the public. There are no exact figures for the scale of drug-related problems in the workplace.

Legal position

Because drug abuse can amount to a criminal offence tribunals have tended to view it as gross misconduct. So be under no illusions: drug abuse at work is not only against the law, it is likely to lead to dismissal. However, in general, an employee's conduct outside work is unlikely to justify dismissal unless the conduct affects the employee adversely at work. For example, a magazine designer was overheard by his boss telling colleagues about a weekend he'd had high on cannabis. When asked to explain himself the designer said he'd never taken any drugs at work but he was dismissed for drug abuse. This is likely to be an unfair dismissal because the drug use did not take place at work and would not impact on his ability to do the job. In some ways drug addiction is like alcoholism and is treated by many employers as an illness for which medical treatment and counselling is offered. As with alcohol, testing for drugs can only take place if the right for employers to test is set down in the contract of employment. In cases where safety is an issue, such as the transport industry, random testing is quite common and seen as reasonable. There are no set rules; it will depend on the exact circumstances that apply.

 Key Questions

Who defines what acceptable conduct is at work?
The definition of what is acceptable conduct comes from two sources: your employer and the courts. An employer's standards are established through custom and practice and are also often found in the written employer's contract or company handbook. These standards themselves derive in part from the courts; over time the courts produce what is called law (decisions and rulings that flow from the courts on a case by case basis which then set precedents for future cases to draw on), and this sets down what constitutes acceptable conduct in the workplace. For example, it is now well established that any form of timesheet fraud or falsification of records is extremely serious and likely to result in a gross misconduct dismissal.

What guidelines should employers follow?
Most employers have a disciplinary procedure and they may form part of your contract of employment. Employers are obliged to follow at least the statutory disciplinary procedure now set out in the law, and it is always advisable to follow ACAS guidelines on discipline at work. A disciplinary procedure generally contains the right to suspend you in order to investigate the matter, details the different sanctions that could apply, and gives details of what constitutes gross misconduct.

What if I am charged with a criminal offence outside of work?
Employers are often tempted to prejudge a person and dismiss them if they are charged with a criminal offence committed outside of work. However, it is important to realize that dismissal is an employment law issue rather than a criminal one. It simply may not be legally fair to dismiss an employee if they have been charged with a criminal offence unrelated to their work. For example, if an administrative clerk is charged with drunk and disorderly conduct, it is likely to be unfair if he is dismissed from work because of this. But on the other hand, if an accountant with access to the company's funds is convicted of theft outside work it may be fair to dismiss him.

What if I commit a serious or criminal offence while at work?

If you steal, commit assault or a sexual offence, are violent, take drugs or commit any other serious offence while at work then this is likely to be gross misconduct. Gross misconduct is a phrase used to describe a serious and unacceptable act, which is inconsistent with you staying at work. Your employer could report you to the police and it is likely that you will be dismissed without any entitlement to notice or payment in lieu of notice. You would also risk your future employment at another establishment.

I'm being accused of sexual harassment. Can I be disciplined?

Sexual harassment of any type can lead you to being disciplined and dismissed. Examples are given in Chapter 15.

Can groups of employees be dismissed even if all were not involved in misconduct?

Four people were in a room when £3,000 went missing. After an investigation all were dismissed even though one of them had not been involved in the theft. This was legally fair because an employer is entitled to dismiss an entire group of suspects if, after reasonable investigation, there is no way of telling which of them actually committed the act.

What if I've lied at work?

It would all depend on what an employee lied about and how significant the lie is. A serious lie about abilities or qualifications can lead to dismissal. A less serious lie may lead to disciplinary action and result in a warning.

What if I've cheated my hours or expenses at work?

Timesheet fraud and fraudulent expense claims are serious matters and likely to lead to disciplinary action and most probably dismissal. Of the many cases reported, it is clear that if a reasonable belief of misconduct is formed after an investigation, then it is very difficult for an employee to defend or to challenge a dismissal. In one case an employee resigned from his job after he had been demoted for falsifying his timesheet. He claimed that he had been constructively dismissed. The court decided that the employee had been guilty of falsifying his timesheet and that the penalty of demotion was reasonable.

Can I be dismissed for disobeying my boss?

An act of disobedience is unlikely to be serious enough to justify dismissal first time round, but it could lead to you being disciplined. However, repeated disobedience could lead to your dismissal. If your boss's orders have been unreasonable the matter is more complicated and you should raise the matter with him. In practice this is often difficult to do so. The alternative is to formally raise a grievance as part of your company's internal procedures. As this is likely to result in a clash between you and your boss you should think about whether there are any less contentious ways of resolving the problem before following this course of action.

I downloaded pornography from the Internet at work. Can I be dismissed?

An offence of this type is a serious matter that is likely to lead to your dismissal (*see* Chapter 20).

Should I be warned before being dismissed?

You are entitled to a fair procedure and your employers are legally obliged to follow a disciplinary procedure which includes warning you and giving you an opportunity to improve and mend your ways. If your employer fails to do this, your dismissal would be automatically unfair, even if your employer has a sound reason for your dismissal in the first place. In cases of gross misconduct, as long as there has been an investigation and you have had a chance to state your case at a disciplinary hearing, a dismissal may be fair without any previous warnings.

What about my benefits?

You are entitled to all your benefits during your notice period unless you are dismissed for gross misconduct in which case you are not entitled to any notice of termination or payment in lieu.

What about my reference?

References are a difficult matter in the case of misconduct since any referral to the misconduct will limit your chances of re-employment (*see* Tactics and Tips below and Chapter 6).

Your Rights

If you have one year's continuous service you have the right to a fair dismissal.

For an employer to act reasonably in dismissing an employee they may need to show:

1 The misconduct was properly investigated.
2 Company's disciplinary procedure was followed.
3 The employee was given the opportunity to state his or her case.
4 The employee was warned of the likely consequences.
5 The employee was not denied the right to be accompanied at a disciplinary hearing.
6 The employee was offered the right to appeal against the dismissal.

Tactics and Tips

Written records
You should keep a written record of all the discussions you have with your employer concerning your misconduct. This will help make your position more robust if you take your case to employment tribunal and claim unfair dismissal.

Seeking information
Be prepared to ask relevant questions and seek information at all stages if your job is at stake. You should ask to see details of disciplinary, grievance, or any other relevant procedures. If there is nothing available in writing your employers are obliged to follow at least the statutory disciplinary procedures set out in the law.

Grievance procedure
If you are not satisfied with the way in which matters are being handled you could raise a 'grievance' against your employer. A grievance procedure is a way of making a formal complaint within your company, and the process is set out in the law and also often set down in your contract or staff handbook, although you can still raise a grievance even if there is no

procedure in writing. In most cases this merely means a letter to your boss raising the complaint.

Right to be accompanied at a disciplinary hearing

This is an important right, particularly if there are allegations that you have been guilty of misconduct. If you request that someone accompany you then it may help you get the support you need to get you through a meeting relating to allegations of misconduct. It will also demonstrate that you know your rights, and that you regard the allegations against you as serious. One further useful tip: if the person that you choose to accompany you is unable to make it, you have the legal right to a postponement of up to five working days from the original date proposed for the hearing.

Right of appeal

You should always be given the right to appeal against your dismissal. Depending on the internal procedures of your firm you may also be able to appeal against warnings given to you under the disciplinary procedure. A dismissal that is not followed by the right of appeal is a breach of statutory procedures and may be unfair on that basis alone.

Gross misconduct

Even if you are being dismissed as a result of an allegation of gross misconduct your employer should still investigate the matter and give you the opportunity to state your case at a disciplinary hearing. You should not be 'instantly' dismissed without your employer first taking these steps. Remember, if you are dismissed for gross misconduct you will lose your right to notice or payment in lieu.

References

The whole business of getting a helpful reference is obviously a particular worry for those facing dismissal for misconduct. If you are in this position it is a good idea to ask your current employer to agree the wording of a reference before you leave. Often an employer will agree to provide just a basic factual reference stating start and end dates and the duties you undertook. Remember they are under an obligation to be honest and may be contacted for further information about the circumstances of your dismissal (*see* Chapter 6).

Contact Points

Alcohol Concern – charity
Address: Waterbridge House, 32–36 Loman Street, London SE1 0EE
Telephone: 020 7928 7377 **Drinkline:** 0800 917 8282
Website: www.alcoholconcern.org.uk

National Drugs Helpline: 0800 776600

Re-Solv – solvent abuse charity
Address: 30a High Street, Stone, Staffs ST15 8AW
Telephone: 01785 817885
Helpline: 0808 800 2345
Website: www.re-solv.org.uk

 What next . . .

If you need advice on workplace misconduct, the first thing you should do is get ahead of the game and take advantage of the tactics and tips every worker and employer should know in Chapter 2. If you need to take things further *see* Part 5: Taking things further. Details of organizations that can assist you and further information are in Appendix B: Contact points.

Legal barrier to work

If you lose your driving licence it could cost you your job too

If your actions result in a situation, or something happens, where you would be breaking the law if you continued to carry out your job you can be dismissed as a result. It will be a legal barrier that prevents you from working in that role.

The most common example of such a legal barrier is the loss of a driving licence. If someone is employed as a minicab driver and gets banned from driving he clearly cannot perform the task he was employed to do. Although this is by far and away the most likely eventuality, a legal barrier can also exist in cases involving failure to achieve certain qualifications, and cases involving some forms of illness.

Unlike a dismissal for under-performance or misconduct, your employer must show that to continue to employ you actually breaks the law, not that they merely formed a reasonable belief that it would.

Your employer would also need to consider the possibility of offering you an alternative job.

Whether or not your employer acted reasonably in dismissing you depends on factors such as the duration of the ban, how much of your work it affects or, in other cases, whether your employer can help you obtain a necessary qualification and whether there is any other job you can be asked to do in place of the job you are banned from doing. You should always be consulted about any alternative arrangements that may be possible.

 What if . . .

- A lorry driver is convicted of drink-driving and disqualified for a year. His employer finds him alternative work driving a lorry on private roads. Six months later there is no further work for him and he is dismissed. The employee wants a redundancy payment.
  Outcome: The court in a similar case said that as the employee was not dismissed for redundancy he was not entitled to redundancy payment. His dismissal was fair.
- A car showroom's used vehicle supervisor is disqualified from driving for 12 months following a motor accident. His employer claims that as driving is obviously an important part of his job he is not able to carry out his duties and he is dismissed.
  Outcome: A dismissal on this basis in a similar case was fair. Although he undertook other duties as part of his job, 40 per cent of his time was spent driving.
- A radiographer was subject to special regulations that meant it was unlawful to employ him if he suffered from certain diseases. When he developed a skin condition that was on the proscribed list of diseases he was dismissed.
  Outcome: A dismissal on this basis in a similar case was fair.
- A trainee was dismissed after he failed to pass a necessary examination.

After being dismissed he successfully applied for an extension to sit the exam again.

Outcome: The dismissal in a similar case was unfair because even though continuing to employ the trainee could have broken the law it did not necessarily make it reasonable for his employer to dismiss him. If his employer had applied for an extension of his training period there was little likelihood of proceedings against the employer.

 ## Key Questions

I've lost my driver's licence – but I don't need to drive for work – can I be dismissed?

If driving is not an essential part of your job, or you can do other parts of your job without a driving licence, then it may be unfair to dismiss you.

What if I conceal that I do not have the right to drive in the UK?

If you are employed to drive and you mislead your employer by concealing that you are not permitted to drive in the UK then your dismissal is likely to be fair. For example, a sales assistant had hidden the fact that she was not qualified to drive in the UK but it was discovered when she was involved in an accident. She was fairly dismissed as a result, and could also have been dismissed for misconduct too. However, if your employer knows you do not have the right sort of licence but dismisses you when the police catch you the dismissal is likely to be unfair.

What if I did not know that my driver's licence does not cover the UK?

A dismissal on this basis is likely to be unfair. For example, a service engineer was dismissed because his employer found out that his New Zealand driving licence was not valid in the UK. He obtained a driving licence in the UK within a few weeks. His dismissal was unfair because his employer should have investigated the matter more thoroughly and acted with less haste.

What if I am dismissed because of a positive breathalyser test but before the court hearing?
If you are dismissed before the outcome of a court hearing your dismissal may be unfair. The factors noted above in the case of a driving ban will also need to be considered by your employer.

What if my wife/a chauffeur can drive in my place?
Your employer should give serious consideration to such proposals before dismissing you. In one case a dismissal was considered to be unfair because the employer rejected, without any consideration, the possibility of the employee's wife doing the driving. Any dismissal without considering the practicality of such proposals is likely to be unfair.

Can I be dismissed for having a health condition?
If there is a legal ban to your working in a particular job when you have a particular health condition, it can be fair to dismiss you. An example of this is the radiographer who was fairly dismissed when he developed a skin condition (cited above). In all cases of this kind the Disability Discrimination Act must also be taken into account.

Am I entitled to be given notice?
Yes, and you are entitled to all pay and benefits including pension contributions during your notice period.

 Your Rights

1 You should be warned about the likely consequences of the legal barrier to your working such as the loss of your licence.
2 You should be considered for any alternative job that may be available.
3 You have the right to be accompanied to any disciplinary hearing.
4 You have the right to appeal if dismissed.

Your employer should also consider the following questions in the case of a driving ban:

a Is driving an essential part of your job, or can you do other parts of your job without a driving licence?
b How much of an inconvenience will it be for them to keep you on?

Tactics and Tips

Seeking solutions

Be prepared to ask relevant questions if your job is at stake because you have lost your licence. It is worth trying to establish how much of your time is actually spent driving and if there is any alternative solution like taking public transport for a while, or even arranging for someone to drive you round.

Grievance procedure

If you are not satisfied with the way in which matters are being handled you could raise a 'grievance' against your employer. A grievance procedure is a way of making a formal complaint within your company, and the process is set off in the law and is also often set down in your contract or staff handbook, although you can still raise a grievance even if there is no procedure in writing. In most cases this merely means a letter to your boss raising the complaint.

 Contact Points

Driver and Vehicle Licensing Authority (DVLA)
Address: Customer Enquiries (Drivers) Unit, Swansea SA6 7JL
Enquiry line: 0870 240 0009

Driving Standards Agency (DSA)
Address: Stanley House, 56 Talbot Street, Nottingham NG1 5GU
Telephone: 0115 901 2500
Website: www.dsa.gov.uk

 What next . . .

If you need advice on legal barriers, the first thing you should do is get ahead of the game and take advantage of the tactics and tips every worker and employer should know at Chapter 2. If you need to take things further *see* Part 5: Taking things further. Details of organizations that can assist you and further information are in Appendix B: Contact points.

Other reasons

> *It's a recession when your neighbour loses his job; it's a depression when you lose yours*
> Harry S. Truman

For people who believe that any old excuse will do for employers to get rid of them this last catch-all category will pander to their prejudices. In fact this category exists to cater for the large number of situations that do not fit neatly into any of the legal pigeon holes so far dealt with. Dismissals in this category are mainly as a result of business restructuring, changes in terms and conditions, and other commercially driven changes. In legal terminology this means losing your job for 'some other substantial reason'.

The main reasons for which you can be dismissed include:

- *Business restructuring or reorganization* – when a change in the structure of the business leads to job losses, the losses may not fit the technical definition of redundancy, but they might still be legal.
- *Changes to terms and conditions* – when an employer has a sound business reason for making changes to the terms and conditions of staff, it may be fair to dismiss those who refuse to accept the changes.
- *Change in the ownership of the business* – special regulations apply when businesses change hands. In such cases a reduction in the workforce may be necessary and dismissals can be fair (*see* Chapter 19).
- *Ending of a fixed-term contract* – although not entirely logical, when a fixed-term contract ends the law regards this to be a dismissal even though the end date of employment was agreed at the outset. While, in theory, such a dismissal can be either fair or unfair, in most cases it is fair when it can be shown that the contract was for a specific purpose and that the purpose has ceased to apply. In practice, the end of a fixed-term contract does not usually cause any problems since there is almost always a clear understanding between those involved.
- *Protecting an employer's business* – if an employee refuses to sign an agreement restricting him from competitive activities for a period of time after he leaves in limited circumstances he may be fairly dismissed.

This only applies if the restriction, known as a *restrictive covenant*, is regarded as necessary for an employer to protect its business interests. In other words, if the employee is junior, or has no client contacts and cannot really do the company any harm, then a restrictive covenant may not really be necessary. The restriction must also be reasonable – it should not be in force for too long after the employee leaves or cover too wide a geographical area.

- *Miscellaneous reasons* – there are numerous other reasons that may be categorized as some other substantial reason for a fair dismissal. These include personality clashes (which might also be classed as misconduct), an employee going to prison, an employee's refusal to switch to cashless pay, and when it is mistakenly but reasonably believed that an employee has resigned.

 What if . . .

- An employee is dismissed following the restructuring of his company's computer services department. Although his actual post remains unchanged the company decides to achieve the necessary staff reductions through redundancies. That means he must undergo competitive selection for his own job but he refuses to do this, claiming he was not redundant and that his dismissal was unfair.

  Outcome: The court in a similar case decided that he had not been made redundant, but had lost his job as a result of his company's reorganization. However, since his employers had presented their case throughout on the basis that his dismissal was a redundancy, it was too late for them to argue that the dismissal could be justified on a different basis. The employee's claim for unfair dismissal was upheld.

- A secretary had worked at a company for about two-and-a-half years when she was dismissed. She got on perfectly well with the first two managers she worked with but not the third manager and this led to her dismissal.

  Outcome: A dismissal on a similar basis was unfair. While the court accepted that it is necessary for a secretary to be able to work with a manager it found that the employer had neither investigated the matter properly nor taken reasonable steps to try and improve the relationship. If an employee's work is satisfactory every step short of dismissal should be taken first.

Key Questions

Can I be dismissed if I refuse to accept changes to my terms and conditions?

If the changes suggested by your employer are for good sound business reasons then they may be justifiable. A sound business reason is one that has a commercial justification. In practice, this does give your employer a wide discretion. Your refusal to accept such changes may, where the commercial reasons can be shown, result in your fair dismissal – providing your employer follows a proper procedure including consulting with you and the rest of the workforce about the proposed changes. Other factors to be taken into account include what proportion of the workforce actually accept the changes and – as crass as it may sound – a comparison of how much you will lose and your employer will gain from your dismissal.

What about personality clashes – can I be dismissed?

If too much disruption is caused by a personal clash with a colleague or customer then you can be fairly dismissed. Your employer must first take steps to try and alleviate the disruption and should not dismiss you until it is reasonable to conclude that the breakdown is irredeemable – rather as in a marriage. If you go to employment tribunal it will consider whether the problem could have been resolved in any other way, and whether objections of your fellow employees were reasonable.

Can I be dismissed for refusing to sign a restrictive covenant?

A restrictive covenant is a means of preventing you from poaching staff and competing for, or dealing with, suppliers and customers for a period of time after you leave. The covenant enables your employer to protect its business interests. If you refuse to sign one when your employer has an overriding business need for the protection, it may be a fair reason for dismissing you.

What about my notice and benefits?

If you are dismissed for some other substantial reason you are entitled to pay and benefits during your notice period or pay in lieu of notice.

Your Rights

Your exact rights depend on the reason for your dismissal, but in most cases you should be entitled to:

1 The chance to explain your position to your employer.
2 Be taken through a fair procedure and be accompanied to any disciplinary hearing.
3 Be considered for any alternative work that may be available.
4 Appeal if you are dismissed.
5 If you have had at least one year's service you may apply to employment tribunal if you consider that you have been unfairly dismissed.

 Tactics and Tips

Written records
You should keep a written record of all the discussions that take place concerning a dismissal, whatever the reason for that dismissal. This will help make an employee's position more robust if you take the case to employment tribunal and strengthen the defence of an employer in the same situation.

Confirmation in writing
Get confirmation of any decisions in writing, particularly in situations such as those detailed above. This prevents misunderstandings and ensures an accurate record of events if the matter proceeds to employment tribunal. A more subtle advantage is that it may make an employer believe you are planning to take the matter further since you are armed with all the relevant information and evidence. Although most employers are fair and reasonable, this may make an unscrupulous employer pause and think carefully before acting unfairly. Employees on the other hand will regard written confirmation as enhancing professionalism and clarity.

 What next . . .

If you need advice on other reasons for dismissal the first thing you should do is get ahead of the game and take advantage of the tactics and tips every worker and employer should know in Chapter 2. If you need to take things further *see* Part 5: Taking things further. Details of organizations that can assist you and further information are in Appendix B: Contact points.

Insolvency

Your employer must pay some employee entitlements before other debts

Insolvency occurs where your employer runs into financial difficulties, and has insufficient funds to pay all its debts, including employees' wages. In most cases this means that employees lose their jobs although there is always the possibility of an injection of funds from a sale or takeover.

If this happens, and you are owed wages and redundancy pay, your position is protected to a limited extent, as your employer is obliged to pay certain of your entitlements, such as wages and accrued holiday pay, ahead of other debts.

If your company is not even in a position to meet these obligations you can apply to the Department of Trade and Industry for compensation from the National Insurance Fund. As well as your wages, you are entitled to claim statutory redundancy payments, statutory maternity pay, and unpaid employer pension contributions.

An application form to make a claim for payment in the above circumstances can be obtained from the DTI, although your employer's representative may complete it on your behalf. If you think the amount you receive from the DTI is wrong, or you are refused payment, then you can ask an employment tribunal to determine the amount you are owed.

 Your Rights

1 To be paid certain of your entitlements ahead of others owed money by your employer.
2 If your employer cannot pay you can apply to the Department of Trade and Industry for compensation.
3 To make a claim to employment tribunal to determine the amount you are owed if you are unhappy with what you receive from the DTI.

Notice periods

If dismissed you are entitled to a maximum notice of 12 weeks

The amount of notice you are entitled to be given or need to give depends on whether your departure is voluntary or forced – have you resigned or has your employer dismissed you? It also depends on what your contract says.

If you resign you must give your employer at least one week's notice; this is the legal minimum which stays the same despite your length of service. However, your contract could stipulate a longer period, and often employers make notice periods longer by requiring employees to give the same length of notice on resignation as the employer has to give on dismissal.

If you are dismissed you are entitled to a minimum amount of notice. This is one week's notice for each continuous year you have worked for your employer, up to a maximum of 12 weeks. You become eligible to claim this once you have been employed for four weeks, unless your contract says otherwise.

Again, in practice, your contract may set out longer periods of notice, and if the amounts in your contract exceed the legal minimum then the longer period applies.

If your contract does not refer to notice entitlements then the statutory minimum periods as stated above apply.

If an employee is very senior, and their contract does not refer to a notice period, either side on resignation or dismissal can go to court to argue that 'reasonable notice' applies. This means arguing that the legal minimum is deemed too short and inappropriate; the court determines whether this is so and what reasonable notice is, taking into account factors such as seniority, age, position and length of service. Typically, a notice period can be anything between three months to a year for middle and senior managers.

 Your Rights

If you have worked for at least four weeks continuously, you have the right to receive statutory minimum notice. This means you are entitled to the following.

The length of time you have worked	Notice entitlement on being dismissed
More than four weeks and less than 1 year	1 week
1 complete year	1 week
2 complete years	2 weeks
3 complete years	3 weeks
4 complete years	4 weeks
5 complete years	5 weeks
6 complete years	6 weeks
7 complete years	7 weeks
8 complete years	8 weeks
9 complete years	9 weeks
10 complete years	10 weeks
11 complete years	11 weeks
12 complete years	12 weeks
More than 12 years	12 weeks – the maximum

Restrictions after you've left

Does your contract have a 'gardening leave' clause?

There are a number of ways your employer can control your activities when you are about to leave or after you have left. These include incorporating restrictive covenants and confidentiality provisions into your contract, as well as the much-misunderstood gardening leave provisions.

Any attempt to restrict your activities after you have left is basically unlawful but, in certain limited circumstances, it is permitted. This is because the law recognizes that you may have gained an unfair advantage from inside information: the contacts, prices and other information that you became aware of when working for your employer. So, to stop you exploiting such advantages if you should work for a competitor, or simply leaving with valuable information about your employer's business, your contract may well have clauses preventing working for a competitor for a period of time or preventing you soliciting customers for a limited period.

Gardening leave

Gardening leave is much misunderstood – it is a means of putting you out of action for a period of time. Normally, if you have handed in your resignation you have to serve your notice. However, your contract can require you not to attend the office, and you do not have to work in that period, the so-called 'gardening leave' clause. It effectively places you at home without work, but unable to start working for another employer. It is fully paid and gives your employer a period of time to take over your work and notify contacts and clients of your departure, thereby limiting the damage you can do, for example, by taking clients with you, when you do actually leave.

Restrictive covenants

Provisions in your contract restricting your activities after you have left work are known as restrictive covenants. Restricting your activities is designed to protect your former employer's business interests as well as its business information. Restrictive covenants can, for a limited period of time after your departure, prevent you from working for a competitor, setting up in competition, contacting any clients or poaching any members of staff still working for your former employer. The restrictions normally apply over a particular geographic region.

The way such a clause is worded must be as clear, precise and as reasonable as possible for your employer to be able to enforce it if it is breached. Such clauses are not always regarded as reasonable. The restrictions may be for too long a period, they may be unclear, the degree of restriction may be excessive or there may be an attempt to restrict activities over too large a geographic region. In such cases the courts are unlikely to allow the restrictions to be enforced.

Confidentiality

Employers often put a confidentiality clause in your contract to prevent employees disclosing sensitive information relating to their businesses. However, in cases of that involve a trade secret, or information so highly confidential that it requires the same amount of protection as a trade secret, both current and former employees are automatically under an obligation not to disclose or use the information.

What constitutes a trade secret and highly confidential information depends on a number of factors, including the context in which the information arises and is used. Factors to take into account include whether you regularly handled the information (if so, it is possible to argue that you may be more aware of the sensitivity of it); whether you were made aware that the information was confidential; to what extent the information was circulated; and whether the information is isolated from information that is freely available to all.

Enforcement

If you breach a restriction in your contract after you have left, your former employer can seek an injunction against you and damages for any losses it has suffered. An injunction is a court order, which restrains the former employee and the new employer from committing any further breach of the restrictions. This sort of case often results in highly publicized court battles.

 Your Rights

1 For any restrictions in your contract to be reasonable and limited to what is needed to protect your employer's business interests, for a reasonable period of time and over a reasonable geographic region.
2 To ignore any restrictions after you have left if you have been dismissed in breach of contract – for example, to be paid in lieu of notice when your contract does not say that you can be paid in lieu of working your notice.

23

When you've had enough: constructive dismissal

'The last straw' is often used to describe the last in a series of small grievances that leads to a claim for constructive dismissal

Constructive dismissal is much misunderstood. In fact it is just a way of describing the way in which a dismissal takes place; when you resign because you feel you have been forced to do so, and have no other option because of the way your employer has acted. It is technically (or in legal terms) referred to as a constructive unfair dismissal, as your actual claim is one of unfair dismissal and/or wrongful dismissal. (So, in order to have a comprehensive grasp of constructive dismissal you should refer to Chapter 22: Being dismissed.)

This is a very important area to understand as it represents one of the few situations where you have the ability to take a lead in bringing a claim against your employer. There should however be a 'health warning' attached to this right. If you do not understand how it works and you go ahead and resign you could be making a very big mistake. But you'll be in good company; many people have resigned to claim constructive dismissal, only to discover after the event that they do not qualify to bring such a claim.

Your contract automatically includes the right for each party to have what's known as *trust and confidence* in the other party. If that trust and confidence is broken then this can mean the relationship is over as the contract has been breached, or broken.

Be warned though that resigning to claim constructive dismissal has to be done in a particular time frame, for particular reasons and, in some cases, in a particular way. So you must be careful to ensure that each one of the requirements below is satisfied.

1 Your employer must have committed a *serious breach* of contract. A breach of contract is where your employer fails to honour the agreement between you. In practice this could arise where your pay is reduced, a

major benefit is taken away, or a significant proportion of your responsibility at work is taken away from you. Your employer's action must amount to more than just unreasonable behaviour, although unreasonable behaviour can sometimes amount to a breach of contract if it amounts to a breach of trust and confidence.

2 You may need to raise a grievance before resigning.

3 You have to leave because of that breach and not for any other reason. The breach must be the effective cause of your leaving, but it does not have to be the only reason. If the real reason for your leaving is that you were offered a better job, then you may have difficulty in showing that it was the action taken by your employer that caused you to leave. You would lose the right to claim constructive dismissal.

4 There should not be too much of a delay between your employer's unacceptable act and you resigning from work. You have to act as soon as possible and in most cases no later than within a couple of weeks. If you do not assert your rights it will be assumed that you have agreed to whatever change has been made to your contract or have waived your right to take action.

If you meet these conditions then you have overcome the first hurdle in claiming constructive dismissal. You now have to prove your dismissal was unfair too, following the procedures outlined in Chapter 22: Being dismissed. And you may also have a claim for your notice period and other contractual benefits. The first 'What if . . .' below shows how someone was constructively dismissed but the employment tribunal then found the dismissal was fair.

So a final warning: most employees would be unwise to regard themselves as constructively dismissed unless the circumstances were clearly unfair, and they had every intention of bringing an unfair dismissal claim at employment tribunal in order to prove their case.

 What if . . .

- Because of a financial crisis a company reduced the number of hours that an employee had to work from 35 to 30. The company's problems were so bad that the appointment of a receiver was imminent. An employee resigns and claims constructive dismissal.
  Outcome: In a similar case an employee had been constructively dis-

missed but the dismissal was fair. The company had no other choice due to its urgent need to reduce outgoings. The dismissal was fair under the category of 'other reasons' (*see* Chapter 22: Being dismissed).

- A receptionist for a van and truck rental company is told that the company has a special policy regarding ethnic minority customers. The company says 'If you get a telephone call from any coloured or Asians you can usually tell them by the sound of their voice. You have to tell them that there are no vehicles available.' The employee is so upset by this policy that she resigns, although she does not immediately give the reason for her resignation. She then claims constructive dismissal and race discrimination.

  Outcome: In a similar case, even though an employee didn't tell her employer the reason for her resignation, she was entitled to resign and claim constructive dismissal on the basis of the unlawful and discriminatory instruction she was given. The court also upheld her complaint of race discrimination. (To find out why *she* could claim race discrimination *see* Chapter 14: Race discrimination.)

- Over the years a typist became the manageress of a small family-owned furnishing company. She'd worked there for 30 years when her employers unilaterally made a number of changes to her terms and conditions of employment. In July her petrol allowance was cut; in August, the non-contributory pension scheme to which she belonged and of which she was a trustee was terminated and, during October, a new manager was appointed and she was notified that one of the directors would be taking over responsibility for the accounts, which constituted a significant part of her duties. Come November she was approached by another furnishing company and offered a job that she decided to accept, and so handed in her notice. As soon as she left she lodged an unfair dismissal complaint with an employment tribunal alleging that she had been constructively dismissed. There was a three-week delay between the final breach by her employer and her resignation.

  Outcome: The employer's actions amounted to a series of breaches of contract and her resignation was because of those breaches. It was the last straw when her employer told her that her responsibility for the accounts was being taken away. This was the case even though there was a three-week delay between the final breach and her resignation, during which time she had been offered another job. The court decided that she didn't resign because of the job offer but had been constructively dismissed. It was then up to an employment tribunal to decide if the dismissal was fair or unfair.

Key Questions

Who qualifies to claim for constructive dismissal?

To have been constructively dismissed you need to satisfy the conditions set out above. When you go on to claim unfair dismissal you must satisfy the qualifying criteria for an unfair dismissal, for example, one year's continuous service with your current employer.

Do I have to resign to claim for constructive dismissal?

Yes, if you do nothing you may be regarded as having accepted your employer's actions. In continuing to work your contract you effectively indicate that you accept the change or variation imposed on you. In most cases you will need to raise a grievance first. In some cases you can write a letter reserving your rights and make a claim at a later date. This would apply when a change to your contract does not come into effect for some time; changes to your bonus where bonuses are paid once a year, for example.

How long can I delay resigning for constructive dismissal?

There is no set period but case law has made it clear that the longer you leave it the less likely it is that you will be able to claim constructive dismissal. Even a few weeks can be too long in some instances.

What if I am literally forced to resign?

This would effectively be a dismissal and you can treat it as such. It would not even have to be presented as a constructive dismissal if you were called into your boss's room and forced to sign a resignation letter and leave.

My boss is irritating and unreasonable – can I regard this as constructive dismissal?

If only! Unless your boss's behaviour amounts to a breach of contract you cannot claim constructive dismissal. Unreasonable behaviour can amount to a breach of trust and confidence in certain cases, but the behaviour has to be very unreasonable.

If I know my employer intends to break my contract in the future can I resign and claim constructive dismissal?
Yes, it may be possible. If your employer threatens or plans to breach your contract in the future you can claim for what is called an *anticipatory breach of contract*.

I've been given a pay cut – can I claim constructive dismissal?
Yes, but you must act quickly. This is the classic reason for employees bringing such a claim as there is a very clear breach of contract.

I've been demoted – can I claim constructive/unfair dismissal?
Yes, you could. You would have to resign and claim to have been constructively dismissed making sure that the requirements detailed above are satisfied.

Do I have to tell my employer the reason for my resignation?
No, you do not have to give a reason for your resignation, although it is often asked for.

 Your Rights

1 To claim unfair dismissal if you are constructively dismissed (and if you have at least one year's service).
2 To claim wrongful dismissal to recover money due to you in your notice period.
(*See* Unfair Dismissal procedure and qualifying periods in Chapter 22: Being dismissed.)

 Tactics and Tips

Take legal advice
If you are considering resigning and claiming constructive dismissal it is particularly important that you seek legal advice before doing so. Resignation in such circumstances is a drastic measure and you will lose your income, so it is best to be as sure as possible that you qualify to bring a claim.

Resignation letter

If you are clear about the reason for your departure you should set it out in your resignation letter as this will be good evidence at employment tribunal.

Reserve your rights

If you do not want to resign but are unhappy with a change being imposed on you, it is a good idea to write a letter to your employer reserving your rights. This means that by formally registering your concern you effectively keep open the possibility of pursuing a claim, rather than losing it. Again, take advice if this is what you choose to do – as you may not be able to successfully reserve your rights for an extended period of time.

Written records

You should keep a written record of all the discussions you have with your employer. This will help make your position more robust if you take your case to employment tribunal and claim unfair dismissal.

Grievance procedure

If you are not satisfied with the way in which matters are being handled you could raise a 'grievance' against your employer. Before claiming constructive dismissal you may be required to raise a grievance first. A grievance procedure is a way of making a formal complaint within your company, and the process is often set down in your contract or staff handbook, although you can still raise a grievance even if there is no procedure in writing. In most cases this merely means a letter to your boss raising the complaint.

Right to be accompanied at a disciplinary or grievance hearing

This is an important right for employees. If you request that someone accompany you then it may help you get through what is undoubtedly a difficult meeting. It will also demonstrate you know your rights. One further useful tip: if the person that you chose to accompany you is unable to make it you have the legal right to a postponement of up to five working days from the date the original hearing was proposed.

Negotiation and compromise deals

It is useful to be aware that you can always negotiate with your employer. This may be particularly important if you feel that you have a legitimate grievance against your employer which may lead you to resign and bring a claim against your employer. One frequently used option is to sign away your rights to bring employment law claims in return for a larger pay-off. This is entering into what is called a *compromise or settlement agreement*.

 ## What next . . .

If you need advice on constructive dismissal, the first thing you should do is get ahead of the game and take advantage of the tactics and tips every employer and worker should know in Chapter 2. If you need to take things further *see* Part 5: Taking things further. Details of organizations that can assist you and further information are in Appendix B: Contact points.

24

Resignation

14 per cent of employees resign each year
Labour Force Survey

Most people have dreamt of marching into their boss's office unannounced and delivering those two simple words 'I resign' at some point. Whether on a matter of principle, because they have found another job, or because they are simply fed up, most employees leave their jobs by resigning.

A recent Labour Force Survey found that out of the almost three-quarters of a million people who had left their jobs in the previous three months, 44 per cent had resigned, 11 per cent had been made redundant, and only one per cent had been dismissed. Around 14 per cent of employees resign each year (from workplaces with over 25 employees).

So resignation comes to all of us in the end and it is often a time of strain and uncertainty: am I doing the right thing? What if I change my mind? Will I get a good reference? These are all questions that are commonly asked and it is important that you know the answers before resigning.

There are basically two types of resignation; voluntary, when you go willingly – because you wish to do so – and involuntarily, when you resign because you feel you have been forced to do so and have no other option – this is known as constructive dismissal and is dealt with in a separate chapter (*see* Chapter 23).

There is also the category referred to as 'heat of the moment' resignations which, as the name suggests, are done in anger or haste. Such resignations can actually be retracted if done so quickly and before the resignation is accepted by an employer.

When you resign the law requires that you give your employer notice of your decision to leave. You then have to work a set notice period, allowing your employer to find a replacement. While this can be annoying if you just want to leave as quickly as possible, it can also work in your favour if an employer is trying to get rid of you as it provides you with a certain amount of security. In practice many people negotiate their leaving date and employers are often willing to be flexible.

Your contract should specify the length of notice that you need to serve in the event of your resignation, and the length of notice your employer must give you in the event of your dismissal (*see* Chapter 22: Notice periods).

...? What if . . .

- An employee lost his temper after a dispute with his boss and said, 'I am leaving, I want my cards.' Later the employee insisted that he had not intended to resign and claimed unfair dismissal.
  Outcome: The court found in a similar case that the employee had resigned and did not have the right to claim unfair dismissal. This is because there was no ambiguity in the words that he used and it is clear how the employer would have understood the words used.

- A security officer is suspended after the discovery that money had gone missing. He responds by saying, 'I am not having any of that, you can stuff it, I am not taking the rap for that.' He notified his boss that he was 'jacking the job in' and then claimed unfair dismissal.
  Outcome: A security officer in a similar case had been dismissed and had not resigned. The court decided he was not tendering his resignation when he told his immediate superior that he was 'jacking the job in' because they were words said in the heat of the moment. In some cases the nature of the exchange can mean there was no real resignation and such exchanges should not be accepted at face value.

- A transport manager is ordered by his company director to obtain a new part for his car that had broken down. The wrong part is obtained and when the employee refuses to go off and get the proper part he is dismissed. Realizing the dismissal was in breach of the disciplinary procedure the director retracts the dismissal and suspends the employee without pay 'to allow time for a rational decision to be made'. The employee despite this regards himself as dismissed and claims unfair dismissal.
  Outcome: There was no dismissal in a similar case as the words were used in the heat of the moment and withdrawn almost immediately. The court felt that it is a matter of plain common sense that either an

employer or an employee should be given an opportunity to retract words spoken in the heat of the moment.

 Key Questions

How do I resign?
There is no set procedure. Most people tell their boss face to face, and then write a letter of resignation that they give to their boss or the human resources department. You do not have to put your resignation in writing unless your contract specifies you must do so. However, even if you fail to put it in writing there is very little your employer can do about it since you're leaving!

Do I need to give the reason?
No, you do not have to give a reason for your resignation although most employers will ask for one. Even if you don't give a reason you can probably still bring a claim for constructive dismissal if you have the grounds for such a claim although you may have to raise a grievance first. In one case a receptionist did not say why she'd resigned from her new job at a van rental firm. The reason was because at her induction training she was told it was company policy to say there were no vehicles available if on the phone the person sounded black or Asian. The court found she had been constructively dismissed and could bring a claim of race discrimination. She won her claim (*see* Chapter 14: Race discrimination for why she could claim race discrimination).

I resigned in the heat of the moment – can I retract my resignation?
You can only retract your resignation if your employer has not yet accepted it. Once your employer has accepted your resignation you cannot withdraw it. In practice the position is unlikely to be clear and if ambiguous words are used it would be a matter of negotiating your position with your employer. The clear lesson is: be sure before you resign. On the other side of the fence, employers may withdraw *words of dismissal* as long as it is done immediately. Employees could argue that a similar principal should apply when they resign.

I was forced to resign – do I have a claim?
If you resign in the heat of the moment because you are outraged by something that your employer has done, or if you are forced to resign,

you may be able to bring a claim for constructive dismissal. It is worth noting that even if you resign in amicable circumstances you may still have the right to make a claim for unfair or constructive dismissal.

I resigned because I knew I was about to be dismissed – what are my rights?

If you resign because you were about to be dismissed it could be a case of constructive dismissal. This means that if you feel forced to resign because your employer does something unacceptable or extreme then the law regards it as if you were in fact dismissed, and you can bring a claim against your employer. Your employer's actions would have to be proved to be in breach of contract or in anticipatory breach of contract (for example, such as your employer telling you that you will be demoted and have a pay cut next month). Remember, if the situation is not a breach of contract you will have no claim; this area of law cannot be used just because you are fed up with your employer. Almost all of us would all make claims on that basis!

My employer won't let me leave prior to the end of my notice period – what if I leave anyway?

You must work to the end of your notice period unless you come to an alternative agreement. If you want to leave early you should try to negotiate with your employer but you do not have the right to up and leave anyway as this would put you in breach of contract, and you could be sued. In reality most employers do not intervene in these cases as they cannot make you come to work against your wishes, and they may not suffer any significant loss by you not working out your notice. Remember, your employer has no obligation to pay you for the part of your notice that you do not work, and that leaving unilaterally does not look good. Your future employers may get to hear of your actions and your employer may refer to your behaviour in your reference.

What about my reference?

Employers do not have to provide a reference (except in the case of some occupations) but if they do, it must be true, accurate and fair (*see* Chapter 6).

Your Rights

1 You are entitled to leave after working out your notice.

2 You might be able to negotiate the exact length of your notice period and reductions are often agreed.

3 Your employer may choose to pay you in lieu of the period of notice you would have worked.

4 If you have resigned because you felt you were forced to, you may have a claim for constructive and/or unfair dismissal (*see* Chapter 23).

Tactics and Tips

Leave on good terms

Whatever the reason for your resignation it is best to depart on good terms (unless you plan on pursuing a claim). If you can't change things by making allegations or criticisms as you depart then it may be better not to make them in the first place.

Put your resignation in writing

Resign in writing to avoid confusion and prevent a dispute about the start date of your notice period or entitlements.

Grievance procedure

If you feel you need to resign because you've simply had enough remember that you could try to resolve the problem through your company's grievance procedure first. This may save your job. A grievance procedure is a way of making a formal complaint within your company, and the process is often set down in your contract or staff handbook, although you can still raise a grievance even if there is no procedure in writing. In most cases this merely means a letter to your boss raising the complaint.

Constructive dismissal

Be very careful if you are resigning because you feel you have a claim for constructive dismissal and, if possible, take advice. Resigning to claim constructive dismissal has to be done quickly, for particular reasons, and in some cases in a particular way. Simply resigning may not work and you do not want to find yourself out of a job with no right to a claim.

Notice periods
Remember often employees negotiate a mutually agreed notice period. Although the law and your contract may specify the exact periods employers are normally willing to be flexible.

Your image in the market place
Remember that other employers may hear about the way in which you resign. Therefore although it may be tempting, it is probably best not to be too melodramatic as you depart.

 What next . . .

If you need advice on resignation, the first thing you should do is get ahead of the game and take advantage of the tactics and tips every worker and employer should know in Chapter 2. If you need to take things further *see* Part 5: Taking things further. Details of organizations that can assist you and further information are in Appendix B: Contact points.

25

Older workers and retirement

19 million people, a third of the UK population, are aged 50 years and over

The rapidly growing proportion of older people in the population is one of the most significant demographic changes in years. Higher life expectancy coupled with a declining birth rate means that 19 million people in the UK are over 50 years, and 11 million are of pensionable age. And if the projections are correct, by 2021 there'll be a further one million pensioners.

But despite the ageing population, over the last 20 years unemployment has been rising amongst older people, with the over 50s more likely to be made redundant. There are currently 6.5 million people over the age of 50 years in full- or part-time employment, one million of these being over 60 years, and about half a million over 65 years.

However, more positive forces are now beginning to be seen in the workplace as attitudes towards older people shift, leading to the proper recognition of their value to employers. Put bluntly, employers now have little choice as they become increasingly dependent on an older workforce.

It is now accepted that many older workers are badly served by the law as there is no specific protection against age discrimination, and voluntary codes of practice have been relatively ineffective. Recognizing this, the government has undertaken to implement a European directive, bringing in age discrimination laws by 2006 to try and improve the situation. The question of how effective such legislation will be partly depends on how many employers manage to win exemptions from such laws.

As things stand older workers have the same basic rights as younger workers, with those over retirement age losing many rights. Until new laws come in, the Department for Work and Pensions code of practice can only be used to support dismissal claims based on age discrimination. This is because the code of practice just sets out recommended practice rather than creating actual legal rights against age discrimination. A European code of practice on ageing in employment has also been

produced in preparation for the outlawing of age discrimination throughout Europe in 2006.

Retirement

The age at which you must retire is usually specified in your contract, or
is the normal retirement age in your organization or industry. If your
contract does not refer to a retirement age then it is likely to be 65 years.

When you reach the retirement age as specified in your contract, your
employment will normally end without any need for either you or your
employer to take any action. Discussions normally take place about
matters like handing over your workload and the recruitment of your
replacement. If there is no retirement age specified in your contract, the
notice of retirement that you are entitled to is either your contractual or
statutory minimum notice – whichever is the longer period (*see*
Chapter 22: Notice periods).

Your pension

The state pension age is currently different for men (65 years) and women
(60 years), but to apply this is unlawful as it discriminates on the grounds
of sex. The state pension age will be equalized to age 65 years in the future.

In occupational pension schemes it is also unlawful for different
retirement ages to apply. You have the right to draw on your occupational
pension scheme on retirement.

What if . . .

- An office manager who is over 50 years applies for a job because he feels
  he is perfectly suited to the requirement in the job advertisement. He
  feels he did a good interview but the job went to someone 20 years
  younger. He believes he's been turned down as a result of his age.
  Outcome: He would not have a claim against the company as the law
  stands at present. This is because the provisions on age discrimination
  are in the form of a code of practice.

- A 57-year-old mechanic is made redundant as his company needs to lay off a number of workers for sound business reasons. He suspects he was chosen because of his age, and the fact he was paid more than a younger worker. He claims unfair dismissal.

  Outcome: If he were able to show that the reason he was selected for redundancy was because of his age his dismissal may be unfair.

- A technician is asked by his company to work past retirement age as he is vital to their business and the company cannot find a replacement, but he is offered less pay.

  Outcome: A drop in salary is a breach of contract unless you agree to it. However, if you are past retirement age or the offer relates to after your retirement, your contract may already be at an end if it states your retirement age. A reduced salary may not, therefore, be a breach of contract. If it is a breach of contract you could lodge a constructive dismissal claim, but beware, it is not a straightforward claim.

- A delivery driver wants to work fewer days each week for the last two years before he retires as he is in poor health and tires easily. His boss refuses.

  Outcome: The real issue here is the health of the driver, not his age. To find out details of rights, if you are seriously or frequently sick *see* Chapter 22: Under-performance and sickness, and Chapter 14.

Code of practice on Age Diversity at Work

The Department for Work and Pensions has a code of practice but it does not amount to a separate legal right that you can enforce. You can, however, use it to support claims such as an unfair redundancy on the basis of age. The code says:

- recruitment should be on the basis of skills and abilities to do the job, as opposed to age;
- selection should be based on merit by focusing on information given on applications about skills and abilities, and on performance at interview;
- promotion should be based on ability, or demonstrated potential to do the job;
- training and development: all employees should be encouraged to take advantage of relevant training opportunities;
- redundancy decisions should be based on objective, job-related criteria to ensure that the skills needed to help the business are retained;

• retirement: employers should ensure that retirement schemes are fairly applied, taking individual and business needs into account.

Ageing in employment: a European code of good practice

Eurolink Age, a non-profit-making European network concerned with older people and issues of ageing, published a European code of practice in anticipation of the anti-age discrimination law to be introduced in 2006. The code is intended to assist employers in managing an ageing workforce, help promote an age-neutral approach to employment and improve prospects for older workers.

 Key Questions

As an older worker do I have the same rights as other workers?
Yes, as an older worker you have the same rights as a worker of a different age, and any claim for unfair dismissal may result in a higher compensatory award. This is designed to compensate you for your future loss and one factor taken into account is that the older you are the longer it generally takes to get another job. However, as you approach retirement age the amount you are awarded in compensation may be reduced since there are fewer and fewer years left in which you could be employed.

I'm being discriminated against in my search for a job because of my age – what are my rights?
You do not have any right to bring a claim against the companies that are interviewing you since the Age Diversity code of practice is just a recommendation, not a separate legal right.

Can I be asked my age at interview?
Yes. There is nothing stopping employers asking your age although the Age Diversity code of practice recommends that you are not asked this at interview, and that age is not a factor taken into account in your recruitment. However, this is only a recommendation and has no legal basis.

I'm being discriminated against because of my age – what are my rights?
If the discrimination results in your dismissal then the fact that age was used as a factor will be taken into account by the tribunal and can mean your dismissal is unfair. This is as a result of the Age Diversity code of practice.

You do not have the right to bring a claim just on the basis of age discrimination, such as not getting a promotion because of your age, but you could raise a grievance. If you have been very badly treated because of your age and you can argue that the trust and respect in your relationship with your employer has been damaged, you could resign and claim constructive dismissal (*see* Chapter 23).

What if my age makes me ill – do I have any rights?
A tribunal has considered whether ailments from natural ageing can give rise to rights such as protection under the Disability Discrimination Act (DDA). The employee had painful ribs, knee and lower back and was suffering from the normal human ageing process. The tribunal ruled that symptoms resulting naturally from ageing do not amount to a disability under the DDA (*see* Chapter 14), so there is no special protection if you suffer from aches and pains, the natural symptoms of getting older. The position is different if the condition is over and above symptoms of natural ageing.

I'm not as fit as I was – should this affect my job?
If your lack of fitness affects your ability to do the work then your job may be at risk due to your incapability to perform the role. This would apply whether your fitness was age-related or not. If your fitness is related to an illness then your employer will need to be reasonable in reaching any decision to dismiss you and will also need to satisfy obligations under the DDA (if that is relevant to your reduced fitness). On a separate but related matter, you may find, as you get older that your ability to deal with new technology, like computers, gets harder. This could give rise to a dismissal for under-performance (*see* Chapters 22 and 14).

Do I have to retire at a certain age?
Arrangements relating to retirement are subject to agreement between you and your employer. If your contract states a retirement age, or you reach the retirement age that it is normal practice to retire at in your industry or company, your contract lawfully comes to an end at this time. However, there is nothing to stop you from negotiating your own deal with your employer if you can.

I've been asked to work beyond retirement age – what are my rights?
There is nothing to stop you from working beyond retirement age, and most of your pre-retirement rights remain. There is no upper age limit for claims for automatic unfair dismissal or discrimination, and you are covered by the same working time and pay rights.

However, you lose the right to claim unfair dismissal if you are over the normal retirement age in your organization or, where there is none, over the age of 65 years. The whole issue of losing employment rights because you have reached a certain age has recently been challenged, so far unsuccessfully, on the grounds of sex discrimination as there are more men than women still working over the age of 65 years.

If I do work past retirement age what is my entitlement to pension/benefits?
There is no requirement for you to stop working to receive a pension. So if you continue to work, what benefits you receive are a question of negotiation and agreement.

Can I retire early?
There is no legal reason why you cannot retire early and your pension scheme may provide for drawing on a pension on early retirement, but you are likely to need the consent of your employer. If you are over 50 years, pension entitlements are sometimes used as an inducement to accept redundancy. Options that may be available include the payment of part of your pension as a lump sum, the diversion of part or all of a termination payment into a pension scheme, the immediate receipt of pension that would have been payable on retirement, or adding further years of service into the computation of the pension.

My company is trying to force me to retire early – what are my rights?
If your employer is trying to force you to retire early, you may be able to leave and claim constructive or unfair dismissal. The reason why you are being put under pressure to retire early would need to be considered since it may be that your employer has a sound basis for making you redundant as an alternative.

Can my employer change the retirement age without my consent?
If your employer changes the retirement age in your contract without your consent it is unlikely to be valid. An employer can change terms in your contract without your consent, but would risk a constructive dismissal or breach of contract claim. However, in practice, employers do

manage to get away with many contract changes because employees fail to take action quickly enough and so lose their rights to bring a claim (*see* Chapter 23).

I have been unwell for some time with a serious condition. Is retirement on the grounds of poor health an option?
Some pension schemes provide for early retirement on the grounds of poor health. Alternatively, your employer may have in place a permanent health insurance scheme, which may cover you, but you should check whether you qualify under the rules of the scheme. If your contract is not well drafted, it may offer the benefit without saying you need to qualify for it. In such cases your employer may need to provide the monetary value of the benefit even if you do not qualify under the scheme rules. A very expensive mistake for employers to make.

After I retire can I keep my company benefits?
Sometimes employers provide benefits that continue after retirement and these are likely to be agreed as part of your original contract.

 Your Rights

To have all the same rights as the rest of the workforce if you are an older worker but under retirement age.

 Tactics and Tips

Raise the matter early
If you want to retire early or work beyond retirement it would be best to address the issue early with your employer, making it clear that you are fully aware of your rights.

Written records
Both employers and employees should keep a written record of all the discussions concerning any agreement on retirement. This will help make the position clearer and evidence more robust if there are negotiations on retirement, or if the matter proceeds to employment tribunal.

Contact Points

Age Concern – charity
Age Concern England: Astral House, 1268 London Road, London SW16 4ER
Telephone 020 8765 7200
Age Concern Wales: Fourth Floor, 1 Cathedral Road, Cardiff CF1 9SD
Telephone: 029 2037 1566
Age Concern Northern Ireland: 3 Lower Crescent, Belfast BT7 1NR
Telephone: 028 9024 5729
Age Concern Scotland: 113 Rose Street, Edinburgh EH2 3DT
Telephone: 0131 220 3345
Website: www.ace.org.uk

 What if . . .

If you need advice on issues relating to age or retirement, the first thing you should do is get ahead of the game and take advantage of the tactics and tips every employer and worker should know in Chapter 2. If you need to take things further *see* Part 5: Taking things further. Details of organizations that can assist you and further information are in Appendix B: Contact points.

26

Internal procedures

Applications to employment tribunals have tripled in the last decade

Sadly for many, events at work escalate to such a stage that they feel they have no choice but to take further action to enforce their rights. Employees in this position have four main options:
1 to try and resolve the matter informally;
2 to use more formal internal mechanisms, such as grievance procedures;
3 to seek redress externally through semi-formal means, such as ACAS arbitration;
4 to seek redress externally at employment tribunal or the courts.
Due to recently introduced statutory discipline and grievance procedures an employer must now go through procedures to avoid an unfair dismissal and an employee may be obliged to go through workplace grievance procedures before they can bring a claim at employment tribunal.

All the options above are likely to involve seeking advice from any one of a range of professional advisers available. Legal proceedings should be the last port of call after all other alternatives have been exhausted. Not only are they costly and time consuming but they can also be unpredictable. The outcome is entirely dependent on how the evidence comes across and who is believed (*see* Chapter 2). In most situations, it is possible for employees and employers to achieve their desired outcome without the need to seek redress at employment tribunal or court.

It is always possible that employers may try to negotiate a settlement with employees. A settlement is effectively a pay-off in return for an employee agreeing not to take any further action against their employer. This will normally take the form of you and your employer entering what is known as a 'compromise or settlement agreement'. A recent case on 'off record' or 'without prejudice' settlement discussions has restricted the circumstances in which such discussions can take place (*see* below).

This Part looks at the options for taking things further including what is involved in going to employment tribunal, guidance on legal advisers available, and other processes by which a settlement between employer and employee may be reached.

Informal resolution

It may just sound like the sort of advice your parents or best friend would give you, but if you have a serious problem at work you should first try to resolve it informally. Often a way forward can be found without the need for the situation to be placed formally on the record – with all the implications that that brings. Think about turning to friends, colleagues, the union or staff representatives for help. Alternatively, Citizens' Advice Bureaux and law centres are excellent sources of objective and practical guidance (*see* below and Appendix B: Contact points).

Raising a grievance

If informal methods don't work your next best option is to turn to your company's grievance procedures. These are procedures prescribed by statute to assist in the resolution of issues internally, and can be used to deal with all manner of problems to do with your work, work environment or work relationships. The statutory procedure requires three steps:
• a statement in writing of your grievance;
• a meeting to discuss the concern;
• the right of appeal against any decision reached.

The exact way in which such procedures operate should be set out in your contract or staff handbook, but even if your contract or staff handbook does not contain such a procedure, you are still entitled to raise a grievance since it is a legal right and an obligation if you want to take things further. The Advisory, Conciliation and Arbitration Service (ACAS), an independent and impartial service charged by law with resolving workplace disputes, produce a code of practice which provides guidance on this law. Many organizations also have special procedures for certain kinds of grievances such as harassment and bullying at work.

Procedures usually require you to outline your concerns in a letter to your line manager, stressing that you are raising a formal grievance, or to a more senior manager where the complaint concerns your line manager.

In general, your letter should clearly state the incident or issue in and state dates, times, witnesses and other relevant facts.

A grievance hearing or meeting is then held between you and your line manager or a more senior manager. The word 'hearing' is used and gives the impression that it is a lot more formal than it really is. Employees have an important statutory right to be accompanied by a fellow employee or trade union official at a grievance hearing, and you could bring an independent claim against your company if you are refused this right. Your issue should be dealt within a reasonable period of time and if the matter is not resolved the procedure should provide for an appeal and the matter would then be referred to a more senior independent manager.

 ## What if . . .

- Jane was receiving rude and abusive e-mails from a fellow colleague, Bob. She did not do anything at first and just tried to ignore them. But later they became aggressive and threatening. She raised it with her boss informally and he just said, 'Come on, you're a big girl now.'

  She therefore wrote to her boss under the company grievance procedure as follows:

  'On 15 September I raised a complaint that I felt I was being bullied and harassed as a result of inappropriate, rude and intimidating e-mails I received from Bob. I had received four by the 15 September. Despite raising this concern, nothing has been done to stop him and I have now received a further three such e-mails which are even more threatening. I now feel it is necessary to raise the matter as a formal grievance under the procedure set out in the company handbook.'

  Her boss should deal with Jane's grievance by following the procedure to address her concern. He should look at the e-mails sent to her, investigate the reasons behind the e-mails being sent, and discipline Bob, perhaps with a written warning if the e-mails prove to be inappropriate.

  If you feel you are getting nowhere despite having raised a grievance, you may have no option but to take the matter further through employment tribunal. If you have not been dismissed, you will first need to establish whether your boss's failure to take action means you can regard yourself as having been dismissed. You should take professional advice on this (*see* Chapter 23).

Being disciplined

Employers can also take matters further if they are dissatisfied with an employee's performance or conduct by implementing disciplinary procedures. Like grievance procedures these are now prescribed in the law. Disciplinary procedures generally set minimum standards of performance and conduct within an organization, and, despite being set out in statute, should also be referred to in your contract or set out in your staff handbook.

A disciplinary procedure is designed to establish the truth and promote fairness, and the process should give you the opportunity to state your point of view and clarify any confusion.

As with grievance procedures employees have the right to be accompanied to any disciplinary hearing by a fellow employee or trade union official. The employee's line manager or a panel of staff, including a representative from personnel, may conduct it. If an employee is found at fault the hearing could result in them receiving a verbal or written warning about their conduct or performance or absence, or even being dismissed.

Sometimes a grievance is raised when an employee feels that inappropriate disciplinary proceedings have been instigated.

27

External procedures

Formal resolution

The three options

If all internal methods and attempts at resolving the matter are exhausted you have the option of enforcing your rights at employment tribunal, through the court in certain cases, or through ACAS arbitration if your complaint is one of unfair dismissal alone.

Employment tribunals or the courts?

Employment tribunals deal with all employment claims with the exception of high-value contractual claims – such as, for example, compensation for a one-year notice period and other contractual losses.

Some years ago employment tribunals could not deal with contractual claims, but their jurisdiction has been extended so they can now hear contractual claims as well. This means that, for example, claims for notice entitlement and contractual bonuses can be pursued in either employment tribunals or the courts. However, employment tribunals are limited to awarding a maximum of £25,000 in contractual claims and amounts in excess of this are usually dealt with by county courts and the High Court.

Generally, employment tribunals are quicker and less costly than going through the courts; however legal aid is available for cases dealt with by the courts. Another difference is that you may be able to recover a portion of the costs you incurred in bringing the claim to court. Such cost orders are not generally available as a matter of course at employment tribunal, although they are occasionally made.

Other employment claims dealt with by the High Court include injunctions to restrain an employee from breaching a restrictive covenant, and personal injury claims for stress.

Employment tribunals

What is an employment tribunal?

Employment tribunals – formerly known as industrial tribunals – are specialist courts that deal specifically with employment problems. In Northern Ireland they are known as fair employment tribunals.

The Employment Tribunals Service has 34 offices across the country and hearings take place at a particular tribunal depending on the location of your employer. The number of people registering claims is dramatically increasing; in 2000/01 there were over 130,000 claims, a 25 per cent rise on the previous year. 2003/4 saw over 197,000 claims registered.

The aim of the Employment Tribunal Service is to 'provide speedy, accessible and relatively informal justice'. It was also originally intended for employers and employees to represent themselves in disputes in a relatively informal manner. But with the increasing complexity of employment law, most employers and a significant number of employees now use a solicitor, barrister or human resources professional to represent them – pushing up the cost of justice dramatically. So it is fair to say that the original aims of the Employment Tribunal Service are no longer being achieved, which is in part the reason for the introduction of the ACAS arbitration scheme. As a result there are now plans to reform the tribunal system to try and speed up the process and, where possible, move dispute resolution back from the courts to offices. The main measures suggested are ones to iron out inconsistencies in tribunal rulings, and deter time-wasters.

How to apply to an employment tribunal

In order to lodge a claim at employment tribunal a form, called an ET1 form, has to be completed setting out your claim. You can get one from the Employment Tribunal Service, law centres, Citizens Advice Bureaux, a solicitor's office or from the Internet (*see* Chapter 28: Contact Points). Remember, for most claims you only have three months from the date of dismissal (or other concern) in which to lodge your claim, although this deadline can be extended in certain circumstances, such as to allow you to complete an internal grievance procedure.

How does an employment tribunal work?

Employment tribunals are presided over by a panel consisting of a legally qualified chairman who has at least seven years' experience, and two non-legally qualified lay members. The lay members are selected from a panel drawn up by the Secretary of State. One of the lay members is usually a representative from an employers' organization, such as the CBI, and the other a representative from an employees' organization, such as a trade union. They do not actually represent the interests of the employer or employee but are meant to be independent and open-minded.

Employment tribunals are supposed to be informal although much depends on the chairman involved. The rules relating to the presentation of evidence are more relaxed and at some tribunals the chairman will take an active part in the hearing, butting in to ask questions during evidence and taking over part of the cross-examination. Others are strict about the rules of evidence and run the hearing as if it were a formal court. Generally, employment tribunals are a little like the American courtroom dramas seen on television, as there are no wigs and gowns and the courtroom is relatively informal.

Although it depends on the nature of the claim, employment tribunals normally begin with an opening statement by the employer. Witnesses usually supply written witness statements, which they read out as their evidence in the witness box, either under oath or affirmation. It is also possible for the written witness statements to stand as the evidence without being read out at all. If the chairman orders this then, after the opening statements (if any), the hearing proceeds straight to cross-examination. After all evidence has been heard each side makes a closing speech, which is the point at which the law is quoted, past cases referred to, and the evidence summarized to assist the tribunal in reaching a decision.

The length of a hearing will depend on the nature of your case. Cases can run from half a day to many weeks.

Decisions can be delivered immediately, or reserved so that the tribunal can consider the issues in further detail. If they are delivered on the day of the hearing the tribunal panel usually takes a break and then, on their return, state their decision – usually backed by their reasons, and the evidence supporting their decision. Sometimes they openly state which of the witnesses they believed and which they disbelieved.

If you're not happy with the outcome there are certain grounds on which the decision can be appealed against at an employment appeal tribunal. Should you have the correct grounds, determination, funds and backing necessary, the matter could, in theory, be referred to higher courts such as the Court of Appeal, the House of Lords, and the European Court of Justice.

What powers does an employment tribunal have?

Employment tribunals have a number of possible options or 'awards' at their disposal, depending on the nature of your claim. In most cases you can claim reinstatement, re-engagement or, like the vast majority of people, compensation.

Research carried out by the Equal Opportunities Review show a large rise in awards, especially in cases of discrimination.

 Key Questions

Can costs of preparing for an employment tribunal be recovered if you win?

Unlike the higher courts, there is no general right at employment tribunal to get your costs paid if you win, although the power to make cost orders has recently been widened. If an employee or their legal adviser has acted vexatiously, abusively, disruptively or otherwise unreasonably, or the claim is misconceived, i.e. has no prospect of success, then a tribunal can make an order that a party pay the costs of the other side, up to a maximum of £10,000 (and more in certain instances). Cost orders can also be made when hearings are postponed or adjourned, or an order of the tribunal has not been complied with. This could apply, for example, if the claimant (employee) does not turn up at the employment tribunal or refuses to withdraw a claim that has no prospect of success. Advisers also need to beware as the power extends to ordering costs against advisers that behave improperly in the conduct of proceedings as well.

Can I represent myself at employment tribunal?
Yes, you can. There is nothing to prevent an employee from representing themselves at employment tribunal and, in such situations, one of the chairman's main objectives is to ensure, as far as possible, that the parties are on an equal footing. In practice this means that the chairman will help the applicant and bend over backwards to ensure that the applicant manages to present his claim as best he can. It is not uncommon in such cases for the chairman to also assist the applicant in cross-examining the other side's witnesses.

Do I have to tell future employers that I made a claim against a former employer, and will it affect my future employment prospects?
If you are asked by a prospective employer whether you lodged a claim against your former or existing employer, you may not get the job or may be dismissed if it is subsequently established that you lied on the application form or at interview.

Tribunal awards

Reinstatement and re-engagement
A tribunal can order employers to reinstate an employee who has been unfairly dismissed, or alternatively re-engage them elsewhere in the organization. It is not entirely uncommon for employers to refuse to comply following the bitterness of a court battle. An award therefore exists specifically for failure to comply with a reinstatement or re-engagement order (*see* below).

Basic award
If you win an unfair dismissal claim you get a *basic* and *compensatory award*. The basic award is monetary compensation for losing the security of a job. It is calculated in almost the same way as a statutory redundancy payment up to a maximum of £8,400 (2005) (*see* Appendix A: Redundancy Calculator).

Compensatory award
The second element of compensation in an unfair dismissal award is the compensatory award. This is usually the largest part of the compensation and is capped at a maximum of £56,800 (2005). It is designed to compensate you for losses – not to punish your employer for the unfair dismissal.

This means if you get a job immediately after your dismissal on the same or a higher salary – you may not get anything other than a basic award.

Additional award
A tribunal makes this award if the employer fails to comply with a reinstatement or re-engagement order. The amount is anywhere between 26 and 52 weeks' pay, with a week's pay capped at a maximum of £280 per week (2005).

Declarations and recommendations
In discrimination cases a tribunal can make a declaration that the employer has violated the employee's rights and can also issue a recommendation that the employer take certain action within a specified period to reduce the negative effect of any discrimination.

Compensation for discrimination
Tribunals have the discretion to award compensation where they think it is just and equitable to do so. There is no upper limit to the amount of the compensation that can be awarded and the compensation aims to put the employee in the position he or she would have been in, as far as possible, had the discrimination not taken place.

Awards for injury to feelings
In discrimination claims, compensation can also be awarded for injury to feelings. In 2000 there was a record payment of over £100,000 in a case of race discrimination.

Little reasonable prospect of success

The payment of a deposit may be ordered at an interim hearing before a full hearing takes place if a claim is unlikely to succeed. The objective is to assess whether the claimant's claim has any reasonable prospect of succeeding. If the employer succeeds in showing that the claimant's claim has no reasonable prospect of success, then the claimant can be ordered to pay a deposit of £500 before he or she can continue with the claim. Needless to say, most claimants withdraw their claim if they fail at such a hearing.

ACAS voluntary arbitration

The Advisory Conciliation and Arbitration Service (ACAS) arbitration scheme is an alternative way of resolving a dispute between employer and employee, but applies only to straightforward unfair dismissal claims which would otherwise go to a full tribunal hearing. It came into force in 2001 and, unlike employment tribunals, is a private as opposed to a public forum. The objective is that it establishes a more informal, speedier and less costly procedure for resolving such disputes. Parties need to opt into it voluntarily as an alternative to taking their case to a tribunal. They then enter an arbitration agreement and ACAS appoints an arbitrator from their 'arbitration panel'.

In contrast with employment tribunals, with the ACAS scheme the two sides are simply invited to submit a written statement of their case before the hearing. At employment tribunals a bundle of relevant documents and witness statements is prepared and exchanged before the hearing. With the ACAS scheme there is no cross-examination or swearing of oaths; the arbitrator will simply ask the witnesses questions. Any decision reached as a result of the arbitration is binding in the same way as a tribunal decision.

A further aspect promoting the informality of the process is that it can take place at any convenient location such as at the office or a local hotel conference facility. As at tribunal, an order for reinstatement, re-engagement or compensation can be made. There are only very select reasons for which the decision of an arbitrator can be challenged. The focus is on general principles of fairness rather than the strict application of law so the principles set out in the ACAS code of practice on discipline and grievance at work are central to an ACAS arbitration.

Getting legal advice

ACAS, law centres, Citizens Advice Bureaux, law firms, or your union can advise you as to the best way of making a claim and where it should be brought. Remember, if your company has a staff association, it may be able to help you with your concerns and issues as well.

Care should be taken in deciding where to get your advice. The main sources all have their advantages and disadvantages.

Law centres and Citizens Advice Bureaux

These sorts of organizations have the advantage of offering free advice. However, you should be careful to ensure that you are actually talking to a specialist in employment law – rather than a general advisor who may need to look up answers to your questions. Having said this some law centres and CABs have developed excellent reputations in certain areas of law, including employment law. It is also quite common for law students and trainee solicitors to spend time at such organizations to gain experience in the real world. Advice from keen students can be excellent.

Specialist niche firms

One of the best sources of advice are niche firms that have a specialist practice in the field of employment law. They tend to have excellent experience, and an added advantage is that their rates can be much more competitive than city law firms.

High-street solicitors

The quality of advice from high-street solicitors can vary tremendously. Again, it is best to insist that the person you are speaking to is an expert in the field of employment law. Solicitors charge an hourly rate, which can work out to be fairly costly, but you should ask if they are prepared to do a fixed-fee initial meeting to discuss your complaint so that you can get an idea of how good your case is and know exactly where you would stand in relation to their charges.

Big city law firms

City law firms will always have employment law experts and, since such lawyers spend all their time on just employment law matters and encounter a large variety of issues, the quality of the advice is always likely to be very high. The main disadvantage is that they can be very costly from the point of view of an individual as such law firms predominantly act for employers. This fact can, ironically, make them very useful, as they know the tricks and strategies employers use in relation to employees. It is advisable to get an estimate of charges, if at all possible, or request to be billed monthly. High hourly rates can mean costs can rapidly escalate.

ACAS and unions

These organizations also have advisers that may be able to assist you. Again the advice may be free, but make sure that you seek advice from an experienced specialist in employment law.

28

Settlements and compromise agreements

Compromise agreements

At all stages of the process – whether still employed or at the door of the employment tribunal – it may be possible to settle your claim. This is often achieved through the process of entering into a compromise agreement. A compromise agreement usually involves you getting a payment from your employer in return for signing away your rights to bring a claim. It is almost always the employer that suggests a compromise agreement. If an employee suggests it, it could look as if he or she is fishing for money.

In order for a compromise agreement to be valid certain requirements need to be satisfied – for example, you have to get independent legal advice. More details on compromise agreements can be obtained from the Citizens Advice Bureaux, law centres and law firms. Recent case law has highlighted that without-prejudice discussions to reach a resolution that are not as a result of a dispute and to cover up something blatantly unlawful may not be protected by the 'without prejudice' label. In other words, the discussions may in certain instances be used as evidence in open court. Advice should be sought before an employer attempts to negotiate a settlement under a compromise agreement.

Settlement agreements

When you lodge a claim at employment tribunal against your employer, an ACAS officer is allocated to the case. The aim is to promote a settlement of the matter at the same time as it is going through the stages of the tribunal procedure. All discussions and correspondence with ACAS is 'off the record' – it cannot be raised in the formal court proceedings or at the hearing itself. This is what is meant by negotiations being 'without prejudice' – any proposals for settling the case cannot be raised at court and cannot therefore prejudice the case. If a settlement is reached through ACAS a conciliated agreement is drawn up which brings the matter to an end. It is not uncommon for argumentative letters to pass between the employer's and employee's representatives while at the same time a payment is being negotiated to settle the matter with the allocated ACAS officer acting as the go-between.

A settlement agreement is different from a compromise agreement. It is used when there are only contractual entitlements to be settled (for example, notice pay, bonuses) as opposed to statutory entitlements, i.e. those arising from acts of parliament, such as unfair dismissal and discrimination.

 ## Tactics and Tips

Deadlines

Always remember that there are deadlines by which you must submit tribunal claims, which is, in most cases, three months from the date of dismissal or the discriminatory act. Even if you are negotiating a settlement, the deadline must be kept in mind because if negotiations proceed beyond the deadline and you have not lodged your claim, you lose your rights and your bargaining position.

Lodging a claim in any event

If you are concerned that you may not complete negotiations for a settlement swiftly, you may wish to lodge a claim to protect your position in the event that the negotiations fail. The claim can be withdrawn once a settlement is reached although there is less chance you will need to do this with the potential to extend time limits in order to, for example, complete the statutory grievance procedure.

Compromise agreements

Negotiations under a compromise agreement – it is not uncommon for your employer to pay a contribution towards legal advice you need to take in order to enter into a compromise agreement. The amount of the contribution can vary depending on how complex your contract is and the nature of your possible complaint. But it is worth bearing in mind.

Choice of adviser

It is entirely your choice who you select to advise you in employment disputes and this is the case even if your employer is making a contribution to your costs. So employees should not feel that they have to use the adviser made available by their employer.

 ## Contact Points

Advisory, Conciliation and Arbitration Service (ACAS) – officially charged with resolving work disputes and promoting good work practice. They produce a guide to their arbitration scheme called *The ACAS arbitration scheme for the resolution of unfair dismissal disputes: a guide to the scheme*, which is also available on the ACAS website.

Address: Brandon House, 180 Borough High Street, London SE1 1LW (check contact details for regional offices in the phonebook or on the Web)

Telephone: 020 7210 3613

E-mail: arbitration@acas.org.uk

Website: www.acas.org.uk

Employment Tribunal Service (ETS)

Enquiry Line: 08457 959775

Law Centres Federation – for advice. Phone for details of your nearest centre

Telephone: 020 7387 8570

Website: www.lawcentres.org.uk

National Association of Citizens Advice Bureaux – over 2,000 outlets dispensing advice. Look in the phonebook or on the Web for your local office

Address: Myddelton House, 115–123 Pentonville Road, London N1 9LZ

Telephone: 020 7833 2181

Website: www.nacab.org.uk

What next . . .

If you need advice on taking things further, the first thing you should do is get ahead of the game and take advantage of the tactics and tips every worker and employer should know in Chapter 2. Details of other organizations that can assist you and where you can obtain further information are in Appendix B: Contact points.

Appendix A: Redundancy Payment calculator

Service (years)

Age	2	3	4	5	6	7	8	9	10	11	12	13	14	15	16	17	18	19	20
20	1	1	1	1	—														
21	1	1.5	1.5	1.5	1.5	—													
22	1	1.5	2	2	2	2	—												
23	1.5	2	2.5	3	3	3	3	—											
24	2	2.5	3	3.5	4	4	4	4	—										
25	2	3	3.5	4	4.5	5	5	5	5	—									
26	2	3	4	4.5	5	5.5	6	6	6	6	—								
27	2	3	4	5	5.5	6	6.5	7	7	7	7	—							
28	2	3	4	5	6	6.5	7	7.5	8	8	8	8	—						
29	2	3	4	5	6	7	7.5	8	8.5	9	9	9	9	—					
30	2	3	4	5	6	7	8	8.5	9	9.5	10	10	10	10	—				
31	2	3	4	5	6	7	8	9	9.5	10	10.5	11	11	11	11	—			
32	2	3	4	5	6	7	8	9	10	10.5	11	11.5	12	12	12	12	—		

Service (years)

Age	2	3	4	5	6	7	8	9	10	11	12	13	14	15	16	17	18	19	20
33	2	3	4	5	6	7	8	9	10	11	11.5	12	12.5	13	13	13	13	–	–
34	2	3	4	5	6	7	8	9	10	11	12	12.5	13	13.5	14	14	14	14	–
35	2	3	4	5	6	7	8	9	10	11	12	13	13.5	14	14.5	15	15	15	15
36	2	3	4	5	6	7	8	9	10	11	12	13	14	14.5	15	15.5	16	16	16
37	2	3	4	5	6	7	8	9	10	11	12	13	14	15	15.5	16	16.5	17	17
38	2	3	4	5	6	7	8	9	10	11	12	13	14	15	16	16.5	17	17.5	18
39	2	3	4	5	6	7	8	9	10	11	12	13	14	15	16	17	17.5	18	18.5
40	2	3	4	5	6	7	8	9	10	11	12	13	14	15	16	17	18	18.5	19
41	2	3	4	5	6	7	8	9	10	11	12	13	14	15	16	17	18	19	19.5
42	2.5	3.5	4.5	5.5	6.5	7.5	8.5	9.5	10.5	11.5	12.5	13.5	14.5	15.5	16.5	17.5	18.5	19.5	20.5
43	3	4	5	6	7	8	9	10	11	12	13	14	15	16	17	18	19	20	21
44	3	4.5	5.5	6.5	7.5	8.5	9.5	10.5	11.5	12.5	13.5	14.5	15.5	16.5	17.5	18.5	19.5	20.5	21.5
45	3	4.5	6	7	8	9	10	11	12	13	14	15	16	17	18	19	20	21	22

46	47	48	49	50	51	52	53	54	55	56	57	58	59	60
22.5	23	23.5	24	24.5	25	25.5	26	26.5	27	27.5	28	28.5	29	29.5
21.5	22	22.5	23	23.5	24	24.5	25	25.5	26	26.5	27	27.5	28	28.5
20.5	21	21.5	22	22.5	23	23.5	24	24.5	25	25.5	26	26.5	27	27
19.5	20	20.5	21	21.5	22	22.5	23	23.5	24	24.5	25	25.5	25.5	25.5
18.5	19	19.5	20	20.5	21	21.5	22	22.5	23	23.5	24	24	24	24
17.5	18	18.5	19	19.5	20	20.5	21	21.5	22	22.5	22.5	22.5	22.5	22.5
16.5	17	17.5	18	18.5	19	19.5	20	20.5	21	21	21	21	21	21
15.5	16	16.5	17	17.5	18	18.5	19	19.5	19.5	19.5	19.5	19.5	19.5	19.5
14.5	15	15.5	16	16.5	17	17.5	18	18	18	18	18	18	18	18
13.5	14	14.5	15	15.5	16	16.5	16.5	16.5	16.5	16.5	16.5	16.5	16.5	16.5
12.5	13	13.5	14	14.5	15	15	15	15	15	15	15	15	15	15
11.5	12	12.5	13	13.5	13.5	13.5	13.5	13.5	13.5	13.5	13.5	13.5	13.5	13.5
10.5	11	11.5	12	12	12	12	12	12	12	12	12	12	12	12
9.5	10	10.5	10.5	10.5	10.5	10.5	10.5	10.5	10.5	10.5	10.5	10.5	10.5	10.5
8.5	9	9	9	9	9	9	9	9	9	9	9	9	9	9
7.5	7.5	7.5	7.5	7.5	7.5	7.5	7.5	7.5	7.5	7.5	7.5	7.5	7.5	7.5
6	6	6	6	6	6	6	6	6	6	6	6	6	6	6
4.5	4.5	4.5	4.5	4.5	4.5	4.5	4.5	4.5	4.5	4.5	4.5	4.5	4.5	4.5
3	3	3	3	3	3	3	3	3	3	3	3	3	3	3

Service (years)

Age	2	3	4	5	6	7	8	9	10	11	12	13	14	15	16	17	18	19	20
61	3	4.5	6	7.5	9	10.5	12	13.5	15	16.5	18	19.5	21	22.5	24	25.5	27	28.5	30
62	3	4.5	6	7.5	9	10.5	12	13.5	15	16.5	18	19.5	21	22.5	24	25.5	27	28.5	30
63	3	4.5	6	7.5	9	10.5	12	13.5	15	16.5	18	19.5	21	22.5	24	25.5	27	28.5	30
64	3	4.5	6	7.5	9	10.5	12	13.5	15	16.5	18	19.5	21	22.5	24	25.5	27	28.5	30

Appendix B: Contact points

Advisory, Conciliation and Arbitration Service (ACAS)
ACAS is officially charged with resolving work disputes and promoting good work practice. It offers impartial advice to all sides in disputes, and acts as an honest broker in any attempt to negotiate a settlement.
Address: Brandon House, 180 Borough High Street, London SE1 1LW. Check contact details for regional offices in the phonebook or on the Web.
Telephone: 020 7210 3613 **Helpline:** 08457 47 47 47
E-mail: arbitration@acas.org.uk
Website: www.acas.org.uk

Age Concern
A charity providing practical help, advice and information for all older people. Runs a wide range of services for the elderly, and produces advice guides and information leaflets.
Age Concern (England): Astral House, 1268 London Road, London SW16 4ER
Telephone: 020 8765 7200
Age Concern Cymru: Transport House, 1 Cathedral Road, Cardiff CF11 9HA
Telephone: 029 2037 1566
Age Concern Northern Ireland: 3 Lower Crescent, Belfast BT7 1NR
Telephone: 028 9024 5729
Age Concern Scotland: 113 Rose Street, Edinburgh EH2 3DT
Telephone: 0131 220 3345
Website: www.ace.org.uk

Alcohol Concern
A national independent charity working to reduce alcohol abuse, Alcohol Concern offers practical help and guidance to all those affected, including 'drinkline' – a telephone helpline.
Address: Waterbridge House, 32–36 Loman Street, London SE1 0EE

Telephone: 020 7928 7377   **Drinkline:** 0800 917 8282
Website: www.alcoholconcern.org.uk

Andrea Adams Trust
Small independent charity set up to tackle workplace bullying. Runs a helpline for those who have experienced bullying, and offers training and guidance for employers.
Address: Hova House, 1 Hova Villas, Hove, East Sussex BN3 3DH
Helpline: 01273 704 900
Website: www.andreaadamstrust.org

BackCare
Helps people manage and prevent back pain by providing advice and specialist resources, and promoting self help.
Address: 16 Elmtree Road, Teddington, Middlesex TW11 8ST
Telephone: 020 8977 5474
Website: www.backpain.org

Chartered Institute of Personnel and Development (CIPD)
Organization for personnel and training professionals producing a wide range of books and reports.
Address: CIPD House, Camp Road, London SW19 4UX
Telephone: 020 8971 9000
Website: www.cipd.co.uk

Commission for Racial Equality (CRE)
Publicly funded body set up under the Race Relations Act to tackle racial discrimination and promote equality. Provides advice to workers and employees, and in some cases helps to bring individual discrimination claims.
Address: St Dunstan's House, 201–211 Borough High Street, London SE1 1GZ
Telephone: 020 7939 0000   **Helpline:** 020 7932 5214
Website: www.cre.gov.uk

Department for Trade and Industry (DTI)
Along with the Department for Work and Pensions the DTI is the government department responsible for the world of work, including the national minimum wage and many employment rights. Its agencies supervise health and safety and employment tribunals. The DTI produces a range of free guides and fact sheets, and runs telephone helplines.

Publications order line: 0870 1502 500
Website: www.dti.gov.uk

DTI Employment Agency Standards Inspectorate Helpline: 0845 955 5105
For complaints about employment agencies.

DTI National Minimum Wage Helpline: 0845 6000 678

DTI Parental Leave Helpline: 08457 47 47 47

DTI Redundancy Payments Helpline: 0845 145 0004

DTI Work Rights Helpline – for working time regulations: 08457 47 47 47

Department for Work and Pensions (DWP)
The DWP is a new department formed after the 2001 general election from parts of the former Department of Social Security and Department for Education and Employment. It is responsible for employment, equality, benefits, pensions and child support and produces a number of helpful leaflets and publications.
Address: Room 112, The Adelphi, 1–11 John Adam Street, London WC2N 6HT
Public enquiries: 020 7712 2171
Website: www.dwp.gov.uk

DWP benefits enquiry line: for people with disabilities 0800 882 200
Website: www.dwp.gov.uk

DWP Disability website
Run by the Disability Unit in the Department for Work and Pensions. The website gives details of existing rights and new initiatives: www.disability.gov.uk

Disability Alliance
Dispenses advice on benefit entitlements for disabled people.
Address: Universal House, 88–94 Wentworth Street, London E1 7SA
Telephone: 020 7247 8763

Disability Rights Commission (DRC)
The DRC is a publicly funded body established in 2000 to help secure rights for disabled people. It provides information and advice and arranges legal advice where appropriate.

Address: Seventh Floor, 222 Grays Inn Road, London WC1X 8HL
Freepost Address: DRC Helpline, FREEPOST MID02164, Stratford upon Avon CV37 9BR
Telephone: 020 7211 4110 **Minicom:** 020 7211 4037
Helpline: 08457 622 633 **Textphone:** 08457 622 644
The DRC also has offices in Manchester, Cardiff and Edinburgh.
Website: www.drc-gb.org

Discrimination Law Association (DLA)
The DLA seeks improvement in law and practice for complainants.
Address: PO Box 6715, Rushden, Northamptonshire NN10 9WL
Telephone: 01933 228 742
Website: www.discrimination-law.org.uk

Driver and Vehicle Licensing Authority (DVLA)
Issues all licences and vehicle registration documents
Address: Customer Enquiries (Drivers) Unit, Sandringham Park, Swansea SA7 0EE
Enquiry line: 0870 240 0009
Website: www.dvla.gov.uk

Driving Standards Agency (DSA)
Agency that supervises driving tests.
Address: Stanley House, 56 Talbot Street, Nottingham NG1 5GU
Telephone: 0115 901 2500
Website: www.dsa.gov.uk

Employers' Forum on Disability (EFD)
National employers' organization with the objective of making it easier to recruit and retain disabled employees and to serve disabled customers.
Address: Nutmeg House, 60 Gainsford Street, London SE1 2NY
Telephone: 020 7403 3020
Website: www.employers-forum.co.uk

Employment Tribunals Service (ETS)
Employment tribunals are judicial bodies established to resolve disputes over employment rights. The service has 34 permanent offices across the UK. For information about how to apply to a tribunal ring the enquiry line or visit the website.
Enquiries
Address: 100 Southgate Street, Bury St Edmunds, Suffolk IP33 2AQ

Telephone: 0845 795 9775
Customer Services
Address: 3rd Floor, Alexandra House, 14–22 The Parsonage, Manchester
M3 2JA
Telephone: 0161 833 6310
Enquiry line: 08457 959 775
Website: www.ets.gov.uk

Equal Opportunities Commission (EOC)
Publicly funded body working to eliminate sex discrimination and pro-
mote equality. Provides advice to workers and employees, and in some
cases helps to bring individual discrimination claims.
Address: Arndale House, Arndale Centre, Manchester M4 3EQ
Telephone: 0845 601 5901
Scotland: St Stephens House, 279 Bath Street, Glasgow G2 4JL
Telephone: 0141 248 5833
Wales: Windsor House, Windsor Place, Cardiff CF10 3GE
Telephone: 029 2034 3552
Website: www.eoc.org.uk

The Equality Commission (N Ireland)
Publicly funded body with responsibility for all types of discrimination in
Northern Ireland. Provides help and advice for all workers and employers.
Address: Equality House, 7–9 Shaftsbury Square, Belfast BT2 7DP
Telephone: 028 90 500 600
Website: www.equalityni.org

Health and Safety Executive (HSE)
Responsible for ensuring that risks to people's health and safety from
work activities are properly controlled. Produces a range of advice leaflets.
If you have a query ring the HSE information line.
Address: HSE Infoline, Caerphilly Business Park, Caerphilly CF83 3GG
Information line: 08701 545 500 – will also give contact details of regional
offices
Website: www.hse.gov.uk

Information Commissioner
Independent supervisory authority for data protection and freedom of
information. If you have queries about how your personal records are
used or stored, or how to access them, you should phone the information
line.

Address: Wycliffe House, Water Lane, Wilmslow, Cheshire SK9 5AF
Telephone: 01625 545 700 **Information line:** 01625 545 745
Website: www.dataprotection.gov.uk

Inland Revenue tax credit Helpline: 0845 300 3900
Website: www.inlandrevenue.gov.uk

Insolvency Service (part of the DTI)

The government agency that deals with financial failure and bankruptcy, and runs the official receiver offices. If you work for a company that goes bankrupt or is in the hands of the official receiver you can contact the Insolvency Service to find out about your rights.
Address: 21 Bloomsbury Street, London WC1B 3QW
Telephone: 020 7291 6895

Law Centres Federation (LCF)

National network of drop-in centres that provide free independent legal advice. Phone or look on the LCF website for details of your nearest centre.
Telephone: 020 7387 8570
Website: www.lawcentres.org.uk

Lesbian and Gay Employment Rights (LAGER)

Gives free and confidential advice to lesbians and gay men who are experiencing discrimination or other problems at work, or while looking for work.
Address: Unit 1G, Leroy House, 436 Essex Road, London N1 3QP
Telephone: Lesbian Helpline and Minicom: 020 7704 8066
Gay Men's Helpline and Minicom: 020 7704 6066
Website: www.lager.dircon.co.uk

Liberty

Independent human rights organization working to defend and extend individual rights. Provides legal advice for the public and lawyers.
Address: 21 Tabard Street, London SE1 4LA
Telephone: 020 7403 3888
Legal advice line: 0845 123 2307
Website: www.liberty-human-rights.org.uk

Low Pay Commission

Advises the government on the national minimum wage. Enquiries about individual cases should be via the DTI Minimum Wage Helpline

Address: 8th Floor, Oxford House, 76 Oxford Street, London W1D 1BS
Telephone: 020 7467 7207
Website: www.lowpay.gov.uk
Inland Revenue helpline: 0845 6000 678
Address: National Minimum Wage, Room 91A, Longbenton, Newcastle upon Tyne NE98 1ZZ

The Maternity Alliance
Charity 'working to end inequality and promote the well-being of all pregnant women, new parents and babies'. Can give advice on the work–life balance and flexible working and publishes free information leaflets and guides.
Address: Unit 1.3, 2–6 Northburgh Street, London EC1V 0AY
Telephone: 020 7490 7639
Information line: 020 7490 7638
E-mail: info@maternityalliance.org.uk

National Association for the Care and Resettlement of Offenders (NACRO)
Helps former offenders rebuild their lives. Gives advice on how to tackle discrimination from employers and get back to work.
Address: 169 Clapham Road, London SW9 0PU
Telephone: 020 7582 6500
Website: www.nacro.org.uk

National Association of Citizens Advice Bureaux
Over 2,000 centres across the UK dispensing free advice on a wide range of issues and problems. Look on the web or in the phonebook for your local office.
Address: Myddelton House, 115–123 Pentonville Road, London N1 9LZ
Telephone: 020 7833 2181
Websites: www.adviceguide.org.uk and www.nacab.org.uk

National Drugs Helpline: 0800 776 600

Parentline Plus
National charity that gives advice and guidance on all aspects of parenting, including advice for working parents.
Parentline: 0808 800 2222
Website: www.parentlineplus.org.uk

Public Concern at Work
Independent charity seeking to ensure that concerns about malpractice in the workplace are properly raised and addressed in the workplace. Gives free legal advice to individuals and guidance to employers on how to implement whistleblowing policies.
Address: Suite 306, 16 Baldwins Gardens, London EC1N 7RJ
Helpline: 020 7404 6609
Website: www.pcaw.co.uk

Race Relations Employment Advisory Service (RREAS)
Offers help and guidance to employers with over 200 staff.
Address: 14th Floor, Cumberland House, 200 Broad Street, Birmingham B15 1TA
Telephone: 0121 244 8141

Recruitment and Employment Confederation
Represents recruitment consultants and employment agencies and sets standards for its members. Complaints about employment agencies should be made via the DTI Inspectorate Helpline.
Address: 36–38 Mortimer Street, London W1W 7RG
Telephone: 020 7462 3260
Website: www.rec.uk.com

Relate
Provides counselling sessions for individuals and groups on a wide range of issues including the pressure put on relationships by work.
Address: Central Office: Herbert Gray College, Little Church Street, Rugby, Warwickshire CV21 3AP (check phonebook or Web for local offices).
Telephone: 01788 573 241/0845 456 1310
Website: www.relate.org.uk

Re-Solv
Charity that tackles solvent abuse and offers practical help and guidance to all affected.
Address: 30a High Street, Stone, Staffs ST15 8AW
Telephone: 01785 817 885 **Helpline:** 0808 800 2345
Website: www.re-solv.org

Royal Association for Disability and Rehabilitation (RADAR)
Charity that provides information and support for disabled people and promotes equality.

Address: 12 City Forum, 250 City Road, London EC1V 8AF
Telephone: 020 7250 3222
Website: www.radar.org.uk

Royal Society for the Prevention of Accidents (RoSPA)
Promotes safety in all areas of life and provides information, advice and training for individuals and organizations.
Address: Edgbaston Park, 353 Bristol Road, Edgbaston, Birmingham B5 7ST
Telephone: 0121 248 2000
Scotland: Slateford House, Lanark Road, Edinburgh EH14 1TL
Telephone: 0131 444 1155
Wales: 7 Cleve House, Lambourne Crescent, Cardiff CF14 5GJ
Telephone: 029 2025 0600
Northern Ireland: Nella House, 4 Dargan Crescent, Dargan Wholesale Park, Belfast BT3 9JP
Telephone: 028 90 501 160
Website: www.rospa.org.uk/www.rospa.com

Scope
Disability organization whose focus is cerebral palsy. Works to beat discrimination and promote equality.
Address: PO Box 833, Milton Keynes MK12 5NY
Telephone: 020 7619 7100
Helpline: 0808 800 3333
Website: www.scope.org.uk

Trades Union Congress (TUC)
The TUC represents its 70 member unions and nearly seven million workers. It offers advice and can put you in touch with its individual members.
Address: Congress House, Great Russell Street, London WC1B 3LS
Telephone: 020 7636 4030
Website: www.tuc.org.uk

UK online
Main website for all government information services, with links to all departments.
Website: www.ukonline.gov.uk

Working Families
Charity with objective of promoting change in the workplace. Works with parents and employers to try and achieve a better work–life balance. Offers practical advice on its website.
Address: 1–3 Berry Street, London EC1V 0AA
Telephone: 020 7253 7243
Website: www.workingfamilies.org.uk

Index of Key Questions

Chapter 4: Applying for a job

Job advertisements
What is an advertisement?
What about the phrase 'This company is an equal opportunities employer'?
What about positive discrimination? Some advertisements say applications are encouraged from women and ethnic minorities, etc.
Do vacancies have to be advertised internally and externally?
What happens if an advertisement is found to be discriminatory?
What if I apply after the closing date?

Application forms and CVs
What can I be asked at an interview or on an application form?
Does is matter if I omit certain facts?
What if I have a criminal record?
Do I have to say if I've been to employment tribunal with a previous/current employer?
Do I have to give the name of a referee?
Does data protection law protect the information I give on an application form?

Interviews and tests
Do I have the right to time off work to go to an interview?
What rights do I have at interview?
Is it legal to ask my age and marital status?
Can I be asked if I'm pregnant or have a child in an interview?
Do I have to reveal my current salary?
What if I have a criminal record?
Are the rules different if I am an internal applicant?
I felt the interview was unfair and unnecessarily confrontational. What are my rights?
Who keeps a record of what went on – should a representative of human resources always be there?
Should the interviewer reimburse my costs for attending an interview?

Chapter 5: Job offers

How long do I have to decide whether to accept a job offer?
What if I change my mind and decide not to accept?
What if the offer is subject to certain conditions, such as references, exam results or passing a medical?
Can the offer be withdrawn because of a bad reference?
Do I need proof of the right to work in the UK, such as work permits, etc.?
What are my rights to negotiate the terms of the offer?
How should I accept a job offer – in writing?
Should I be offered a contract or a written statement of my employment terms?
What if I need adjustments because I'm disabled?
What if I'm bound by a restrictive covenant?
Does the disciplinary procedure apply during the probationary period?
What if I already work for the company?

Chapter 6: References

Do I have the right to see my reference?
What if my employer refuses to provide a reference?
What points should a reference cover?
What format should a reference take?
Can my prospective employer insist on a reference?
What if my boss gives me a really bad reference and, as a result, my job offer is retracted?
What if an employer gives an unrealistically good reference to get rid of an employee?
Are there any rules about who I can choose at a referee?

Chapter 7: Your contract

Should I get a written contract before I start work?
What if my employer refuses to give me a Section 1 statement of particulars?
If I am not given a contract what should I do?
What if my employer has reneged on what we verbally agreed?
What if there is a dispute about what is 'custom and practice'?
What about changes to my contract – can they be made without my consent?
What are my rights to negotiate changes to my contract?
What if my contract entitles me to four weeks' notice of dismissal but I am dismissed without receiving it or getting the opportunity to work the four-week period?
Can my contract still have any bearing on me even after I have left?

Chapter 8: Hours and holidays

Working hours

Does the 48-hour maximum apply to me?
What if I want to work longer hours?
How are averages calculated?
Who logs the hours I work?
What about collective or workforce agreements in my organization?
If I work longer hours can I take some off in lieu?
I feel forced to work longer hours to keep my job. What are my rights?
I was dismissed for not agreeing to sign an opt-out – what are my rights?
I'm a younger worker under 16/18 years – do I have the same rights?
Is there an automatic right to overtime payment?
What about work involving heavy physical or mental strain – are there any special provisions?

Rest breaks and time off

What about part-time, agency, freelance and contract workers, etc.?
Are days off in addition to annual leave?
Am I paid during my breaks?
Do I get more breaks if my work is monotonous?
Are rest breaks in addition to meal breaks?
Can my boss force me to give up my breaks or time off?
If I don't take my breaks can I go home earlier/get overtime/take time off in lieu?
Should access to any facilities be provided (for example, food and hot drinks in the middle of the night)?
Do I have to take my break?
What records does my employer need to make?
Do I have the right to the same day off each week?
Do younger workers (below the age of 18 years and over the minimum school leaving age) have additional protection?

Night working

Are there different rights for those who work occasional night shifts and dedicated night workers?
So what are my rights if I do some night shifts, say one week in three?
But what if I regularly finish work at 1 a.m.?
How are averages of night hours worked out?
I must work no more that eight actual hours if my work involves a special hazard – what is a special hazard?
Must my employer take into account my health in asking me to work nights?
How much time off a week am I allowed?
Should I be paid more for working nights?
Does my employer have to provide transport to and from work?

Holidays

Who qualifies for four weeks' paid holiday?

What about agency/contract/part-time workers, etc.?

Is there a minimum qualifying period of employment before I can take holiday?

How much notice do I have to give my employer before taking holiday?

Can I be refused holiday?

Can an employer rule out me taking my holiday during some periods and insist that I take it during other periods?

What about religious festivals?

What if I don't think my employer is being fair?

What about bereavement, maternity, parental emergencies?

How is my holiday pay calculated?

Can my employers insist that I take my leave?

Can I carry holiday over to next year?

If I don't take my holiday entitlement can I be paid instead?

What about my holiday entitlement if I am leaving work?

Can I still get holiday pay if I am off work due to sickness throughout the whole holiday year?

Chapter 9: Family-friendly rights

Becoming a parent

What notice must I give for maternity leave? And what about paternity leave?

What if I am sick as a result of my pregnancy before my leave is due to start?

What if the environment in which I work could be dangerous for my unborn child?

What about my pay and benefits on maternity leave?

What about my pension?

How much notice do I need to give of my return?

Do I have the right to return to the same job?

Can I add holiday to my maternity leave?

What if I am made redundant during maternity leave?

What about men going with their partners to scans and other antenatal appointments – are they entitled to any statutory time off?

Do gay and lesbian couples have any rights?

Parental leave

Do I qualify for parental leave?

Is there anything that my employer needs from me before I can take parental leave?

Do both men and women have the right to this leave?

I am due to go on maternity leave – can I add my parental leave entitlement to the end of my maternity leave period?

How much notice do I need to give to my employer that I wish to take leave?

Can my employer postpone my planned parental leave?

What if my child is disabled?

My child was injured at school – can I take parental leave?

Other flexible work patterns
Do I have the same rights as other workers?
What about pay benefits and overtime?
If I'm working from home do I have the same rights as at work?
Can I be forced to become a shift worker?
What sort of recovery time is allowed between day/night shifts, etc. – if I'm
    changing shifts continually?
What about nights – do I have extra rights?
What are my rights to share my job?
Can I be forced into job-sharing?
Am I liable for my job-sharer's mistakes?

Chapter 12: Sickness

Genuine frequent short-term sickness
Am I entitled to any sick leave?
I am frequently off work for a couple of days just due to being sickly – what is my
    position?
Do I have to get a doctor's report if I am frequently off sick for short periods?
What if it is alcohol-related?
How much paid sick leave am I entitled to?
Am I entitled to more paid sick leave if I have a serious illness or need an operation?
Does my employer need to get a doctor's report if I am off sick with a serious condition?

Statutory sick pay
Will I still be paid if I am seriously ill?
Whatever my illness, will my company help with the costs of treatment?
What if I am sick and it is related to my disability?
What if my sickness is related to my pregnancy?
What if my GP's report and the company doctor's report conflict?
Do I have the right to see the medical report?
If I get caught out pulling a 'sickie' what can I do?
Am I entitled to permanent health insurance?

Chapter 13: Pay

The national minimum wage
Who is eligible for the minimum wage?
How are 'hours' and 'pay' defined?
How are the hours calculated?
What if my employer doesn't comply?
What if I'm having difficulty in getting paid?
Do I have the right to a written pay statement?
What if I don't get a pay statement?

Chapter 14: Discrimination

Disability discrimination
Am I covered by the Disability Discrimination Act?
Which types of employees are excluded from protection?
How am I protected?
Do I have to reveal I'm disabled in my application?
Do I have to be registered disabled to get my rights?
Do I need to be diagnosed as having a disability for my employer to recognize
    that I am protected?

Religion and sexual orientation discrimination
What is a religion or belief?
What is religious discrimination?
Can my employer refuse to, for example, let me pray at work?
There is a real drinking culture at my work, and often promotions are discussed
    at the pub, but as I don't drink alcohol, I feel that I am excluded. Is there
    anything I can do?
What is meant by sexual orientation?
Although I am not gay, I have an effeminate manner and as a result I am constantly
    harassed and taunted at work. Do I have any rights?
Is there anything my employer should do to prevent a breach of this law?

Chapter 15: Harassment and bullying

Harassment
Who does the law protect against harassment?
What is harassment?
What if I was harassed on only one occasion?
If a colleague harasses me, who is liable?
What if a client harasses me?
Should my employer have an anti-harassment policy?
Are there any exemptions?
If I complain it may affect my standing at work. What do I do?
I've been having an office romance. Now he/she's harassing me. What is my position?
When does harassment become a criminal offence?

Chapter 16: Trade union membership

Do I have the right to belong to a union?
Must my employer recognize my union?
What about staff associations – what is their status?
Can I be sacked for taking industrial action?
Can I negotiate on my own behalf for pay or does the union do all bargaining?

Chapter 18: Stress at work

What is stress?

Isn't my employer obliged to look after my well-being?

I have to take time off because of stress – what are my rights?

Stress made me difficult to deal with, or less productive, at work and I was dismissed. What are my rights?

What if I am stressed but my employer does nothing to help?

What should my employer do?

I've suffered ill-health since I left work because of stress at work – do I still have a claim?

How do I prove stress-related illness or injury?

I am being bullied and harassed at work and it is really stressing me out – do I have a stress claim?

Chapter 19: Business transfers: when your employer changes hands

Am I protected when my employer changes hands?

Is there a qualifying length of service for rights under a protected transfer?

Are any transfers excluded?

Who is not protected?

What information must unions or employee representatives receive?

What should union/employee representatives do with this information?

What claims can I make if my employer doesn't inform and consult?

What about contracting out and privitization?

How long are my terms and conditions specially protected by TUPE?

What if I am dismissed prior to the transfer?

Can I refuse to be transferred?

Are there any rights or liabilities that do not transfer?

In reality, mergers and takeovers lead to changes and redundancies. What are my rights?

Chapter 20: Privacy: e-mail and the Internet

In what circumstances can my employer monitor my e-mails and calls?

What can I do if my rights are breached?

What if I discover that my employer has been monitoring my private communications at work without any notification at all that this may be happening?

Should my company have a privacy and monitoring policy?

Can I see the records that they keep on me?

Chapter 21: Whistleblowing

Who qualifies for protection under the Public Interest Disclosure Act?
What is a protected or qualifying disclosure?
What if I wanted to make a qualifying disclosure on a future event?
How can I be sure I am protected under the Public Interest Disclosure Act?
What do I do if my contract contains gagging clauses?
What if there is a clause on confidentiality in my contract?
What if, by making the disclosure, I am breaking the law?
What is a detriment?

Chapter 22: Losing or giving up your job

Being dismissed
Can I bring a claim for unfair dismissal?
What if I am dismissed for what is clearly an unfair reason?
Do I have the right to know the reason why I'm being dismissed?
Am I entitled to warnings before being dismissed?
My final payment – what am I entitled to?
I've been unfairly dismissed – what do I do next?
What sort of compensation might I be entitled to?
Could I be reinstated in my job?

Redundancy
What is a fair redundancy dismissal and procedure?
How should I be told that I've been made redundant?
How long should I be consulted prior to my possible redundancy?
Can I get compensation for the way I was told about being made redundant?
How much notice should I get prior to my redundancy?
Do I qualify for a redundancy payment?
Who is excluded from claiming a redundancy payment?
What if my employer decides to move to a different location?
How is my statutory redundancy payment calculated?
Does my employer have to offer me another job?
What about voluntary redundancy?
Can I be made redundant during maternity leave?
What if I think my employers have used redundancy as an excuse?
Are the rules different if lots of people are being made redundant?
Can I leave before my notice period is completed?
Am I compensated for my loss of benefits due to being made redundant?
What about my reference?

Under-performance and sickness
What constitutes under-performance?

How much of a chance to improve should I be given?
Who decides if I've improved – and how?
I've been off sick intermittently – can I be dismissed?
What if I am seriously ill?
How long can I be off sick before I can be dismissed?
Can I be dismissed for pulling 'sickies'?
Can my employer dismiss me for being 'difficult'?
Can I be dismissed for one action alone?
What if my employer says that I am capable – but just being lazy?
What if my appraisal suggests that I've performed well?
What if my employer is just using poor performance as an excuse?
What if I lied about my qualifications?
Should I be offered alternative employment?
What about my pay and benefits if I am dismissed?
What about my reference?

Misconduct
Who defines what acceptable conduct is at work?
What guidelines should employers follow?
What if I am charged with a criminal offence outside of work?
What if I commit a serious or criminal offence while at work?
I'm being accused of sexual harassment. Can I be disciplined?
Can groups of employees be dismissed even if all were not involved in misconduct?
What if I've lied at work?
What if I've cheated my hours or expenses at work?
Can I be dismissed for disobeying my boss?
I downloaded pornography from the Internet at work. Can I be dismissed?
Should I be warned before being dismissed?
What about my benefits?
What about my reference?

Legal barrier to work
I've lost my driver's licence – but I don't need to drive for work – can I be dismissed?
What if I conceal that I do not have the right to drive in the UK?
What if I did not know that my driver's licence does not cover the UK?
What if I am dismissed because of a positive breathalyser test but before the court hearing?
What if my wife/a chauffeur can drive in my place?
Can I be dismissed for having a health condition?
Am I entitled to be given notice?

Other reasons
Can I be dismissed if I refuse to accept changes to my terms and conditions?
What about personality clashes – can I be dismissed?
Can I be dismissed for refusing to sign a restrictive covenant?
What about my notice and benefits?

Chapter 23: When you've had enough: constructive dismissal

Who qualifies to claim for constructive dismissal?
Do I have to resign to claim for constructive dismissal?
How long can I delay resigning for constructive dismissal?
What if I am literally forced to resign?
My boss is irritating and unreasonable – can I regard this as constructive dismissal?
If I know my employer intends to break my contract in the future can I resign and
    claim constructive dismissal?
I've been given a pay cut – can I claim constructive dismissal?
I've been demoted – can I claim constructive/unfair dismissal?
Do I have to tell my employer the reason for my resignation?

Chapter 24: Resignation

How do I resign?
Do I need to give the reason?
I resigned in the heat of the moment – can I retract my resignation?
I was forced to resign – do I have a claim?
I resigned because I knew that I was about to be dismissed – what are my rights?
My employer won't let me leave prior to the end of my notice period – what if I
    leave anyway?
What about my reference?

Chapter 25: Older workers and retirement

As an older worker do I have the same rights as other workers?
I'm being discriminated against in my search for a job because of my age – what
    are my rights?
Can I be asked my age at interview?
I'm being discriminated against because of my age – what are my rights?
What if my age makes me ill – do I have any rights?
I'm not as fit as I was – should this affect my job?
Do I have to retire at a certain age?
I've been asked to work beyond retirement age – what are my rights?
If I do work past retirement age what is my entitlement to pension/benefits?
Can I retire early?
My company is trying to force me to retire early – what are my rights?
Can my employer change the retirement age without my consent?
I have been unwell for some time with a serious condition. Is retirement on the
    grounds of poor health an option?
After I retire can I keep my company benefits?

Chapter 27: External procedures

Employment tribunals

Can costs of preparing for an employment tribunal be recovered if you win?

Can I represent myself at employment tribunal?

Do I have to tell future employers that I made a claim against a former employer, and will it affect my future employment prospects?